Lee Krasner: A Retrospective

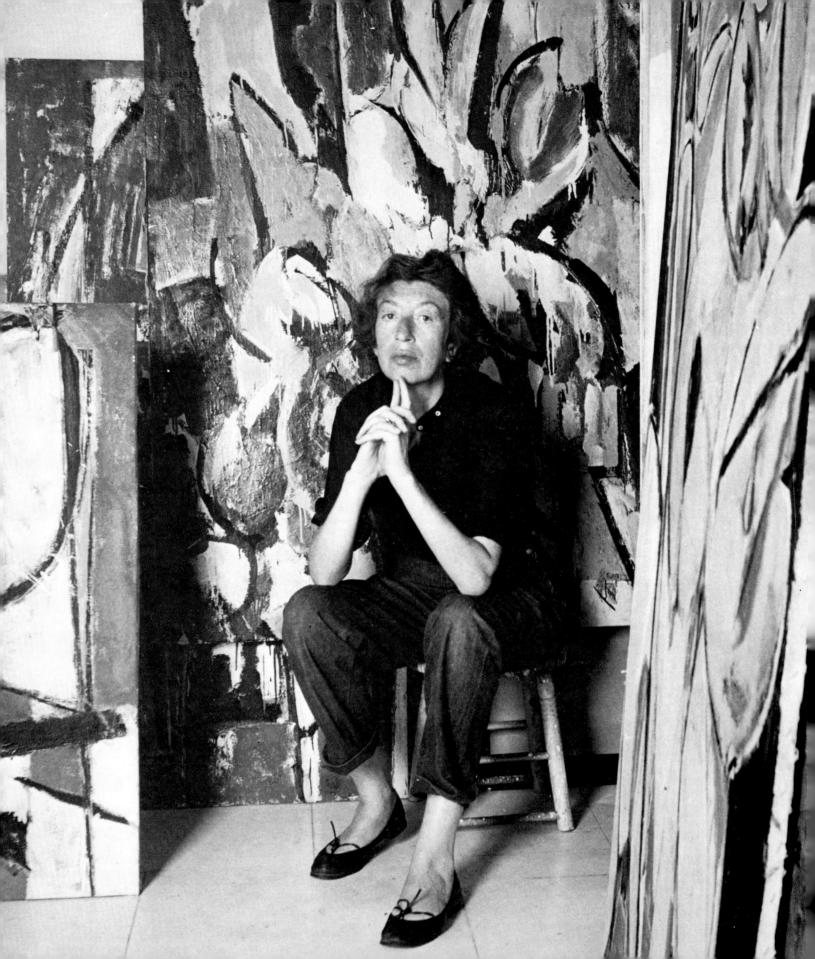

Lee Krasner: A Retrospective

Barbara Rose

The Museum of Fine Arts, Houston, and
The Museum of Modern Art, New York

This book and the exhibition which it accompanies have been
sponsored by Shell Companies Foundation, Incorporated.

Additional assistance for the exhibition has been provided by
The Jesse H. and Mary Gibbs Jones Exhibition Endowment
Fund and the National Endowment for the Arts.

Additional assistance for the catalogue has been provided by
the DeWitt Wallace Fund #3 in Community Funds, Inc.

The educational component of the exhibition has been
sponsored by The Rockefeller Foundation.

Library of Congress Catalog Card Number 83-62554
ISBN 0-87070-415-X

The Museum of Modern Art, 11 West 53 Street, New York 10019

The Museum of Fine Arts, Houston, 1001 Bissonnet, Houston, Texas 77005

Frontispiece: Lee Krasner, August 30, 1956.

Contents

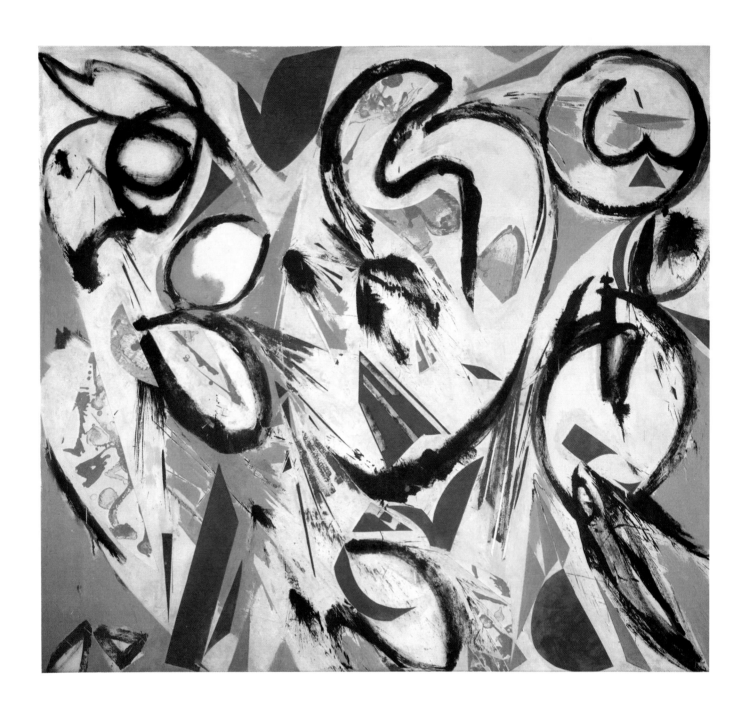

Twelve Hour Crossing, March Twenty-first. 1981. Oil and paper collage on canvas. 68 x 75″ (172.7 x 190.5 cm). Courtesy Robert Miller Gallery.

Foreword

Seeing paintings at three miles an hour—the way gallery and museum goers most often experience them—is not likely to tell us much about a major virtue of Lee Krasner's art: its staying power. Her pictures not only "hold the wall," they hold our interest. And go on holding it. This is certainly a matter of their aesthetic density, which has nothing to do with literal painterly density, but is a richness born of plastic invention reinforced by an intangible we might call "painting culture." Krasner absorbed the latter in the course of a long apprenticeship that gave her an in-depth sense of earlier twentieth-century modernism unmatched in her own Abstract Expressionist generation except, perhaps, by that of Arshile Gorky. Indeed, she and Gorky were notable in being "late bloomers." But when they hit their individual strides, both produced work that was all the richer for their protracted struggles.

And the coming of age of any truly independent painter *is* a struggle. Picasso struggled with Cézanne. And Pollock struggled with Picasso. But he didn't have to share a home with him, as Krasner did with Pollock. To a painter of less conviction, integrity, and personal vision than Krasner, continuous intimate dialogue with the most challenging artist of the age would surely have been a crushing experience. Yet she was able not only to keep working, but admirably to progress. Pollock got more out of this dialogue, I believe, than she. Most artists must bear with wives who react conservatively to new stylistic departures; Pollock, on the contrary, not only profited from Krasner's sublimely "hard" eye, but drew support in moments of doubt from her instinct for his most daring options. From Pollock, Krasner, in her turn, got encouragement and a few pictorial ideas. But such ideas were being absorbed by many other painters at lesser psychic cost. Is it any wonder, then, that the final liberation of Krasner's art should have taken place only after Pollock's death (although the fact

of their marriage continued for some years, I am convinced, to impede her professional recognition).

Krasner's grip on the nature of modern painting as centered between Picasso and Matisse inspired the pendulum-like dynamic of her explorations remarked by Barbara Rose in this book. To conceive modern painting that way is to locate one's self between two extremes: "North pole, South pole," as Picasso quite rightly characterized Matisse and himself. In painterly terms, the magnetism of the Picasso pole pulled Krasner toward light-dark compositional armatures, exploitation of collage, and the predominance of drawing (usually in the form of bold, improvisational brushwork); that of Matisse drew her to construct directly in color, and to an airy, unconstrained sensuousness of expression. It took time, but out of this polarity Krasner made something very personal and deeply moving (as did, after an even longer struggle, her teacher, Hans Hofmann—though in quite another way). In those superb large pictures of the last twenty-five years that show Krasner at her best, we are struck by the sustained "pneuma," or breathing, of her compositions, whose unique color gamut and Matissean ease is in no way undercut by their electric gestural drawing.

There are artists who are wise. And there are artists who are "painting wise." Lee Krasner is both. A long life of vicissitudes, personal and artistic, has contributed to the remarkable wisdom with which she faces challenges. In her mature work, this wisdom is in happy conjunction with her "painting culture," and the result has been some of the most exhilarating work of the last decades—an art that has reassured us during a period, happily now over, when many were pronouncing the death of painting.

WILLIAM RUBIN
Director, Department of Painting and Sculpture
The Museum of Modern Art, New York

Introduction

The difficulty in assessing the role of Lee Krasner as a pioneer first-generation New York School artist of primary importance has been twofold: First, there is Krasner's own idiosyncratic character. Like most complex artists she can be self-contradictory. On the one hand, she has been so self-effacing regarding the art she continued to practice, despite any obstacle, for the past half-century that she kept little documentation regarding her own work. On the other hand, there is her aggressively contentious personality, which alienated every major critic of her generation. Second, although it is still arguable who does or does not belong to the so-called "heroic first generation" of Abstract Expressionists, Krasner was certainly among the first to emerge as a full-fledged abstract artist with an early understanding of Matisse, Picasso, and Miró as well as Mondrian. Indeed, she and Ad Reinhardt were the only two New York School painters working in completely abstract styles prior to World War II. Why then has Krasner not been acknowledged as a charter member of the group that successfully challenged the authority of the School of Paris to create the first major innovations in modern painting since Cubism?

The answer, it seems, is that she did not appear in the photograph of the "Irascibles," the celebrated 1951 group portrait of the major figures of the New York School who protested the refusal of The Metropolitan Museum of Art to exhibit modern art.[1] This photograph, published in *Life* magazine, came to be interpreted as the definitive honor roll of the New York School. Krasner, who had just shown a painting in the historic "Ninth Street Show" and had had a solo exhibition at the Betty Parsons Gallery, where others in the group, including her husband Jackson Pollock, and Tony Smith, Barnett Newman, Mark Rothko, and Clyfford Still, also exhibited, was not in the photo.

Later, Krasner refused to attend meetings of the Artists Club, where reputations were made, or to frequent the Cedar Bar, where, she recalls, "women were treated like cattle."[2] Her aloofness from "the scene" did not help her reputation much, and her sharp criticism of everything she detected as mere rhetoric went a long way to nearly destroying it. To this day, she has little use for most of her contemporaries, although she respected and was respected by Bradley Walker Tomlin and Franz Kline. She also remained one of the few painters able to maintain relationships with the two artists who were perhaps even more critical than she, Clyfford Still and Ad Reinhardt. Indeed, when Reinhardt was buried in 1967 in the same Springs, Long Island, cemetery as Pollock, Krasner held the wake. In a sense it was appropriate: Reinhardt's acerbic tongue and moral rigor had managed to alienate many of the same power brokers and taste makers who disliked Krasner. Her colleague since the WPA and the American Abstract Artists, Reinhardt had assessed "the scene" as caustically as had Krasner.

No matter how supportive she may have been of Pollock's efforts, Krasner was otherwise abrasive and strongly opinionated in her judgments, which she kept no secret.[3] She fought bitterly with the leading critics of the time over virtually every issue. Nor should one discount the enmity of those who would perhaps have wished to share her intimacy with Pollock, who listened to her views, some thought, too much.[4] In any event, when the telephone rang in the Krasner-Pollock household and it was, as usual, Krasner who answered, she was not asked to join the "Irascibles," although it was well known that she had a long history of protesting, picketing, and signing petitions. In this connection, it is ironic to note that her last major picketing venture was joining the lines of those who marched in 1972 against The Museum of Modern Art because it did not show enough women artists. Her complaints were for others more than for herself, however, since among the first to recognize the quality of her painting was William Rubin, director of the Department of Painting and Sculpture at the Museum. As a result of Rubin's appreciation, three works by Krasner were acquired for the Museum's collection significantly before other museums began, as they now have, to make major purchases. Another early admirer, English critic and curator Bryan Robertson, was also responsible for encouraging Krasner, organizing a retrospective exhibition of her paintings for London's Whitechapel Gallery in 1965 that was far more enthusiastically received by the London press than her works had been in New York.[5]

Krasner respects her work, but to say she appreciates its significance is not correct because she does not look at art history as a series of sensational breakthroughs. For her it is a continuum encompassing Eastern as well as Western art, and within this collective body, which transcends the individual genius, forms may appear and reappear centuries or millenia later in another context.[6] Her outlook is closer in this sense to Henri Focillon's approach in *The Life of Forms in Art* than it is to any strict Western chronological approach equating quality with innovation.[7] Krasner's idea was never to make art history but to make good and durable paintings. However, in retrospect, it appears much in her art prefigures the Expressionist styles of the eighties. She was involved at an early date with problems regarding the relationship between abstraction and representation and classic and baroque formats, upon which we shall elaborate later. Today, one of her greatest gratifications is seeing her work understood, not by her own generation, who were blind to its qualities, but by serious young painters mining the depths of Abstract Expressionism for an understanding of the poetic and lyric base of the metaphorical content lost in the literalist sensi-

bilities of the sixties and seventies. During this period, when the media focused on the slick novelty-oriented styles of Pop, Minimal, Conceptual, and other styles, Krasner painted some of her most beautiful and haunting paintings. However, the climate was as hostile to their appreciation at that time as it is favorable to her passionately energetic style today.

My own interest in Lee Krasner was awakened by seeing her two shows of mural-size canvases—really big pictures—at the Howard Wise Gallery in 1960 and 1962. As a young art historian, I was astonished by their power and authority, their technical mastery, and emotional and physical intensity. In 1963, John Bernard Myers introduced me to the artist. Her work at the time was not acknowledged sufficiently, although Bryan Robertson, Gene Baro, William Lieberman, and William Rubin all spoke highly of it to me. Later, younger curators such as Marcia Tucker, who organized a show of Krasner's large-scale works in 1978 at the Whitney Museum of American Art, and Gail Levin and Robert Hobbs, who first identified Krasner as a first-generation Abstract Expressionist in their influential historical exhibition "Abstract Expressionism: The Formative Years" at the Herbert F. Johnson Museum at Cornell University, looked at her work freshly and without prejudice.[8] They began the necessary reassessment of Krasner's role, both as a painter and as a significant behind-the-scenes theoretician who refused to write or to promote herself in any way, but whose opinions and tastes carried great weight, by their own admission, with both Pollock and critic Clement Greenberg.

Once, Lee Krasner was asked how she thought Jackson Pollock's work should be regarded. She answered: "I think if you took a cross-section of all world art, you would get Pollock." That is how I have come to feel about Krasner's equally synthetic and ambitious art as I have studied it and its complex and multiple sources over the years. In my search to understand her work, to make sense of a career whose continuity was buried by the myth of Jackson Pollock, whose wife she was for fourteen years, I have been encouraged and aided by Arnold Glimcher, who helped me make a film on Krasner working and supplied material for this publication; John Bernard Myers, exigent friend and critic; Robert Miller, whose love of Krasner's work equals my own; and especially William Rubin. The enthusiasm of Henry Hopkins, William C. Agee, and Peter Marzio has also helped greatly to realize this difficult undertaking. Jill Flake, curatorial assistant at the Museum of Fine Arts, Houston, Ginna Grimes, Joanna Bobrowicz, and Darby Cardonsky have been of inestimable assistance in collating material and helping to organize this retrospective exhibition.

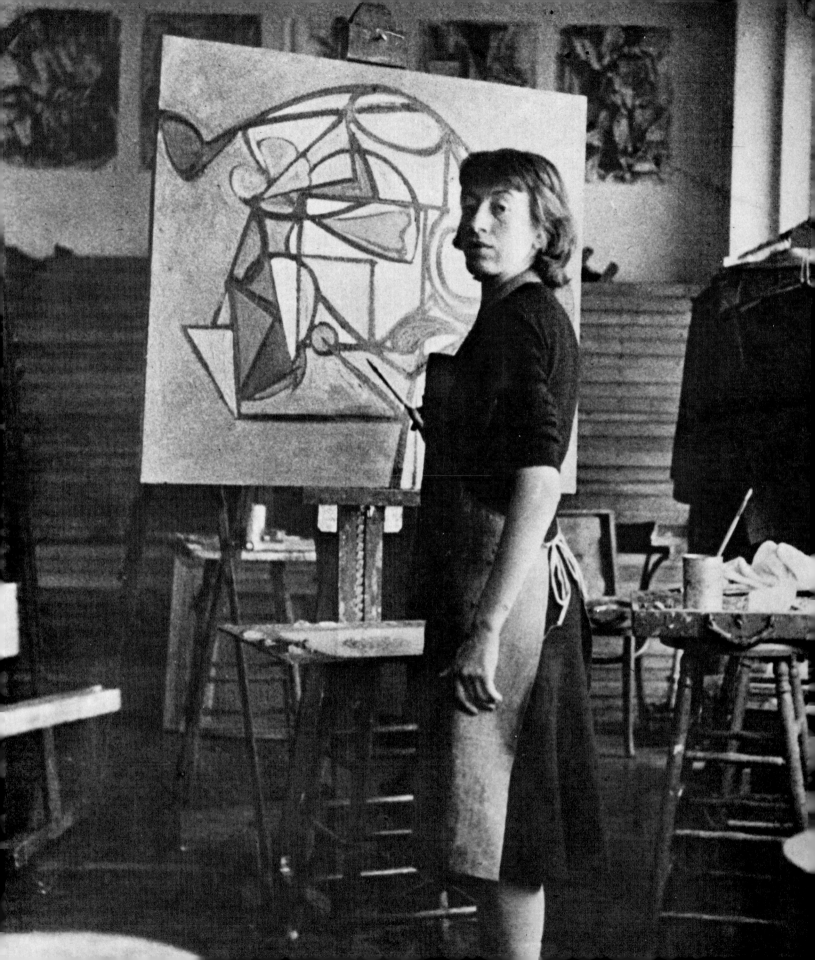

I. Portrait of the Artist as a Young Woman

This is so good you would not know it was done by a woman.

HANS HOFMANN, in class to Lee Krasner, 1937

Lee Krasner in Hans Hofmann's studio, early 1940s.

Lee Krasner does not recall deciding to be a painter; she simply never thought of being anything else. Of course, preparing herself for a career at all for a woman of her generation, born in the first decade of this century, was an anomaly. However, the strength of character that sustained her throughout her life as an artist—an artist, moreover, married to Jackson Pollock, the mythical hero of American art—manifested itself at an early age.

She was the fourth of five children of a Russian immigrant family who fled the persecutions of the Cossacks and the poverty of Odessa for the rich promise of Brooklyn. The family, whose name was spelled "Krassner" on the immigration documents, valued learning and culture above all material considerations, as did many Eastern European Jews. The daughter they named Lenore was their first child born in the United States. It was thought that as an American, she would have opportunities—which such families construed principally as educational opportunities—the Old Country could never offer. Certainly no one dreamed, though, that she would become one of the leading painters of her age, for it was assumed that a woman could not be a great artist. Moreover, it has often occurred to the author that there are very few important visual artists[9] even among Jewish men, and that this is a consequence of the ancient Jewish prohibition against making graven images. We have speculated that abstraction enabled them to overcome their reluctance to depict images, and that it was as abstractionists that many Jews, including leading members of the New York School, such as Newman, Rothko, Gottlieb, as well as Krasner, could realize their art.

The Krassner family followed the classic pattern: Father Joseph was an introspective, sensitive man rooted in the Talmudic tradition of critical inquiry and philosophical debate. He owned a small produce store in Brooklyn, which was essentially run by his wife Anna, a practical, outgoing woman of strong character and constitution. Typically in such families, the women took care of business and worldly affairs. It was a motif Krasner would see repeated later in life when many members of the New York School survived the lean years by having wives who worked. Although Lee Krasner did manage business and worldly affairs after her marriage, she made sure to choose a husband who would insist she continue with her own painting. Throughout her life, she went through problematic periods with her work, as she struggled to find new styles that would satisfy her constant search for fresh means of expression, but she never stopped painting, even during the most turbulent years of her marriage. Her tendency constantly to re-evaluate her own past production, to criticize, reject, destroy, or rework paintings she deems unsuccessful, has produced an oeuvre that is remarkably consistent in quality, but full of lacunae created by the absence of lost or destroyed transitional works. Tracing her evolution as an artist of major ambition and achievement is made harder by her propensity for ruthless self-criticism—a propensity she shared, incidentally, with Pollock.

Impatient with stasis and inertia, Krasner irritated many by constantly moving on to new challenges. Adopting a dialectical mode, she would swing back and forth between the polarities of classic, architectonic structure and baroque action, open form and hard-edge shape, brilliant color and monochrome. Like Pollock, who also worked in image cycles rather than in series, Krasner refused to become a serial painter with a repeated trademark format. A painting by Krasner is recognized by its style, its rhythm, its mastery of color and nuance, its fine detail, and its floral, naturalistic, or organic imagery. However, each painting is different in mood, content, texture, emotional state. This has been a source of considerable consternation to those wishing to see art history as a series of neat packages, easily identified, compartmentalized, and labeled. Krasner does not make it simple to play the matching game, to enjoy being able to identify a work as "a Krasner." On the contrary, one has the sense of a stark confrontation with "Lee Krasner," not an object but a psychic and emotional state—often raw and disturbing. These states themselves, moreover, fit into no prefabricated categories. Krasner has a confrontational personality, and she is equally challenging as a painter.

Although Krasner is a powerful and dramatic artist, she attempts not to overwhelm but to engage. Then, within the terms of this engagement, there is an element of interactive struggle, of a visual and kinesthetic combat we experience empathetically, which requires substantial energy from the viewer to sustain. Her paintings are never loud or raucous in a vulgar way, but they are not easy or quiet either. However much she may be attracted to the ornamental and the filigreed, to the densely patterned and richly detailed, she concedes nothing to decoration per se. Her paintings are no relaxed picnics on the grass; they are direct, vigorous, demanding encounters between the psyche of the artist and that of the viewer.

Given the independent, unconventional personality Krasner had already demonstrated as a child, added to the immense battle she fought struggling to free herself from the influences of her teacher, Hans Hofmann, and her husband, Jackson Pollock, her art could hardly have been otherwise. Her unflinching dedication to finding her own way would win out.[10] A stubborn if good-natured child, Krasner was berated for her willfulness. Like many artists, she was not a good student. Her family did not oppose her decision to become a painter, possibly because she showed no other promise. They quietly assumed that a woman who wanted to be an artist would end up as an art teacher. Lee Krasner knew from the outset she had no intention of ever teaching.[11] However, she did earn a degree in art education, which she never used. She supported herself entirely, but by illustrating, decorating hats or porcelain in factories, and waitressing. She preferred waitressing because it gave her freedom to paint during the day.[12]

Krasner attended technical art schools and not an academic college. She had perhaps the most extensive and thorough artistic education of any of the members of the New York School, including a knowledge of the Old Masters and their techniques and compositions, as well as a grasp of modern art theory and its practice. There was no art in her immediate everyday surroundings, her family's interests being literary, political, and philosophical rather than artistic; however, she was so determined to pursue an art career that she commuted from Brooklyn to Manhattan to attend the Washington Irving High School for Girls because they offered a studio art major. She was already painting seriously as a teenager. After high school, she won a scholarship to Cooper Union, in those days comprised of two divisions, an art school that trained women to be teachers and an engineering school for men. Krasner completed the course work for a teaching certificate, but by this time she had, as she puts it, discovered art "with a capital A." The Metropolitan Museum of Art, which now owns several of her works, was her beacon.

Despite her ambition and talent, Krasner was modest enough to know that years of apprenticeship were necessary to lay the foundations for great art. It was a price she was ready to pay. She was prepared to spend the time and energy necessary to learn the lessons of the masters. Armed with her life drawings done at Cooper Union, she applied to the prestigious National Academy of Design. Admission to the academy was on the basis of talent; once accepted, students paid no fees. The academy was the closest institution in America to the Ecole des Beaux-Arts in Paris in its curriculum and goals. Students first drew from plaster casts, graduating to life drawing if they were proficient enough, and then ultimately to oil painting. This slow step-by-step mastery of a tradition rooted in the study of classical art and the Old Masters provided solid training in drawing, composition, and technique.

Lee Krasner enrolled in the National Academy in 1929. She was nineteen years old and she had been drawing and painting all her life. Her first extant works are her academy drawings after casts. She has also preserved a few portraits and still lifes that she produced during her last two years at the academy. The life drawings were mostly done in sanguine chalk. A self-portrait is typical of her careful, academic style (fig. 1). It is one of the few surviving life drawings Krasner made at the academy; the rest were burned in a fire.

Krasner still owns the self-portrait she submitted to qualify for admission to the academy life drawing class (fig. 2). The defiant expression was characteristic of her tough-minded attitude: She would submit to any discipline she deemed necessary to achieve her goals of acquiring the techniques and skills needed to produce great art, but she would do it her own way and on her own terms. At first, the judges questioned the veracity of the portrait, refusing to believe that she had been able to produce a plein air self-portrait, a difficult task for the most experienced artist. "I explained to them that I had tacked a mirror to the tree, and they finally accepted the work." Even at this early stage of her development, Krasner pictured herself surrounded by nature. Indeed, the forms of nature were to become her major subject when she became a mature abstract artist.

In 1929, The Museum of Modern Art opened in the Heckscher Building on Fifth Avenue and Fifty-seventh

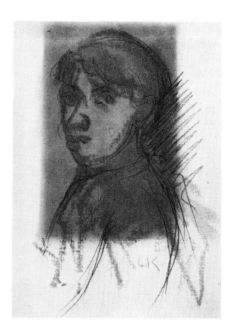

Fig. 1.
Self-Portrait. c. 1933.
Oil on linen.
17¾ × 15¾″ (45.1 × 40 cm).
Collection the artist.

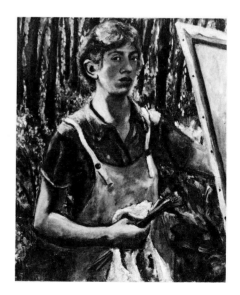

Fig. 2.
Self-Portrait. c. 1930.
Oil on linen.
30⅛ × 25⅛″ (76.5 × 63.8 cm).
Collection the artist.

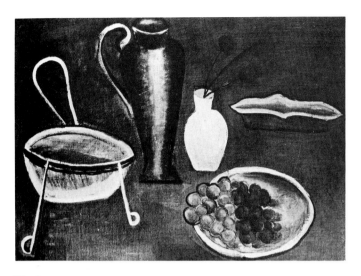

Fig. 3.
Untitled. 1935.
Oil on canvas.
19¾ × 27¾″ (50.2 × 70.5 cm).
Collection the artist.

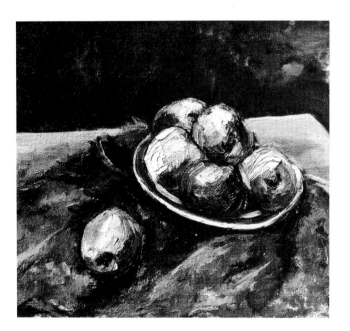

Fig. 4.
Still Life with Apples. 1932.
Oil on canvas.
18 × 9½″ (45.7 × 24.1 cm).
Private collection.

Street. Krasner was among the first to visit the new museum. Although still a student at the academy, painting traditional still lifes and floral arrangements, she had already begun to criticize academic notions of style (fig. 3). Her initial modern idol was Henri Matisse. Imitating Matisse's own development, she began investigating new ways of adumbrating form, creating volume through color rather than through chiaroscuro modeling by studying the still lifes of Paul Cézanne closely. Cézanne was among the four masters in the opening show of The Museum of Modern Art along with Georges Seurat, Vincent van Gogh, and Paul Gauguin, and Krasner was clearly affected by all of them in one way or another. This first encounter with Post-Impressionism had an immediate impact on her art even while she was still a student at the academy. In a number of still lifes of fruit with their heavy impasto, individual brushstrokes are used to build up and outline form sculpturally, reflecting the influence of Cézanne (figs. 4, 5).

Krasner's academic drawings of male nudes are especially noteworthy for their candor and anatomical accuracy. Within their context, they are probably unique works by a woman artist of her generation. (In fact, women were only first permitted to draw male nudes in the same classes as men when Krasner was still a student at the academy.) In comparison with Krasner's matter-of-fact treatment of male nudes, figure drawings by other artists of her generation look puritanically stilted and artificial.[13] It is obvious from her early life drawings that Krasner was uninhibited in her attitude toward the body. As a mature artist, this general lack of inhibition expressed itself in her willingness to experiment with new materials and techniques and to search for images that frequently expressed a potent sensuality. Indeed, it was her generation of American artists, especially those of Eastern European or Mediterranean backgrounds, who first sought to introduce the sensuous into American art, previously reticent to express enjoyment of the body.

Ilya Bolotowsky and Giorgio Cavallon, fellow students of Krasner's at the National Academy who also later became abstract artists, remember Krasner well as a talented, forceful redhead who was always trying to drag her fellow students to modern art exhibitions.[14] Like Bolotowsky, Igor Pantuhoff, Krasner's special friend at the academy, was a White Russian who had fled the Bolsheviks. His father had been a Czarist officer; Pantuhoff, who later became a successful society portrait painter, was, however, interested in Marxist political writings, to which he introduced Krasner. Much to Krasner's disappointment, Pantuhoff's political ideas were more advanced than his aesthetics, and they drew apart as she became more involved with the modern movement. They remained close during the Depression because of similar interests in politics and literature, but Krasner went her own way regarding art. Determined to develop her talents as fully as possible, but in a modern rather than an academic direction, she studied throughout the thirties, mastering the elements of composition, technique, and theory that would form the art she had chosen as her life's work.

Krasner studied life drawing for a semester in 1933 with Job Goodman at Greenwich House. Goodman taught a version of realist Thomas Hart Benton's aesthetics. He emphasized the heroic male nude, which he posed in class in Michelangelesque positions. A drawing by Krasner done from a live model in Goodman's class is reminiscent of Michelangelo's *ignudi* in its muscularity and twisted *contrapposto* (fig. 6). Later, in Hans Hofmann's classes, Krasner would use what she had learned of anatomy as the means to diagram action in her remarkable charcoal drawings of nudes, in which lines of motion and muscular tension take precedence over literally descriptive representation (fig. 7).

It is worth noting that both Krasner and Jackson Pollock were exposed to Benton's system of diagramming motion and anatomy. As a long-time student of Benton's art at the Art Students League, which Krasner attended only for one month in the summer of 1928, Pollock was more familiar with the method of reducing Old Master compositions to lines of action and to dealing with multifigure compositions. However, before their meeting, both artists practiced abstracting dynamic lines of "action," which could eventually be converted into gestural abstractions. In other words, Lee Krasner's education prepared her as much to be an "action painter" as it did to become an outstanding colorist. Indeed, her education was so thorough that the synthesis of action and color she ultimately achieved in her figurative abstractions of the late fifties and her monumental mural-size canvases of the sixties and seventies was arrived at relatively late in her

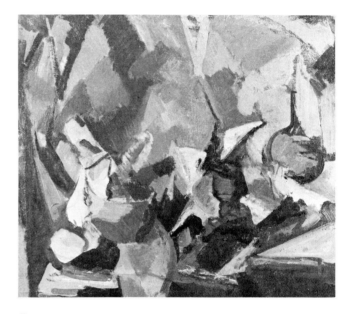

Fig. 5.
Untitled. c. 1938.
Oil on canvas.
20 × 24″ (50.8 × 61 cm).
Collection Joseph Glickman, Palm Beach.

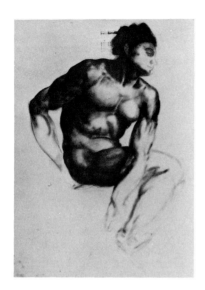

Fig. 6.
Nude Study from Life. 1933.
Conté crayon on paper.
31 × 25″ (78.7 × 63.5 cm).
Collection the artist.

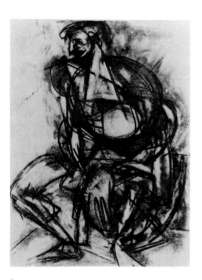

Fig. 7.
Nude Study from Life. 1939.
Charcoal on paper.
25 × 19″ (63.5 × 48.3 cm).
Collection the artist.

career. This was also true of her future teacher, Hans Hofmann, who did his finest and most original paintings at the end of a long career which stressed synthesis rather than innovation for its own sake. Indeed, one could argue that Krasner and Hofmann were the only two major New York School artists to remain completely untouched by any Dada-inspired wish to attract attention through shock or novelty.

We have seen that Krasner's brief studies at the Art Students League with George Bridgman during the summer of 1928 turned her toward a more abstract conception of the figure. Bridgman's analyses of the figure were not intended to lead students toward abstract art; however, his method of simplifying the body into geometric volumes that were twisted in space and his insistence on identifying the main lines of a physical action were a step in the direction of abstraction through diagramming the figure. On the other hand, the Cubist method of progressive abstraction from reality was demonstrated in Theo van Doesburg's celebrated series of drawings in which a cow is gradually transformed into a series of rectangles. This drawing was included by Alfred Barr in his epoch-making catalogue accompanying "Cubism and Abstract Art," the show which he organized at The Museum of Modern Art in 1936. Krasner saw and studied both show and catalogue intently. By 1936, the year Barr also organized the exhibition "Fantastic Art, Dada, Surrealism," Krasner had become a full-fledged convert to the aesthetic of the School of Paris, which The Museum of Modern Art was gradually imparting to American artists. Once again her own best critic, she knew she did not have the training yet to express what she felt. Hearing that the German painter Hans Hofmann had opened an art school in Greenwich Village, Krasner signed up to study with the man who had actually known Matisse, Robert Delaunay, Wassily Kandinsky, and Piet Mondrian. Hofmann's important service to the American avant-garde was to transmit the essence of their ideas, often synthesized in his own novel manner, to the New York School.

Hofmann was quick to recognize Krasner's talent. He offered her a partial scholarship. She still had to wait tables every night in a Greenwich Village restaurant named Sam Johnson's. There she met a young poet named Harold Rosenberg, with whom she struck up a life-long friendship, which had its tense moments, since both had volatile personalities. Rosenberg never wrote of Krasner's paintings, although at one point she rented a room in the cold-water flat where he and his wife lived in the thirties.

Krasner invited Rosenberg's friend, another young writer named Clement Greenberg, to attend Hofmann's Friday evening lecture series. During these lectures, Hofmann expounded his version of Matisse's color theories. Hofmann's celebrated "push-pull" was shorthand for the spatial tension set up by the property of warm colors to project and cool ones to recede. Essentially, it was an updated account of Delaunay's interpretation of Eugène Chevreul's theories concerning the optical interaction of adjacent colors.

Both Greenberg and Krasner were fundamentally classicists who shared Hofmann's distaste for Surrealism. This antagonism toward Surrealism is reflected in Greenberg's writing as well as in Krasner's painting. Following Hofmann, Greenberg defined the essence of modernism as the artist's involvement with the physical properties of the medium.[15] "Picasso, Braque, Mondrian, Miró, Kandinsky, Brancusi, even Klee, Matisse and Cézanne," he wrote, checking off the Pantheon revered in the Hofmann School, "derive their chief inspiration from the medium they work in." In a note to the article, he added: "I owe this formulation to a remark made by Hans Hofmann, the art teacher, in one of his lectures. From the point of view of this formulation, Surrealism in plastic art is a reactionary tendency which is attempting to restore 'outside' subject matter."[16] Throughout his career as a critic, Greenberg avoided any discussion of subject matter in general. Krasner, on the other hand, became increasingly involved with content and images derived from the unconscious.

We have seen that Krasner had already learned how to do anatomically correct drawings at the National Academy. Her powerfully muscular nudes, although done from nature, have as we have noted the heroic proportions of Michelangelo's athletic figures (figs. 8, 9). Thus, by the time Krasner came to Hofmann, she was already steeped in an appreciation of the grand manner of a heroic and epic style. The athletic bodies engaged in heroic actions and a monumental architectonic sense of pictorial construction of Old Master painting were the context within which she interpreted the form and structure of Cézanne and Post-

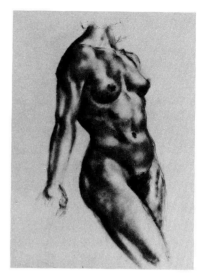

Fig. 8.
Nude Study from Life. 1933.
Conté crayon on paper.
31 × 25″ (78.7 × 63.5 cm).
Collection the artist.

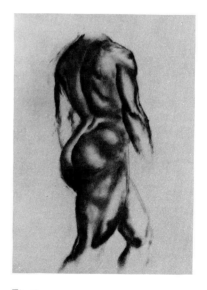

Fig. 9.
Nude Study from Life. 1933.
Conté crayon on paper.
31 × 25″ (78.7 × 63.5 cm).
Collection the artist.

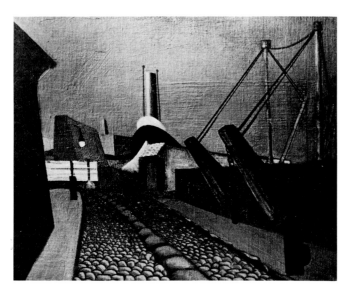

Fig. 10.
Gansevoort I. c. 1934.
Oil on canvas.
19¾ × 24¾″ (50.2 × 62.9 cm).
Collection the artist.

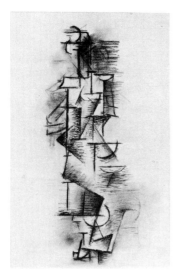

Fig. 11.
Pablo Picasso.
Nude. 1910.
Charcoal.
19¹⁄₁₆ × 12⁵⁄₁₆″ (48.4 × 31.3 cm).
The Metropolitan Museum of Art, New York.
The Alfred Stieglitz Collection.

Impressionism. Then, through Hofmann, she made direct contact with Matisse, Mondrian, and Pablo Picasso, which enlarged and modernized the artistic conceptions she had formulated through her previous academic training.

When Krasner enrolled in Hofmann's classes in 1937, she had already been looking at modern painting for eight years, analyzing Cézanne's structure, Picasso's drama, and even the metaphysical poetry of Giorgio de Chirico. The latter is reflected in *Gansevoort I* (fig. 10), an early surreal painting of a silent pier at night, as eerily lit and ominously vacant as a de Chirico piazza. In this work, Krasner painted one of her few genuinely biomorphic shapes, for when, as a mature painter, she became involved with the theme of organic growth, she did not refer to the vocabulary of gourdlike shapes that the Surrealists had appropriated from Jean Arp. Indeed, as Krasner continued drawing from the figure in Hofmann's studio, her interests turned more and more toward the concerns of pictorial structure: the placement of the body in space, the axial lines of motion, the sense of spatial illusionism. However, this type of illusionism was not that of the deep space of Old Master art which had typified her figure drawings at the National Academy. Krasner's drawings of the late thirties were grisaille, but their space was shallow and value contrasts referred to Cubist *passage,* not Old Master chiaroscuro. She had progressed considerably in learning the vocabulary of Cubism since the fully rounded sculptural realistic figure drawings she made from casts and models at the academy. She was drawn to Picasso's work, intently studying both his Analytic and Synthetic Cubist works during her frequent visits to The Museum of Modern Art. She recalls seeing the Picasso figure drawing that Alfred Stieglitz gave The Metropolitan Museum of Art, which dissects the figure into a series of linear axes and geometric planes (fig. 11). This drawing had a profound effect on her own conception of the figure as a point of departure for abstraction (fig. 12).

Hofmann published his lecture notes, but there is still some question regarding what, in fact, he was actually teaching in his class.[17] His students had no idea what Hofmann was doing himself. Hofmann did not exhibit his own work until 1944, when Krasner and Pollock finally persuaded Peggy Guggenheim to show Hofmann—over the objections of the Surrealists. The Surrealists' hostility

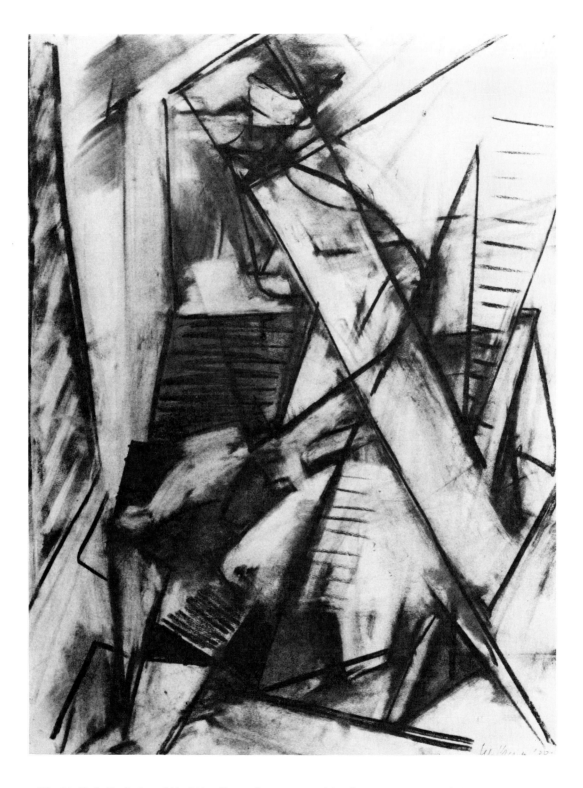

Fig. 12. *Nude Study from Life*. 1938. Charcoal on paper. 31 × 25″ (78.7 × 63.5 cm). Collection the artist.

to the German painter-pedagogue was certainly understandable since the one modern movement he absolutely excluded from his teaching, on both aesthetic and moral grounds, was Surrealism. His objective as he defined it in the essay published as part of his 1948 retrospective was "the search for the real."[18] No one has really ever been able to make sense of Hofmann's theories for the good reason that they are a kind of jumble of early modern Continental aesthetics, a personal synthesis he created of Cézanne as seen by Matisse, Matisse as seen by Delaunay, Expressionist improvisation as defined by Kandinsky. To these Hofmann added a liberal dose of Mondrian's structuralist and formalist Neo-Plastic doctrine of formal purity and geometric clarity. It was a rich mixture, a complex synthesis of the cross-currents of modernism, both stimulating and confusing to his students.

Since Hofmann made no effort either to impose his own style on his students or to cause them to work in any given manner, the styles they developed were extremely varied.[19] There seems no question today that, of Hofmann's students, only Krasner developed independently into an artist of the first rank. While she studied with him, however, she resented his heavy Germanic pedantry, feeling that art was more a matter of intuition than theory. Nevertheless, two elements of Hofmann's teaching stayed with her throughout her life: his insistence that the interaction of color could create a spatial illusion that was purely optical and hence more abstract than the illusion of sculptural space created in academic and Old Master art; and his emphasis on the importance of structuring the composition in relationship to the frame to create a greater sense of monumentality.

Normally, it is with German Expressionism that one associates Hofmann, who was born and schooled in Germany, where he met Kandinsky. Kandinsky's Bauhaus period had been geometric, but the legacy of his early Expressionist style had lived on in Munich, where he painted his early abstractions, the open-form lyrical Improvisations. Unquestionably, outside of the German Expressionist content of the art of Marsden Hartley and Arthur G. Dove, Hofmann was the main channel for bringing American artists into intimate contact with an aggressive, activated Expressionist style that stressed thick paint, visible brushwork, and intense color. However, the artist

Hofmann spoke about most, besides his revered heroes Picasso and Matisse, was Mondrian. There is some irony in the fact that Mondrian first became a cult figure for American artists among Hofmann's students as a result of Hofmann's intense admiration for the Dutch purist.

Hofmann stressed Mondrian's emphasis on "relationships" as the basis of art and insisted that the figure be seen as a totality, in relation to the space around it. "Monumentality," Hofmann wrote in *Search for the Real*, "is an affair of relativity. The truly monumental can only come about by means of the most exact and refined relation between parts."[20] Years later, while Hofmann was painting the abstract relationship between objects in space, critics would praise Barnett Newman as a "nonrelational" painter who disposed of the relationships of form to form within the pictorial field in favor of the single relationship of the whole image to the rectangular frame. By the sixties, Hofmann's insistence that the relationships between colors and forms were the basis of painting seemed a Cubist convention that could be discarded. Krasner, on the other hand, remained faithful to Hofmann's precepts that drawing and relationships—of both color and structure—were fundamental to great art, although her interpretations of these elements diverged more and more from Hofmann's style.

For Hofmann, the two great revolutions in modern art were that of the Impressionists, who "discovered the full plastic significance of the picture plane as a two-dimensional entity" and that of the Cubists who "broke with tradition by changing from a line to a plane concept."[21] By the time these teachings filtered down to American artists of the sixties, the popular misconception that painting should be literally flat and that linear drawing was a relic of Cubism that ought to be jettisoned along with internal relationships between forms and colors was the doctrine of "advanced" art. The results were paintings far from the synthesis of Impressionism and Cubism that Hofmann advocated. How and why these misconceptions gained currency is a story too long to tell here, but one thing is certain: Those who, like Krasner, heard Hofmann firsthand had a great advantage over those who received garbled thirdhand versions of the gospel.

In fact, what Hofmann taught was not very different from what Matisse had taught him: a method of arranging shifting color planes and abstracting from nature *devant le motif.* Hofmann had seen the Cézanne retrospective in Paris in 1907 and probably knew Matisse's interpretation of Cézanne's work. He was in Paris during the years the art magazines reported Matisse's writings and accounts of conversations with Cézanne. Hans Hofmann was, in many respects, Matisse's most faithful and intelligent disciple. From him, Hofmann took his concern with the creation of plastic volumes and of a kind of tension balanced out by the adjustment of color volumes finally set into an equilibrium that did not "poke holes," i.e., create deep space, in the painting, but instead preserved the sense of the two-dimensionality of the plane. Krasner thoroughly understood this concern. Although she painted few oils on canvas while actually studying with Hofmann, she produced many oil-on-paper still lifes and figure studies in which she applied Hofmann's precepts of "push-pull" balancing out of spatial tensions by contrasting warm and cool colors (figs. 13, 14, 15). These are extraordinarily accomplished works, done with a finesse and technical mastery few, if any, could equal in New York at the time (figs. 16, 17).

In Hofmann's class, Krasner also produced many charcoal drawings of both male and female nudes, as well as a series of still-life drawings (fig. 18). It was Hofmann's practice to arrange studio setups (fig. 19) for his students in a manner he composed, perhaps unconsciously, with an eye to the architectonic structure of Cézanne's monumental still lifes. The human body was treated in an equally architectonic and structural manner.

When Krasner enrolled in Hofmann's school in 1937, her aim was to study with someone who could teach her more about modern art than she could learn just by visiting exhibitions and looking at reproductions. Hofmann, who had been teaching in New York since 1933, already had a reputation as the man who, as Clement Greenberg put it, "could teach as much about Matisse's color as Matisse himself."[22] Among the small group of serious students of modern art in New York, it was well known that Hofmann, who had closed his Munich school because he quickly understood what Hitler had in mind, was the leading anti-Bauhaus force in Germany and a direct link to German Expressionism.

In his writings, Hofmann was overtly critical of the Bauhaus: "It was the tragedy of the Bauhaus that, at the

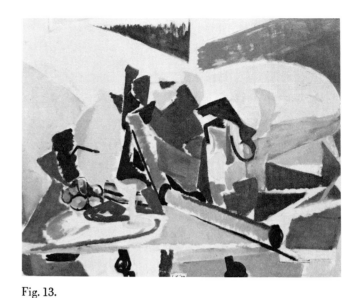

Fig. 13.
Still Life. 1938.
Oil on paper.
19 × 25″ (48.4 × 63.5 cm).
The Museum of Modern Art, New York. Acquired with matching funds from the Edward John Noble Foundation and the National Endowment for the Arts.

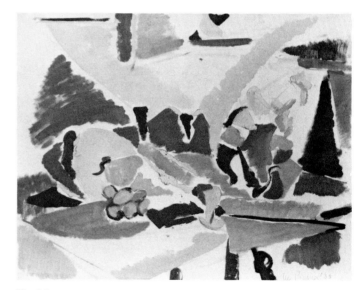

Fig. 14.
Untitled. 1938.
Oil on paper.
18¾ × 24″ (47.6 × 61 cm).
Collection the artist.

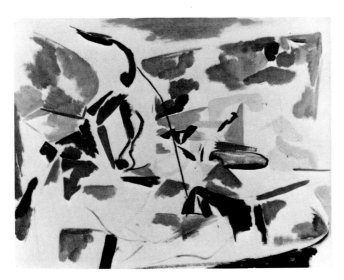

Fig. 15.
Still Life. 1938.
Oil on paper.
19 × 24¾″ (48.3 × 62.9 cm).
Private collection.

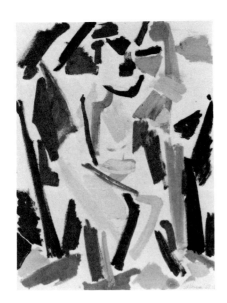

Fig. 16.
Untitled. 1938.
Oil on paper.
19 × 24¾″ (48.3 × 62.9 cm).
Private collection.

beginning of its existence, it confused the concepts of the fine and applied arts."[23] Hofmann distinguished Bauhaus geometric decoration from the mystical abstract art of Paul Klee, Kandinsky, and Mondrian, whom he considered particularly misunderstood. "It is the greatest injustice done to Mondrian," he wrote, "that people who are plastically blind see only decorative design instead of the plastic perfections which characterize his work."[24]

Krasner did not actually study formally with Hofmann the entire time she was registered at the school. She found it a convenient and convivial place to paint, and left her easel and materials there until she got her own studio. She vividly recalls the routine at the Hofmann School:

The classes were conducted in the most orderly sense. You drew from a model on a platform in the morning, and you drew still life in the afternoon. You had the model again if you went to the evening class.

Hofmann would come in twice a week and criticize every student. He would come up to each easel and say what he had to say, or do what he chose to do with the work in front of him. When he wasn't there, a monitor would be in charge. Essentially I learned the rudiments of Cubism in Hofmann's class. I later realized that he himself would swing from Picasso to Matisse: the criticism would change, depending on what was influencing him more at the moment.

He also gave public lectures once a week. There'd be fairly good attendance, the classroom would be pretty well filled. I imagine each student brought one or two other people. About thirty or forty people would attend. The lecture would be part of what he was teaching: the two-dimensional surface had to be punctured and then brought back to two-dimensionality again. As I try to look back, I would say that the most valid thing that came to me from Hofmann was his enthusiasm for painting and his seriousness and commitment to it. That is the most I got from Hofmann.

Even today, speaking of the years she spent as a Hofmann student, she can work herself into a rage recalling Hofmann taking her charcoal and redefining the contour of a figure or still life she was trying to translate into an arrangement of lines and planes. As dogmatic as Hofmann

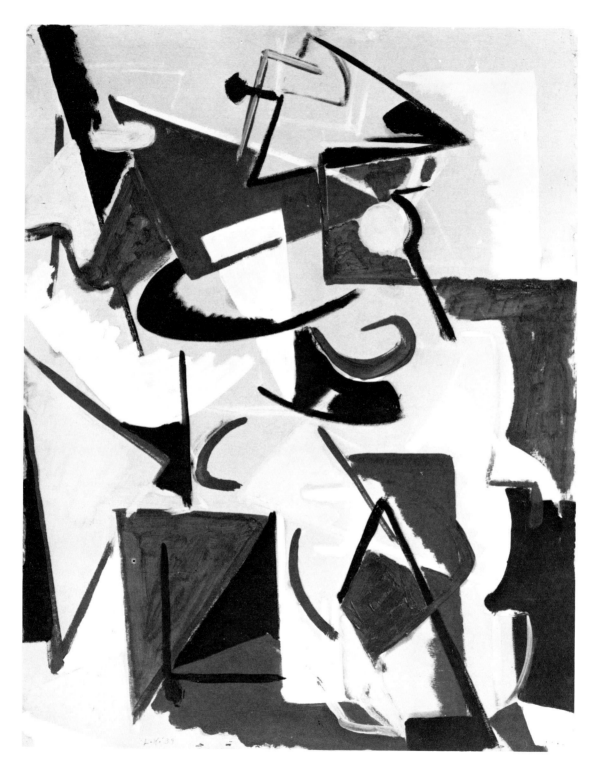

Fig. 17. *Brown Green White Yellow Black*. 1939. Oil on gray paper. 25½ × 20″ (64.8 × 50.8 cm). Collection the artist.

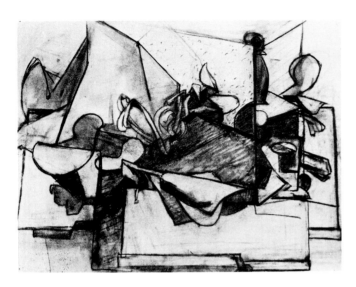

Fig. 18.
Still Life. 1937.
Charcoal on paper.
25 × 31″ (63.5 × 78.7 cm).
Collection the artist.

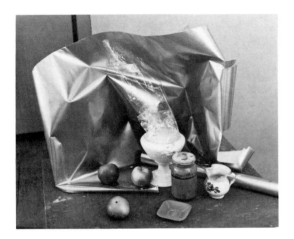

Fig. 19.
Still-life composition setup at the Hans Hofmann studio.

might have been about "push-pull," he did not inhibit his students or impede them from evolving styles more abstract than his own. Essentially he taught a synthesis of rational Cubist design, an architectonic sense of composition that related what was depicted to the right angle of the framing edge and the emotional qualities of Fauve color. Previously, the major impediment to a synthesis of Fauve color with Cubist design was the persistence of the traditional polarization between *disegno* and *colore*. The continuing split between drawing and color is reflected in the fact that Hofmann assigned two different types of class exercises: drawing lessons to depict space through the relationship of lines to each other as well as to the framing edge; and painting lessons to create space by using the properties of warm colors to advance and cool colors to recede.

As a result of the continued separation of design from color in the Hofmann School, Krasner's works of this period are basically of two types: charcoal drawings from the model and oil-on-paper color studies from still life (figs. 20, 21). Hofmann, of course, insisted on working from nature.[25] As we know, painting from nature meant, for Hofmann, depicting what one saw, with some Expressionist distortion. At the time, it did not mean for him, as it did for Krasner, transforming nature into an abstract arrangement of lines and colors (figs. 22, 23, 24). At this period, Krasner was in the ideal position to translate her drawings into paintings, yet something kept her from enlarging these provocative abstract drawings and turning them into paintings. For "action painting" is essentially a style that translates the graphic into the pictorial gesture through an enlargement of scale and a change of medium. The radicality of Pollock's paintings of the early forties was that he was able to do what Krasner could not: take the images from his automatic Expressionist drawings executed during the same period Krasner was drawing abstractions from the figure and translate them into paintings. He eliminated the dichotomy perpetuated by Hofmann's method, and by drawing directly in paint, married color to line. Because she was on the verge of making a similar move, it is not strange that Krasner was the first to understand fully the significance of what Pollock had done. That Krasner was the first is a point that no one has disputed.

Hofmann emphasized still life, the favorite subject of the Cubists. Typically, he would set up a still life in class, instruct the students to draw it in terms of the relationship of the edges and planes to one another and to the space around them—as opposed to copying it—and wait for the results to criticize (figs. 25, 26, 27). Cynthia Goodman, who interviewed his students, has described Hofmann's method:

Circulating through the classroom, he applied himself to an unsuccessful student drawing, adding "corrections" —a Cubist study in the margin, a diagonal line to indicate the axis of the body or the direction of movement in space, or a caricature of a face if he noticed a student straying too far from nature in an abstraction. Usually students accepted such alterations with respect, but occasionally Hofmann's assertiveness disturbed them. As a startled student looked on he would rip a drawing in two, demonstrating another way of visualizing a rigid spatial composition by shifting the paper.[26]

Later, not only Krasner, but Willem de Kooning as well, would emulate Hofmann and create abrupt and dramatic spatial disjunctions by tearing up drawings and pasting them back together.[27] Through these hands-on critiques Hofmann's students learned the essence of what he was teaching, since few of them could understand what he was saying because of his heavy German accent. Krasner, for example, said that George McNeil, an abstract artist who was the class monitor, usually translated for her. Hofmann had written a treatise, *The Painter's Primer*, in German which summarized his method, but it was unknown to his American students. *The Search for the Real*, an abbreviated version of the treatise, appeared in English in 1948. By that time Krasner was already a fully formed artist who had moved away from her teacher.

When one compares Krasner's work as a Hofmann student with what he himself was doing in 1937–40, one realizes that she was working in a more advanced style of Cubism, derived directly from Picasso and Matisse, than her teacher, who resisted total abstraction until the later fifties. This curious fact is explicable in terms of a split within Hofmann's own school. There were essentially two factions. One was more closely tied to Kandinsky and

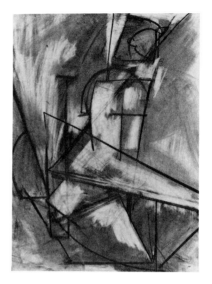

Fig. 20.
Nude Study from Life. 1938.
Charcoal on paper.
31 × 25″ (78.7 × 63.5 cm).
Collection the artist.

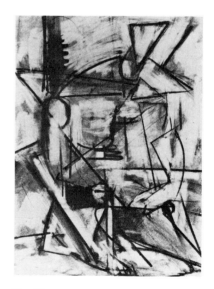

Fig. 21.
Nude Study from Life. 1938.
Charcoal on paper.
31 × 25″ (78.7 × 63.5 cm).
Collection the artist.

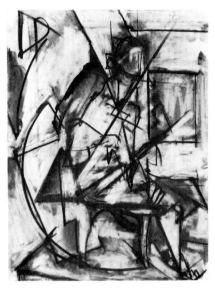

Fig. 22.
Seated Nude. 1940.
Charcoal on paper.
25 × 18⅛″ (63.5 × 48 cm).
The Museum of Modern Art, New York.
Gift of Constance B. Cartwright.

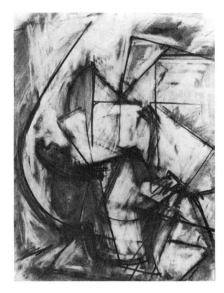

Fig. 23.
Nude Study from Life. 1938.
Charcoal on paper.
31 × 25″ (78.7 × 63.5 cm).
Collection the artist.

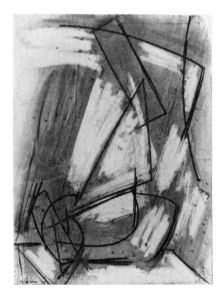

Fig. 24.
Nude Study from Life. 1938.
Charcoal on paper.
31 × 25″ (78.7 × 63.5 cm).
Collection the artist.

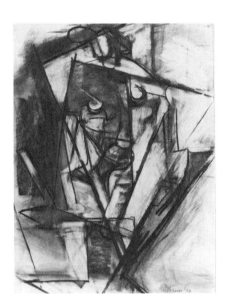

Fig. 25.
Nude Study from Life. 1938.
Charcoal on paper.
31 × 25″ (78.7 × 63.5 cm).
Collection the artist.

Expressionism; it centered around Hofmann's student Mercedes Carles, the daughter of Arthur B. Carles, the Philadelphia-based painter, who visited Stieglitz in New York and studied Matisse at the Barnes Foundation outside Philadelphia. Carles had created an original style uniting Matisse's color with Expressionist painterliness which prefigured the styles of the New York School. Carles's work was not well known in New York, but Hofmann was certainly familiar with his sophisticated still-life paintings. Indeed, in 1935 Mercedes Carles had persuaded Hofmann, who had stopped painting and was drawing nudes and landscapes, to paint still lifes. Krasner knew Carles and his work and was very friendly with his sister, Sarah Johns, a fashion illustrator for whom she sometimes modeled.[28]

The other faction was led by Harry Holtzman, who became Mondrian's principal champion in New York. Unappreciated in Paris, Mondrian was enthusiastically collected in New York by A. E. Gallatin, Solomon Guggenheim, and Alfred Barr. His paintings were admired by the small circle of avant-garde American artists even before Holtzman set off to Paris to meet the great Dutch Neo-Plastic painter. When the Germans marched on Paris, Mondrian left for London. After his studio was bombed during the Blitz, Holtzman persuaded him that New York was the only safe refuge, where Mondrian already had a circle of disciples. These young admirers of Mondrian were the nucleus of the American Abstract Artists, a group Krasner joined when she left the Hofmann School.[29]

Krasner recalls her last days as a Hofmann student: "There was a sense of wanting to rebel against Cubism, but if you rebeled sufficiently you wouldn't be in class." For her, it was impossible to go on with Hofmann. She remained on good terms with Hofmann, however, painting in his Provincetown studio in the summer of 1943. She continued working on this painting in the studio she shared with Pollock in New York (fig. 28). Later, after Pollock's death, Hofmann remembered her with affection as one of his best students; he added, "She gave in all the time. She was very feminine."[30] This was an odd assessment considering that Krasner's figure drawings and paintings based on the figure, done while she was a Hofmann student, point forward to a muscular, athletic gestural style of "action painting."

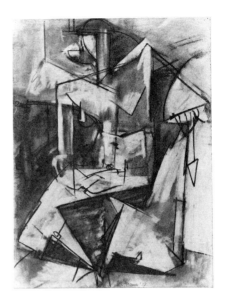

Fig. 26.
Nude Study from Life. 1938.
Charcoal on paper.
31 × 25″ (78.7 × 63.5 cm).
Collection the artist.

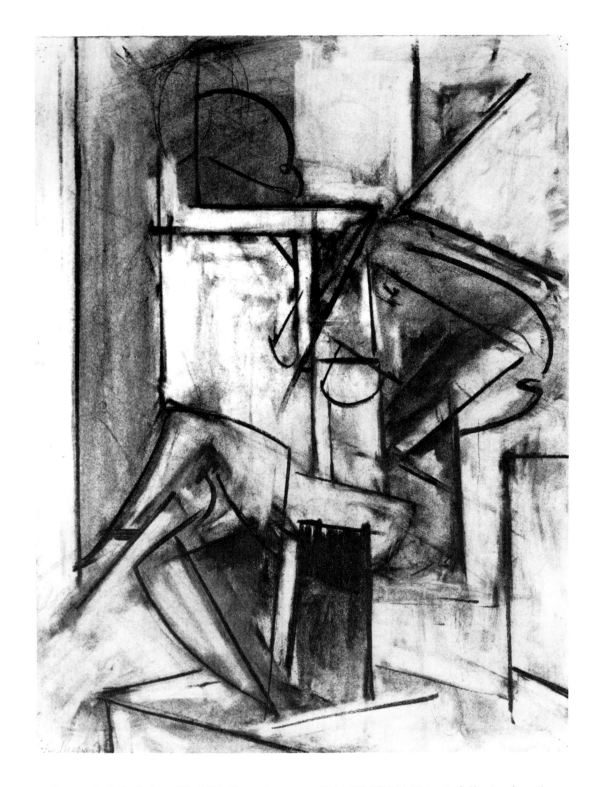

Fig. 27. *Nude Study from Life*. 1938. Charcoal on paper. 31 × 25″ (78.7 × 63.5 cm). Collection the artist.

Hofmann counseled a rhythmic approach to drawing that remained the basis for Krasner's art. "Everything rhythmically organic is true," he wrote.[31] The duty of the art teacher, as he saw it, was above all to develop the student's "sensibility and his power for 'feeling into' animate, or inanimate things with sympathy."[32] Reading these lines we realize that Hofmann was as influenced by the theory of *einfühlung* or empathy with the human body and its gestures as the realist Benton. It was virtually the only point—outside of their emphasis on drawing—on which he and Benton concurred. The focus on the human body, its motions, rhythms, and élan vital common to Benton and Hofmann would eventually be translated by the artists of the New York School into the bold physical gestures of "action painting," which in the hands of its leading practitioners involved enlarging drawings into monumental abstractions which evoked a strong physical as well as optical response.

A generation older than they, Hofmann himself remained true to his own teachings and backed away from "action painting," conceivably because he was too old for the physical exertion it required. The younger gestural abstractionists enlarged their own figure drawings—in Kline's case literally—extending movement from wrist to arm.[33] Pollock was the first to expand the act of drawing to monumental physical gesture on a grand scale, but it was a move that Krasner, for reasons we have mentioned and others we shall examine, eventually found natural to follow.

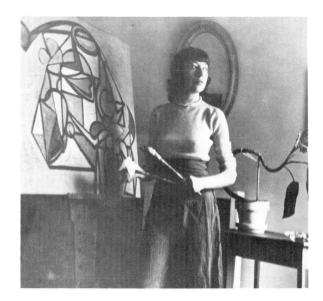

Fig. 28.
Lee Krasner, early 1940s.

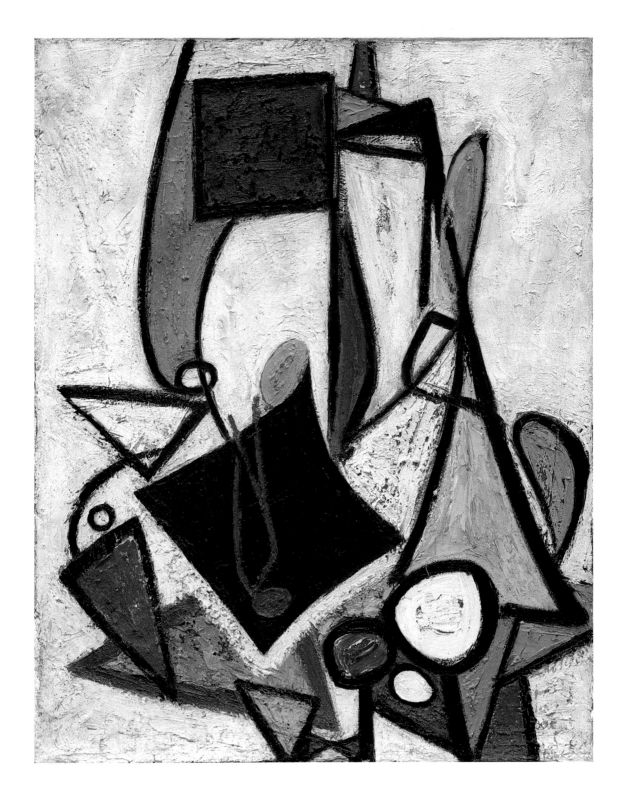

Fig. 29. *Blue Square*. 1939–43. Oil on canvas. 30 × 24″ (76.2 × 60.9 cm). Collection the artist.

II. Art Workers and American Abstract Artists

Miss Lenore Krasner had . . . charge of the project within the War Services Office and I know something of the difficulties she encountered in coordinating all of the work in spite of academic and other temperaments. The fact that all those who worked on the displays still seem happy about them, is not the least of the things to Miss Krasner's credit, it seems to me. . . . As for the artists, I would like to mention each of them by name, for they patiently attempted to get hold of a vague idea and did materialize it. . . . Miss Ray Klein, Mr. Xceron, Mr. Jackson Pollock, Mr. Frederick Hauck, Mr. Ben Benn, Mr. Agostino, Mr. Greco, Mr. Trubach made a fine crew.

PEARL BERNSTEIN, letter to
Audrey McMahon, October 1, 1942

During the summer of 1933, when Krasner studied for a month with Job Goodman at Greenwich House, it became more difficult to support herself as a waitress. The economic situation in the United States continued to worsen. By the time Franklin D. Roosevelt was elected in 1932 to save the country from economic collapse, it was obvious a vast program of government employment would have to be created. Roosevelt, a cultured patrician, was sympathetic to the plight of artists. To keep them alive and working during the period of mass unemployment, his New Deal inaugurated the first subsidized federal art project, the Public Works of Art in 1933–34. Its function was to commission decorations for government buildings. In 1935, a broader based agency, the Federal Art Project, a branch of the Works Progress Administration (WPA), was established. The project hired artists to make paintings, sculpture, mosaics, stained glass, and so on, for the thousands of buildings being erected by the New Deal, as well as to teach art and to illustrate books on American crafts.

Lee Krasner joined the Federal Art Project of the WPA in 1935, the year it was initiated. About this time she began calling herself "Lee" instead of Lenore, and dropped the second "s," simplifying her family name as Krasner. She had no difficulty proving the financial need required, and since it was financial need, not sex, religion, or color, that was the determining criterion for WPA employment, minorities and women were for the first time given equal opportunity as artists on the project, where women like Lee Krasner, black artists like Norman Lewis, and Cubist abstractionists like Ad Reinhardt could meet and become friends. Krasner's first job on the project was to assist a City College professor in executing illustrations of *forminifera* for his textbooks on marine biology. This was her second job illustrating textbooks and she learned from both experiences, enjoying especially the attention to structures of organic forms that was required of her.

There were three divisions in the Federal Art Project: mural, easel, and educational. Krasner was assigned to the mural division, where she and her poet friend, Harold Rosenberg, were to assist Max Spivak, who specialized in painting clowns for children's hospitals, in executing his murals. Krasner's own work at the time consisted of still-life easel paintings that attempted to come

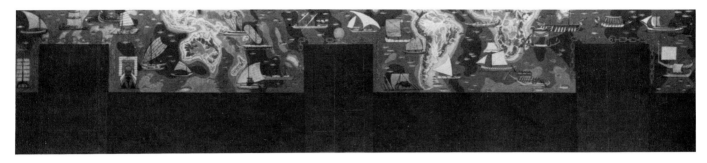

Fig. 30.
Leonard Jenkins. *History of Navigation.* c. 1938.
Mural sketch for a children's library in Brooklyn.
Whereabouts unknown.

to terms with the simplification and deformation of form introduced by Matisse in the interest of greater expressiveness. She was still working from nature, but beginning to transform it in accordance with a conscious will to Expressionism.

This style of incipient modernism had little or no place on the project, whose mandate was to produce a democratic "art for the millions." As Rosenberg later pointed out, the democratic principle in art meant that no distinctions of quality or significance were made. "It didn't matter," he reminisced, "if you were a portrait painter or you painted bears in a shooting gallery on Coney Island."[34]

Krasner recalls the somewhat arbitrary way artists were hired to work on the Federal Art Project. While she was studying with Job Goodman, a government official entered the class and asked if there were any indigent artists needing jobs. Krasner immediately raised her hand and was instructed to report for an examination. On the basis of her skills, education, and proven financial need, she was hired to work on the Federal Art Project. Later in 1935, during mass layoffs, she was let go, for equally arbitrary reasons. When she was hired again on the project in 1937, she gave her address as the Hofmann School to prove that she had a studio; and in fact, she continued her studies with Hofmann while working on the project. This caused a certain dichotomy in her art life, since Hofmann was teaching the principles of Fauvism, Cubism, and easel painting from individual motifs of nudes or still lifes, whereas realistic mural painting was the heart of the WPA art. As part of the mural division of the project, Krasner was responsible for enlarging sketches of epic themes into murals. These huge portable murals, the best known of which is the *History of Aviation* Arshile Gorky executed for Newark Airport, dealt with heroic themes in American history.[35] The evolution of the mural-size "big picture" as well as epic and heroic aspirations of the New York School are in some degree attributable to these experiences in the WPA of so many of its members. Krasner's job consisted of blowing up sketches by other artists and directing their execution as murals. This process of enlargement was done by projecting the drawing onto the canvas with a lantern projector. Her work enlarging drawings to epic scale formed a precedent for her later mural-size abstractions.

Krasner was happy to be working on the WPA, but unhappy to be involved with other people's art. One of her major jobs was supervising the execution of Leonard Jenkins's 100-foot-long *History of Navigation*, destined to decorate a children's library in Brooklyn (fig. 30). One should not exaggerate the influence of this lost mural on Krasner's later work, since the original design was not her own; however, one notes that the flat local color and hard-edge graphic shapes of the map of the Americas have certain affinities with hard-edge shapes and large areas of unbroken local color she used in her mature work (fig. 31).

Except for the abstract maquette her friend de Kooning designed as a mural for the Williamsburg Housing Project, which Krasner was assigned to blow up into a mural, she was obliged to work on representational subjects. This irritated her a great deal, as did the fact that she was required to transform de Kooning's sketch into a wall painting, instead of painting her own mural. During the late thirties and early forties she executed a number of gouache sketches for abstract murals, hoping finally to receive a commission for an abstract mural herself (figs. 32, 33). These gouaches are stylistically related to the Cubist paintings she began producing while studying with Hofmann (fig. 34).

One reason Krasner was so angry at having to blow up de Kooning's sketch is that her own ideas were quite different from those of de Kooning, who was involved with static biomorphic forms, transparent pastel tints, and figurative motifs at the time. Krasner's paintings of the late thirties, on the other hand, were heavily impastoed, rhythmically activated, and dramatically focused on a few large forms, which adhered to the picture plane itself, as opposed to receding behind it. She worked on her own time in the studio she kept in the Hofmann School and later in her own studio on Ninth Street rather than on the West Side pier where the murals were collectively executed by teams of art workers. She did two series of abstract geometric gouaches she thought would be appropriate mural paintings for Radio Station WNYC, where her friend and fellow activist Stuart Davis had painted two murals commissioned by Burgoyne Diller, head of the easel painting division of the New York Federal Art Project. None of Krasner's sketches for abstract murals is dated, but it appears that the series based on Picasso's hard-edged Synthetic Cubism antedates the series of more freely painted curving forms with its improvised painterly passages. Krasner's struggle to find a freer, looser style of painting is also reflected in the difference between the two sets of mural maquettes (figs. 35, 37).

Burgoyne Diller was Mondrian's principal disciple in America. Diller was already painting in a purist Neo-Plastic style in the thirties which reflected Mondrian's strict reductivist geometry. Through a series of adroit political maneuvers, Diller was able to gain control of the mural commissions of several municipal buildings in New York, which he quickly filled with the first abstract murals ever painted. According to Krasner, abstract art per se was not discriminated against; the problem was simply that critical and aesthetic judgments on the WPA were made by bureaucrats and were essentially a function of political

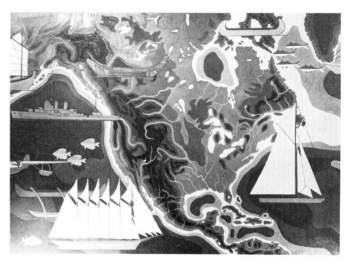

Fig. 31.
Leonard Jenkins. *History of Navigation.* Detail.

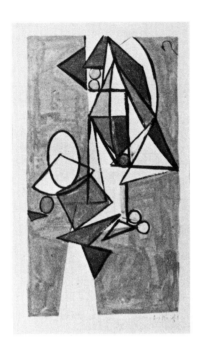

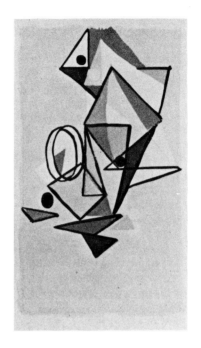

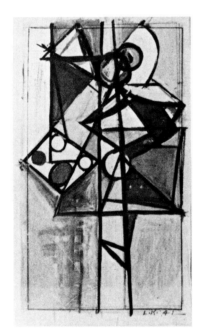

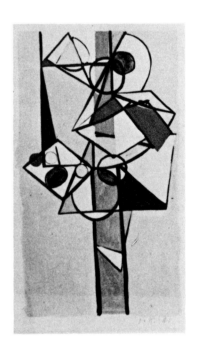

Fig. 32
Four sketches for mural for Station WNYC, Studio A. 1941.
Gouache on paper.
9¾ × 13⅜″ (24.7 × 34 cm) each.
Collection the artist.

power. As the Communist Party gained strength in the project bureaucracy, the possibilities of the abstract artists diminished, since the party held to the Stalinist line that the purpose of art was to instruct the masses in a realist propagandistic style that exalted images of labor.

Krasner recalls the political climate on the Federal Art Project vividly:

There was the Spanish Civil War, the clash of Fascism and Communism. In theory, we were sympathetic to the Russian Revolution—the socialist idea as against the fascist idea, naturally. Then came complications like Stalinism being the betrayal of the revolution. I, for one, didn't feel my art had to reflect my political point of view. I didn't feel like I was purifying the world at all. No, I was just going about my business and my business seemed to be in the direction of abstraction.

One of Krasner's WPA activities was organizing protest demonstrations for the Artists Union, the trade union to which all the project artists belonged. On the project, artists were government workers, but their status was ambiguous. Theoretically, they were white-collar workers, yet most did manual labor. In defending artists' rights as workers, the Artists Union was more like a medieval craft guild than a labor union, although it was affiliated with the CIO. It negotiated neither hours nor wages, but intervened for individual artists in danger of being dropped from the project. The Artists Union held regular meetings where many artists met for the first time. These meetings of American Abstract Artists of the late thirties and forties were the precursors of the Artists Club meetings of the fifties. Both Stuart Davis and Harold Rosenberg wrote for *Art Front*, the Artists Union publication. Aesthetics were not discussed as such, but it was inevitable that discussion regarding so volatile a problem as subject matter should be taken up, if not at the meetings themselves, then later, when groups of like-minded artists retired to the local bar or cafeteria or the benches in Union Square to talk things over. Articulate and enthusiastic, Krasner was frequently part of these conversations. She remembers the discussions of the time:

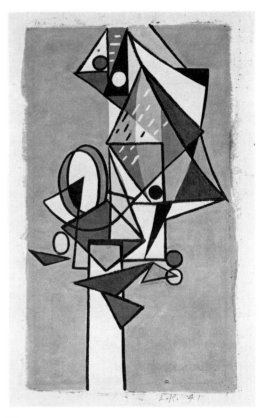

Fig. 33.
Untitled (Gouache #4). 1941.
Gouache on paper.
9¾ × 13⅜″ (24.8 × 34 cm).
Collection the artist.

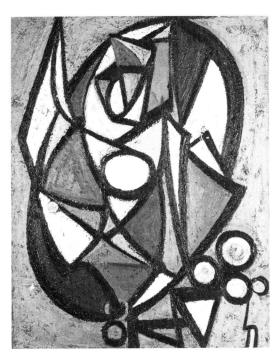

Fig. 34.
Untitled Still Life (Gray Ground).
c. late 1930s.
Oil on canvas.
29¾ × 24" (75.5 × 61 cm).
Private collection.

*Talk would vary. At one point we might be bellyaching
about some imposition the WPA forced on us. At another
time, it might be a completely aesthetic discussion—
whether we had just seen a new Picasso reproduction, and
it would take off on that. The discussion was mainly about
new French painting—a show or an article or a reproduction.*

By the late thirties, Picasso had become the new god of the
emergent New York School. The paintings by the Spanish
master acquired and exhibited by The Museum of Modern
Art, together with the arrival of *Guernica* in New York in
1939, had an enormous impact on virtually every member
of the American avant-garde. Lee Krasner was no exception. Although she appreciated the bold drawing of
Guernica, she rejected its brutal, deformed Expressionist
style, tempering her views with a continuing admiration
for Matisse's color and a growing allegiance to the disciplined rational classicism of Mondrian. The style of her
early Cubist paintings is certainly influenced by Picasso's
cloisonné Cubism of the twenties, which utilized thick
black lines to frame planes of color, but the flatness of
her space is related to the manner in which Mondrian
used his grid structure to diminish space behind the picture plane. Krasner did not confine herself to the primary
colors of Neo-Plasticism in most of these paintings, but
continued to mix her own odd palette of shades and tones
of both primary and secondary colors, as well as browns
and grays. Mondrian's grids, Picasso's cloisonné Cubism,
and possibly the steel armatures for stained-glass windows,
which she saw being made on the WPA, provide sources
for such remarkably forceful geometric paintings as *Blue
Square* (fig. 29).

 During the late thirties, Krasner was actively involved
in discussing art with two groups: her fellow students at
the Hofmann School, and her fellow artists in the WPA
like de Kooning, Gorky, Davis, and Reinhardt. Sometimes
they exchanged studio visits. One evening, in particular,
summed up the discouragement of the New York avant-
garde in the face of Picasso's monumental achievement.
Arshile Gorky called a meeting in de Kooning's studio.
Krasner remembers:

Gorky announced, "We must admit we are defeated." He

38

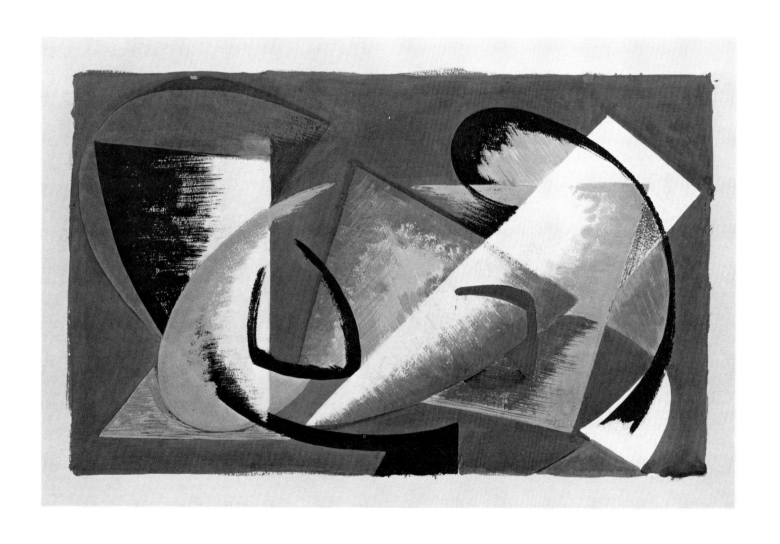

Fig. 35. *Gouache #5*. 1942. Gouache on paper. 10 × 15″ (25.4 × 38.1 cm). Collection the artist.

thought perhaps we would do better as a group than we could alone. Gorky suggested we work on a group painting. . . . When we asked, "What do you mean?" he said, "Well, here we are about six or seven of us and one person could draw better, another person has better ideas, another is better at color. What we have to do is sit and talk this over and come up with a thought. Then we'll all go home and do our separate things and bring them back and decide who should draw, who should paint, who should do color."

The collaboration was never realized. "We never got too far," Krasner recalls. "I don't think there was a second meeting." Krasner was more optimistic than Gorky regarding a point of departure for a new art in geometric abstraction. She joined the American Abstract Artists, a group that included a number of her fellow students from both the National Academy and the Hofmann School who were more interested in Mondrian than Picasso. The AAA members were all American Cubists, many of whom combined biomorphic with geometric shapes. Although Krasner painted some bright Expressionist gouaches during her years with Hofmann, she ultimately aligned herself with the pro-Mondrian faction, who worked in nonobjective geometric styles. This pro-Mondrian splinter group from the Hofmann School, including Holtzman and Krasner, Perle Fine, and Giorgio Cavallon, joined the "Park Avenue Cubists"—led by A. E. Gallatin and George L. K. Morris—to exhibit together under the name American Abstract Artists and to promote the cause of abstract art in the United States through educational lectures and publications.

The American Abstract Artists held annual public exhibitions of works by the minority of American painters and sculptors painting in abstract and nonobjective modes. Its criteria were fairly rigid with regard to what constituted "abstract" art. These were so rigid, in fact, that Gorky and de Kooning, initially interested in the group, walked out, rejecting the AAA's total denial of subject matter as overly dogmatic. A. E. Gallatin, a wealthy Cubist painter whose collection of School of Paris painting, The Museum of Living Art, was housed in New York University and regularly visited by modern artists, articulated the AAA position with regard to subject matter:

By completely eliminating all subject-matter, which was a necessity for the Old Masters, historical and documentary recorders as they were for the most part, and propagandists for the Church, such artists as Mondrian have purified painting, have given us painting for its own sake in the same sense that music exists for itself alone, as it is also possible for architecture.[36]

"Art for art's sake" was the credo of the American Abstract Artists, and at the time Lee Krasner subscribed to it. Unquestionably, exhibiting with like-minded artists gave younger painters like her the kind of moral support and sense of community they desperately needed. The works she showed in the three AAA exhibitions in which she took part in the early forties were all Cubist still lifes in the black-gridded cloisonné style. These were distinctly easel pictures painted and repainted until coats of subsequent revisions were built up into an almost relief-like texture. Their dense, airless quality was redeemed by the excitement of the physical gesture recorded in the swinging, looping circuit of black tracery bordering the flat planes of color. Already in these paintings, there is a hint of dissatisfaction with the static imagery of Neo-Plastic design, an aggressive, energetic attack on the canvas and a piling up of paint that indicate the direction New York School painting would take in a more romantic, open, calligraphic, painterly, and baroque style.

The stylistic battle, which would result in the emergence of a synthesis of Expressionism and abstraction, was already being fought in the late thirties. Those who stayed loyal to Mondrian's clean surfaces and precise hard edges, like Diller, Bolotowsky, and Fritz Glarner, would remain Neo-Plastic purists. On the other hand, Krasner, Cavallon, McNeil, and a few others, who intuited from Hofmann that impasto was not only tolerable but desirable, would develop freer, more painterly styles.

The AAA members admired Mondrian and invited him to join their group soon after he arrived in New York in 1940. Krasner met him at a party given by George L. K. Morris, president and founder of the group. Krasner and Mondrian shared an interest in boogie woogie. Sometimes they went dancing together. "He had a very strange staccato rhythm," she once observed. Mondrian saw a Cubist still life by Krasner at the annual American Abstract Art-

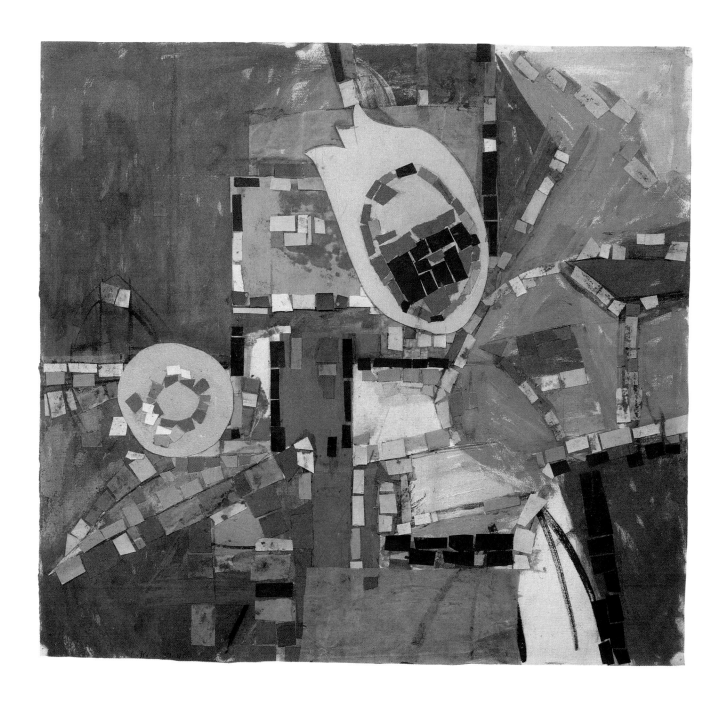

Fig. 36. *Mosaic Collage*. 1939–40. Collage on paper. 18 × 19½″ (47.7 × 49.5 cm). Collection the artist.

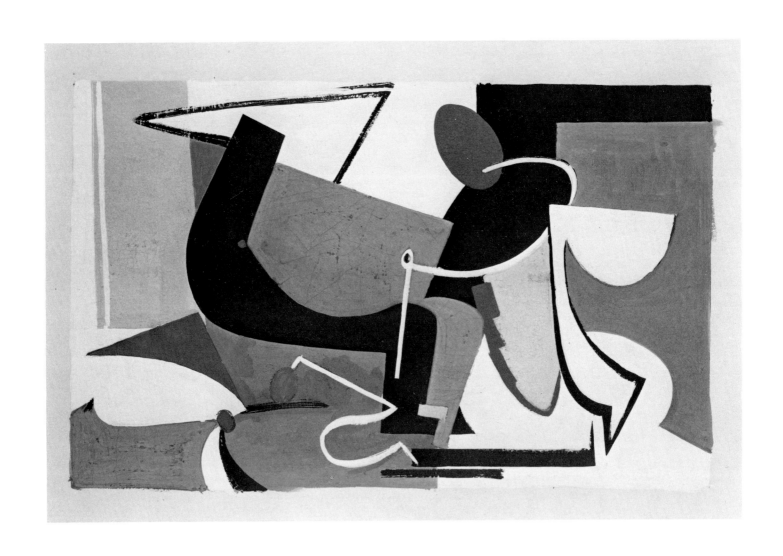

Fig. 37. *Gouache #4.* 1942. Gouache on paper. 10 × 15″ (25.4 × 38.1 cm). Collection the artist.

ists exhibition and complimented her on the strength of her own "inner rhythm," which he advised her never to lose. Mondrian's advice consolidated what she already knew from her training with Hofmann. The rhythmic, swinging quality of Krasner's drawing was already evident in the charcoal sketches she had produced in Hofmann's classes. Indeed, one of Hofmann's main points was that art had to express a definable rhythmic quality. Although the rhythm of Kandinsky's polyphonic Improvisations is different from the staccato beat of Mondrian's New York boogie woogie paintings or from Stuart Davis's Dixieland swing for that matter, the importance of the active, dynamic movement of rhythm to all these painters paralleled Krasner's own natural inclination to express strong, abstract rhythms in her painting. An excellent dancer, Krasner was conscious of the importance of the rhythmic quality of her drawings and paintings, which Mondrian was the first to comment on, as a constant of her work throughout her career.

Krasner's drawings, as well as gouaches and oils on paper of the late thirties—a moment when the other members of the New York School with the exception of Reinhardt, who was a geometric painter, were still representational artists—were thus both abstract and Expressionist. However, the drawings were more developed than the gouaches and oils in the direction of a genuinely gestural abstraction that records the rhythmic movements of the human body. Because they were executed on a relatively small scale, the gesture in Krasner's drawings is not that of the arm or the whole body, but the motion of the wrist passing rapidly over the page, recording the changing pressure of the hand applying the charcoal.

At about the time Krasner joined the AAA and met Mondrian, she executed a prophetic work, a "mosaic" collage (fig. 36). Mosaics were one of the medieval crafts like stained glass and jewelry-making being revived as part of the WPA's attempt to teach artists skills. Indeed, Pollock actually executed a mosaic on the WPA. Krasner's mosaic collage was not, strictly speaking, a study for a mosaic. The cardboard tesserae, painted in various shades of red and yellow, indicate she was acquainted with Mondrian's way of working at the time with tiny painted rectangles. However, the palette was closer to Matisse's than to Mondrian's, and the dominant motif was not geo-

metric but floral. The cut-out shape points toward Krasner's collage paintings of the mid-fifties, which would be directly influenced by Matisse's découpages. Indeed, this little-known unique work is Krasner's first collage painting. Her tendency to oppose warm and cool color creates a spatial tension, and her faultless sense of scale makes even this small work implicitly monumental. The variable saturation of color is exactly the opposite of Mondrian's uniformly opaque rectangles of primary colors. The date of this work, 1939–40, suggests that Krasner has reworked the original painting, which was a WPA assignment, to transform the work of painter Harry Bowden into a mosaic. It is typical of Krasner that she kept up a running critique of her paintings, reviewing them periodically to decide whether to sign, change, destroy, or cut them up for use as material for future works. At times, years would pass before she would rework a painting or recycle its contents in another form, which suggests a remarkable continuity of memory. Indeed, Krasner's grasp of dialectical thinking, which she had encountered in her reading of Karl Marx, was so thorough that she naturally subsumed the elements of her past and of preceding work within each successive stylistic synthesis. Krasner's capacity to keep intact the continuity of historical memory, the contact with a tradition that is transformed even as it is subsumed, is a major reason her work grows increasingly rich and complex while at the same time remaining extraordinarily fresh and contemporary.

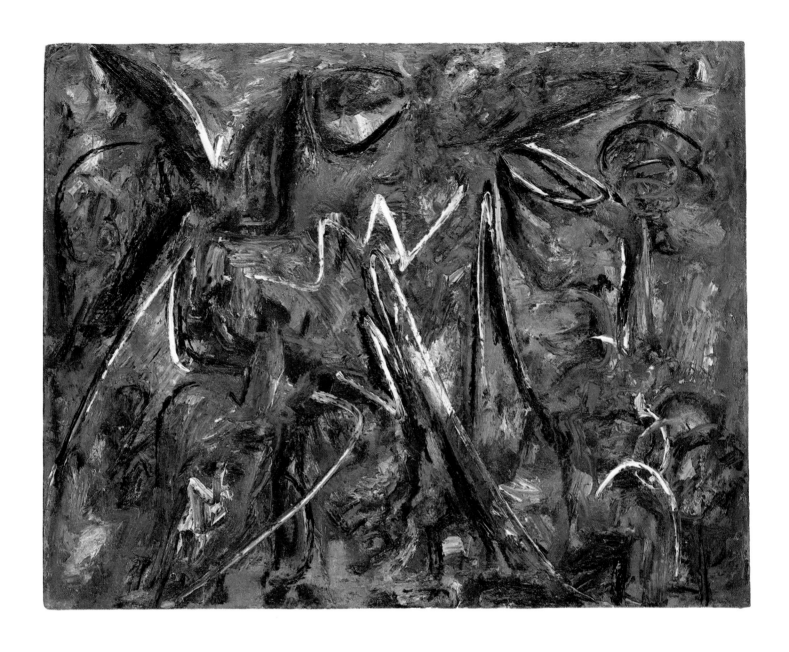

Fig. 38. *Blue Painting*. 1946. Oil on canvas. 28 × 26″ (71.1 × 66 cm). Private collection.

III. Search for the Real

Art opens access to the unconscious mind.

JOHN GRAHAM, *System and Dialectic of Art*, 1937

Although the WPA Federal Art Project became part of the War Services Office when the United States entered World War II, Lee Krasner was able to retain her job, becoming a supervisor of exhibits urging participation in the war effort. Sometimes these large poster photo-collages were exhibited in department store windows to attract attention to the war effort (fig. 39). Cutting and pasting these displays gave her yet another experience with the cutout shapes of collage. Moreover, these graphic designs suggested that several different types of material and image could be combined. This was a technique Krasner used in her painted paper collages and collage paintings a decade later.

Krasner had exhibited in several important shows by this time, including the AAA Annual; she was unquestionably well respected by her peers. Many members of the American Abstract Artists were women so her work was shown on an equal ground with that of her male counterparts. Krasner was living alone on Ninth Street now, very much part of the Village bohemian artists' and writers' community. One day, shortly before Pearl Harbor, she was taking a stroll when she spotted a friend, Greek-born painter Aristodemus Kaldis. He was accompanied by a small, dapper, bald man whom he introduced as John Graham. Scrutinizing Krasner, Graham deduced from the paint stains on her clothes and shoes that she was an artist. He immediately asked to see her work. Impressed by what he saw, he invited her to participate in an exhibition of French and American painters, to be held in January, 1942, at the McMillen Gallery.

John Graham was, like Igor Pantuhoff, another of the cultivated White Russians who played a large role in Krasner's life. She had already read Graham's book *System and Dialectics of Art* when it was published in 1937. Although many of his lapidary pronouncements remained mysterious to her, she was attracted to his views on primitive art, the unconscious, and automatic *écriture* or personal "handwriting" as the basis for modern art imagery. Graham's emphasis on psychological content and imagery and on technical experiment rather than exclusively formal concerns coincided with Krasner's growing criticism of the strictures of Hofmann's thinking. Graham held many novel views. One idea of consequence for Abstract Expressionism was that the barrenness and lack of ex-

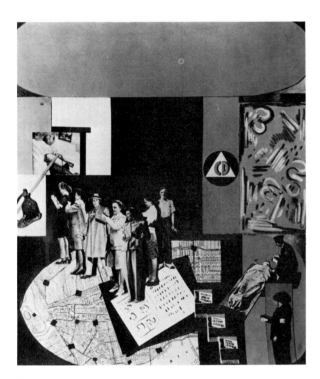

Fig. 39.
Photograph of lost window display.
c. 1942. Collage and mixed mediums.

pression of American art was a result of the puritanical Anglo-Saxon obsession with hygiene. In Graham's view, accidents should be cultivated, not avoided, and a dramatic, emotional painterly style was preferable to pristine surfaces and hard edges. To a large extent, Graham's influence, especially on painters like Gorky, de Kooning, Pollock, and Krasner, helped to point them in the direction of loose, gestural Expressionist painting styles.

For Krasner, Graham's liberating theories were an antidote to Hofmann's rigidity. One can see from her charcoal figure studies that she was anxious to invest line not only with space-creating potential, but also with an emotional and psychological content as well. She absorbed Hofmann's lessons, but she felt, even as his student, that there was more to say about art. In John Graham's ideas, she found what she felt Hofmann had missed. Hofmann taught that color was the basic means for communicating emotion; for Graham, on the other hand, *drawing* —which he defined as *écriture*, or automatic writing—was the record of physical gesture, hence the principal means of expression. Comparing Krasner's drawings of the late thirties with the Analytic Cubist compositions of Picasso and Mondrian that inspired them, one is struck by Krasner's greater emphasis on the physicality of gesture and her use of line as a dynamic trajectory moving and cutting through space as a dancer leaps across the stage (fig. 40). Krasner's superimposed transparent planes and controlled automatic drawing already reflect the influence of Graham on her work at this time (fig. 41).

Like the other first-generation Abstract Expressionists who were her contemporaries and friends, Krasner was never entirely satisfied with the Cubist emphasis on art as a purely objective and distanced aesthetic experience. Indeed, the New York School's romantic rebellion against Cubism was posited on a new view of painting as not primarily an object but a record on canvas of an experiential struggle that was both emotional and formal. Cubism had been an essentially classical style, presupposing an objective ideal, a resolution of relationships in a static equilibrium of rhythmic forms. This was a definition of art that the restless, romantic young Americans could not continue to accept.

John Graham's repeated insistence on the emotional expressiveness of the abstract gesture was the first formu-

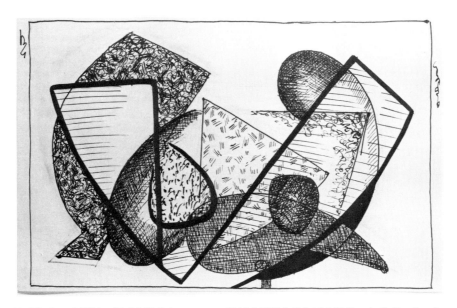

Fig. 40. *Black and White* #2. 1942. Ink on paper. 7¼ × 11¾″ (18.4 × 29.8 cm). Collection the artist.

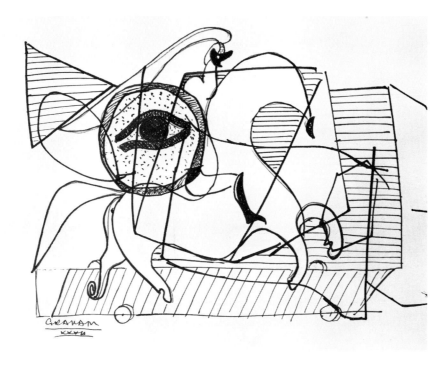

Fig. 41. John Graham. *Soldier on Horseback*. 1932. Pen and ink on paper. 8⅞ × 11⅞″ (22.5 × 30.2 cm). Private collection.

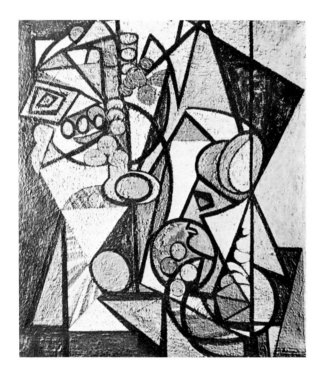

Fig. 42.
Untitled. 1941.
Oil on canvas.
40 × 36″ (101.6 × 91.4 cm) approx.
Whereabouts unknown.

lation of "action painting." In her figure drawings of the late thirties, Krasner had already begun to use gesture as an independent abstract element. Her variable and rhythmic line was a record of a specific physical event, not a representation of a given external object, the basis of realism. Inspired by Graham, Krasner took the step from abstracting from nature as Hofmann had taught her to do to conceiving of line as an autonomous abstract element. This was essentially the same process by means of which de Kooning and Kline arrived at abstract styles in 1950.

The painting Krasner showed in the 1942 McMillen Gallery exhibition (fig. 42) was a Picassoid abstraction. Other American painters in the show, such as Stuart Davis and Graham himself, also showed Cubist works largely indebted to Picasso. Although de Kooning was included, he exhibited a figurative painting. A painting entitled *Birth*, by one of the young Americans, selected by Graham to hang opposite Picasso, Matisse, and André Derain, was totally different in character from the rest. It was a raw, brutal, churning Expressionist image which fused the imagery of primitive art with that of Mexican mural painting. The title of the painting was appropriate to its generative imagery. *Birth* opposed the disciplined boundaries, right angles, and closed forms of Cubism with a swirling baroque composition of gyrating movement. Its passionate intensity was the opposite of the cold mechanical forms of abstract Cubism. Krasner immediately recognized the originality of *Birth*. The name of its author, Jackson Pollock, was new to her. Her reaction to genuine innovation was immediate: She got Pollock's address and knocked on the door of his studio on Eighth Street, only a block from her own. She recognized the balding Midwesterner who answered the door as a fellow painter she had once spurned at a WPA loft party. Now her excitement over his art was the overriding consideration.

Between 1937, the year she began studying with Hofmann, and 1945, the year she married Jackson Pollock, Krasner exhibited Cubist abstractions at nine major group shows. The first, "Pink Slips over Culture," was an exhibition held in 1937 to protest the firing of a number of artists (Krasner included) who had been working on the WPA. It was sponsored by the Artists Union and the Citizens Committee for Support of the WPA and took place at the ACA Gallery in New York. Krasner was one of its organizers. In 1940, after joining the American Abstract Artists, she exhibited in the "First Annual Exhibition of the American Modern Artists" at the Riverside Museum. The following year, she showed in the "Fifth Annual Exhibition of the American Abstract Artists" at the Riverside Museum, and in "Abstract Painting," organized by the WPA, which traveled all over the United States.

In early 1942, as we have seen, she exhibited a Cubist abstraction in John Graham's historic group show of French and American paintings. Later that year she showed another Cubist abstraction in the "Sixth Annual Exhibition of the American Abstract Artists" held at the Fine Arts Gallery. She also exhibited in the AAA Annual in 1943. In 1944, she participated in the exhibition "Abstract and Surrealist Art in America" at the Mortimer Brandt Gallery. The exhibition was based on the Harriet and Sidney Janis book bearing that title, published the year before World War II ended. Krasner's heavily impastoed Cubist abstraction, illustrated on a full page of the book, made a freer use of geometry than she had previously been willing to permit (fig. 43). With its anthropomorphic configuration, it appears to be a continuation of Krasner's gradual transformation of the figure into an abstraction. Bolder, denser, and more activated than the works of the Constructivists, it nevertheless still has its point of departure in nature. Now, however, the hybridized forms suggest a human-bird *personnage* rather than the typical mechanical Cubist abstraction from the figure. All Krasner's extant paintings of this period have obviously been reworked many times, to the point that a simply clear image emerges. The record of the struggle to find form has been effaced. This is a clarity Krasner would shortly sacrifice in the interest of a more open, painterly, and spontaneous style.

Although it is popularly supposed that Krasner stopped painting and devoted herself solely to her relationship with Pollock, we find ample evidence that she continued to work and to exhibit in the early forties. In a photograph of the Eighth Street studio they shared, taken about this time, Jackson Pollock is seen surrounded not only by his paintings, but by those of Krasner as well.[37] Although the snapshot is too dim to make out which works of hers were on the walls, we may assume they were the heavily impastoed, black-gridded Cubist figure paintings that were becoming more and more like *personnages* re-

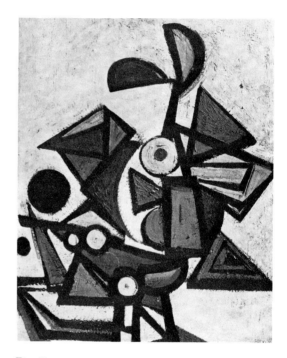

Fig. 43.
Composition. 1943.
Oil on canvas.
30 × 24" (76.2 × 61 cm).
Collection the artist.

sembling the illustration in the Janises' book. When it was published in 1944, *Abstract and Surrealist Art in America* was a very daring study. It attempted an encyclopedic roundup of advanced art in New York at the time. The division of avant-garde American art into two categories, abstract and surreal, was based on a distinction made between works that were figurative, i.e., abstracted from nature and to varying degrees representational (Davis, Graham, Hofmann, de Kooning, Krasner, and Robert Motherwell were placed in this category, which was extended so far as to include the entirely nonobjective abstractions of Reinhardt) and those that were sprung from the mind (Pollock was thus placed with the Surrealists). "It is evident," Harriet and Sidney Janis wrote, "that in the recent past the tendency has been away from pure geometric art." They were right about the New York School in general, although Mondrian's most faithful disciples among the American Abstract Artists remained Constructivists throughout their lives. They were especially right about Lee Krasner, who began to a greater and greater degree to employ spontaneous gesture in works no longer based on abstraction from nature, but on forms spontaneously generated by the artist's imagination. Undoubtedly, her style changed as a result of her encounter with Pollock, as well as her continuing relationship with Graham, who admired and recognized her art at the same time he identified Gorky, David Smith, de Kooning, and Pollock as the young Americans whose art was good enough to challenge the School of Paris.

The effect of Pollock's art on Krasner was to cause her to question everything she was doing. She had just finished a painting in a freer, more painterly style that challenged Cubism (fig. 44). She was unsure of where to go next. From 1942 to 1945, Krasner shared Pollock's Eighth Street studio. It had always been set up for two artists, so when Pollock's brother Sanford moved out, it was convenient for Krasner to use his space. It was one of the most productive periods in Pollock's life and one of the least in Krasner's. Legend has it that she permitted him to drain her, pouring her own energy and ideas into his art and career. It is more accurate to say that in the early forties, Krasner took the advice Hofmann had passed on from Matisse: "Study the reigning master." For a decade she had apprenticed herself to Matisse, Picasso, and Mondrian. Now, the first to recognize Pollock as the new "reigning master," she tried to understand the new post-Cubist style he was creating. The matter is complicated by the fact that Krasner was going into an artistic crisis at precisely the moment that Pollock had found a way to move beyond Cubism into a more dramatic, symbolic, and physically expressive art. She felt obliged, as she puts it, to "get rid of Hofmann, get rid of Cubism." However, she also had to do it on her own terms, and at her own pace. While Pollock turned out his great early figurative work, Krasner scraped down her paintings, working and reworking them until, she recalls, they were nothing but "gray slabs." At a later date, these slabs might have been acclaimed as the precursors of what John Graham was the first to term "minimal art."[38] At the time, they depressed Krasner. She saw Pollock using his unconscious as a source for potent psychologically charged imagery based on what Carl Jung had called universal myth and metaphor. She, too, was interested in Jung and had read *The Psychology of the Integration of Personality* before she met Pollock, but she was perhaps too well grounded within an academic tradition to let go of "reality" so completely.

As much as Krasner searched for some new form to evolve from the sludge, she could accept nothing that was happening in her studio until 1945, when she painted *Image Surfacing* (fig. 45). In this predominantly pink, white, and blue work, a protean *personnage* begins to emerge from primordial gray slime—a metaphor for artistic creation. This painting is closely related to the untitled *Composition* of 1943 that the Janises chose to illustrate their book. In *Image Surfacing*, Krasner has already begun to use the background as an active rather than a passive element, brushing white into shapes as she erased out areas in her charcoal drawings. This leveling of distinction between foreground and background interlocked the two on the plane of the picture. This approach became a characteristic of the New York School not found in Cubism. These images, pushed up against the picture plane, had more of the "closeup" look of Mondrian's flat rectangles, which filled and divided the field. Rather than being depicted, as in conventional representational art, as shapes silhouetted against a background, indicating a plane or planes behind the picture plane, New York School pictures like Krasner's had a more dramatic and imme-

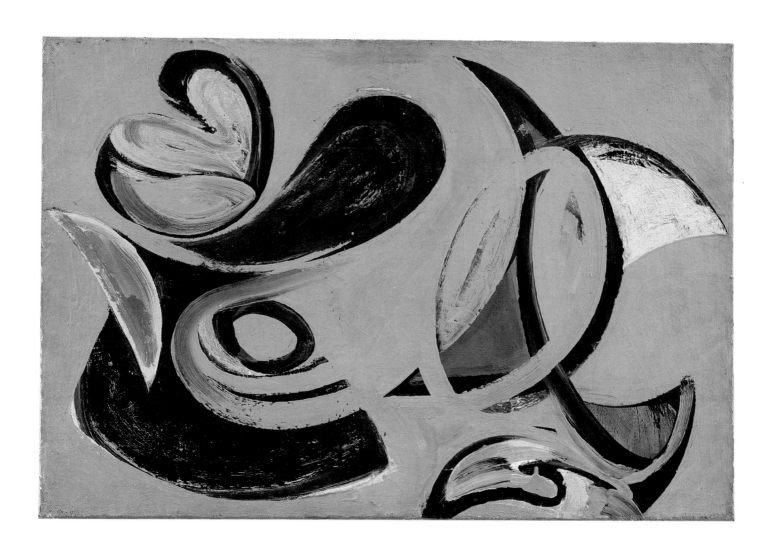

Fig. 44. *Igor*. 1943. Oil on canvas. 18 × 24⅞″ (45.7 × 63.2 cm). Collection the artist.

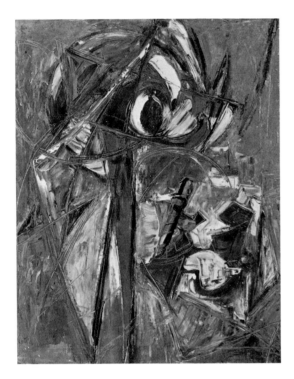

Fig. 45.
Image Surfacing. 1945.
Oil on linen.
27 × 21¼″ (68.6 × 54 cm).
Collection the artist.

diate impact. Her early commitment to locating the image *on* the plane, and not behind it, indicates how advanced her style was before she met Pollock.

During the early years of her relationship with Pollock, which was always based on aesthetic dialogue, Krasner tried to interest him in Mondrian and Matisse, the gods she had learned to worship through Hofmann. Her allegiance to Mondrian's strict grid contrasted with Pollock's interest in Miró's and Kandinsky's improvisational styles. Their different sources explain to a great extent the divergence of their styles in the forties. The early forties were also the years that Pollock received his initial notoriety as the star of Peggy Guggenheim's Art of This Century Gallery, which he joined in 1943. The gallery and Miss Guggenheim herself were dominated by the tastes of the "Surrealists-in-exile," as the group of artists who fled Europe with poet André Breton to take up residence in New York were called. Krasner was still acknowledged as a foremost avant-garde New York artist. However, after 1945, Krasner did not exhibit in New York again until 1951. Certainly, the misogyny the Surrealists passed on to the New York School did not help her.

By her own admission, Peggy Guggenheim had no use for women. "I prefer the company of homosexuals," Miss Guggenheim wrote in her autobiography, *Art of This Century*. She and Krasner tolerated each other, but barely. When Krasner and Pollock decided to marry in 1945 and invited her to be a witness, she declined on the basis that she had a luncheon date. After Howard Putzel, Miss Guggenheim's secretary, who is credited with making many of her decisions, opened his own gallery in 1945, he invited Krasner to participate in the opening show, "A Challenge to the Critics." Putzel's sudden death later that year deprived Krasner of a close friend and supporter.

Krasner was treated with contempt by many who may have been jealous of her exclusive intimacy with the difficult, introspective master. On a visit to Pollock's studio, Peggy Guggenheim exclaimed with irritation: "Who is this L.K.? I did not come to see L.K.'s paintings!" When Miss Guggenheim finally asked Krasner to exhibit a work in a minor group show of all women artists, Krasner considered it an insult and refused to participate.

Most difficult of all for Krasner was the condescending attitude of the Surrealists toward women, which began to rub off on the members of the New York School. Krasner thought the Surrealists treated women as objects, dressing up their wives and showing them off as prize poodles. She also considered their conception of eroticism perverse and hostile to women. Recent studies have proved her intuition correct. We have already seen how Hofmann instilled in his students antagonism toward Surrealism; we can imagine how this antagonism was exacerbated into outright hostility toward any Surrealist idea on Krasner's part. Since the thirties, Pollock had been using automatic drawing as a way of eliciting imagery from his unconscious. He had also been experimenting with automatic techniques at the workshop of David Alfaro Siquieros. Krasner, on the other hand, distrustful of anything related to the Surrealists, undoubtedly inhibited her own development in the forties by refusing to emulate any process or imagery she associated with them. There is no question that living with Pollock she was well acquainted with both; thus, one must conclude, her rejection of full-scale automatism at this time was related to her general disdain for the Surrealists because of their well-documented misogyny.

In the spring of 1945, Krasner and Pollock moved from Manhattan to Springs, East Hampton, Long Island. The move was Krasner's idea: She thought Pollock would be less agitated and drink less in the peaceful countryside. She was right. Once they had cleaned up the Springs farmhouse to the point where it was habitable, Pollock began painting in the upstairs bedroom. There he painted his first canvas done on the floor, *The Key*, in 1946. In the spring of 1947, he moved his studio to the barn they had renovated next to the house. Krasner began using the bedroom as her studio. Clearly, she could have painted works as large as *The Key*, a horizontal picture about six by seven feet, but she did not choose to. Instead, she confined herself to the format of small easel paintings. Between 1946 and 1949, she painted three significant cycles of works. She refers to them as her Little Image paintings. Curiously, they are much tighter and more controlled than the few works that immediately preceded them, such as *Igor*, *Image Surfacing*, and *Blue Painting*.

Blue Painting (fig. 38) was probably the first painting Krasner made in Springs. It developed naturally from *Igor* and *Image Surfacing* and points toward a fully improvisational style of "action painting." However, it

appears Krasner was not yet ready to give up the secure, rational, logical structure of the grid. Consequently she did not pursue the implication of *Blue Painting* at this time. Because there was no public context for her work—she showed it only to Pollock and a few close artist friends like Bradley Walker Tomlin—she was deprived of the feedback a painter needs to confirm the pursuit of a new direction. Pollock counted heavily on Krasner's eye, sometimes asking her if what he was doing was a painting. After her first approval, however, he had the opportunity to place his work in the world, to have it seen by other artists, critics, museum people, and collectors. Krasner, on the other hand, worked in virtually total isolation, except for her dialogue with Pollock, throughout the forties and early fifties.

By the spring of 1946, the working and living situations in Springs were sufficiently well organized for both Krasner and Pollock to become highly productive. Heating remained a problem that determined how much and what kind of work could be done since the house was heated only downstairs with wood fires and a coal stove, and the barn was so poorly warmed by a kerosene stove that Pollock could not work there during the coldest days of winter. Pollock was painting upstairs in the bedroom, preparing for his third show to take place in April, 1946, at Art of This Century. The eleven oils he showed were all figurative works in which the brush was used to draw in color on canvas. During that summer he painted the series known as Sounds in the Grass. In the course of painting this series, Pollock became involved for the first time with the problem of allover composition, which he eventually resolved in a radically new fashion in his poured paintings.

Krasner was engaged in concerns close to Pollock's by this time. She had begun to paint regularly again and to synthesize her dual concerns with color and structure in completely abstract works. Here it is important to note that one of the essential lessons Krasner learned from Pollock was how to leave behind the motif and to work in a strictly nonobjective way, without using a model. Her struggle to forget everything she had learned from Hofmann about working only *devant le motif*, i.e., from the model and nature, and to look within her own imagination rather than to the external world for inspiration had at last

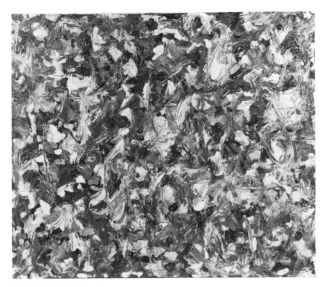

Fig. 46.
Night Life (first version). 1947.
Oil on linen.
20¼ × 24″ (51.4 × 60.9 cm).
Private collection.

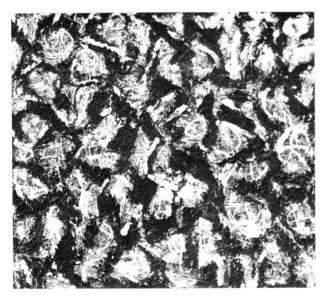

Fig. 47.
Abstract #2. 1946–48.
Oil on canvas.
20½ × 23¼″ (52.1 × 59 cm).
Collection the artist.

been won. Accepting the transcendence of the "reality" of painting over that of the world of actual forms, she embarked on a new direction that no longer depended on abstracting from nature or the model.

In 1946, both Krasner and Pollock began to be preoccupied with allover compositions as a way to break with the structure of Cubist composition. William Rubin has pointed out that one of the sources of Pollock's allover compositions were Mondrian's plus-and-minus paintings and drawings, in which forms were dispersed across a surface in a regular rhythmic pattern. Krasner had clearly succeeded in drawing Pollock's attention to Mondrian, whose work continued to play an important role in her own thought in the late forties (fig. 57). The three series of Little Image paintings—mosaic (divisionist), webbed, and grid (hieroglyph)—Krasner executed in the late forties are different solutions to the problem of allover composition. They differ considerably from Pollock's interpretation. They remain tied to the easel painting tradition Pollock was in the process of rejecting and revising in favor of largescale environmental works he described as "somewhere between the easel and the mural." Although Pollock surely invented a new kind of allover composition, it appears likely he first became interested in the conception of the allover as a result of Krasner's divisionist preoccupation with splintering, fracturing, and dispersing color across the whole field of the canvas in her first Little Image paintings like *Noon* painted in 1946 (fig. 48).

At this point Krasner's firm anchoring within the mainstream of modernist painting became as much a limitation as it was an advantage. The type of alloverness she achieves in her first Little Image paintings is related both spatially and structurally to the mosaic-like *taches* of color that make up the forms of Neo-Impressionist painting. The atomized spots of color are enlarged, and the image is carried forward to be located on the plane of the picture. The brilliant sparkle of interacting hues is more dramatic than that of Neo-Impressionism, referring to reflective mosaics and stained-glass colors (figs. 46, 47, 49, 50, 51). The strokes are large and bold and the impasto thick and opaque. No shapes are depicted, and the image is unquestionably thoroughly abstract, but the rhythmic regularity, size of the brushstrokes, absolute frontality of the image with its decisive single orientation, and shallowness of the

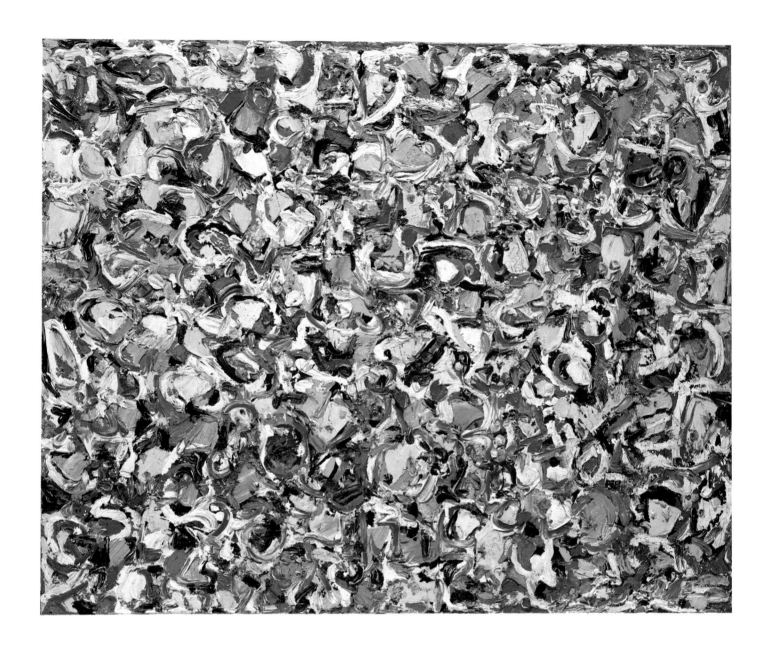

Fig. 48. *Noon*. 1946. Oil on linen. 24 × 30″ (76.2 × 60.9 cm). Collection the artist.

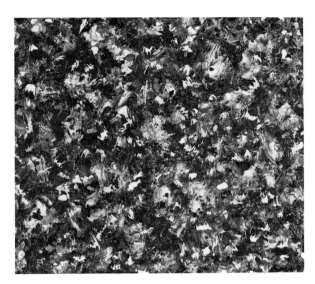

Fig. 49.
Night Life (second version). 1947.
Oil on linen.
20¼ × 24″ (51.4 × 60.9 cm).
Collection the artist.

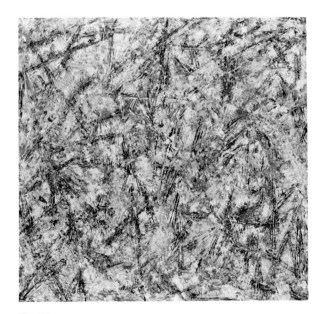

Fig. 50.
Untitled (Little Image). 1946.
Oil on linen.
27¾ × 30¼″ (70.5 × 76.8 cm).
Whereabouts unknown.

space of these luminous paintings have their roots in Post-Impressionism. Pollock's allover paintings, on the other hand, introduce new elements not found in earlier modern art. Toward the end of 1946, Pollock began to pour and trickle paint directly onto the unstretched canvas surface. The kind of alloverness he produced in this manner, although it treated the canvas as a single unified field, had a degree of irregularity and indeterminate space suggesting a metaphysical infinity rather than any physically measurable space.

Early in 1947, as soon as the weather was warm enough, Pollock began to work in the barn, producing a steady stream of his "classic" drip paintings: the pulsating, webbed images for which he is best known. Krasner, too, began to drip paint in her second series of Little Image paintings, executed in 1947–49. Pollock poured paint from the can as well as from sticks and brushes. Krasner was more cautious and continued to use a brush, working close to the surface of the painting, permitting the accidental effect to occur, but always within a context of an iron discipline (figs. 52, 55).

It has been suggested that Krasner was inhibited in her evolution as an "action" painter because her studio was the small bedroom, not the large barn; however, as we have seen, she could easily have worked on the floor on the bedroom studio and painted a picture as large as *The Key*. The decision to continue to work small and retain maximum control was her own; she was not yet psychologically free enough to let go of both the model and the sense of architectonic structure that was the legacy of Cubism.

In the second series of Little Image paintings, Krasner emphasizes the calligraphic elements one also recognizes in the subtle paintings of Reinhardt and Richard Pousette-Dart in the forties, and in the way that Tomlin, a house guest of Krasner and Pollock, accommodated allover painting to a Cubist grid structure. Both Krasner and Pollock, like Reinhardt, Tomlin, Adolph Gottlieb, Kline, and Motherwell, were interested in calligraphy and picture writing. Mark Tobey exhibited his "white writing" paintings based on Oriental calligraphy in New York at the Willard Gallery in the mid-forties. However, John Graham's idea of automatic *écriture* was a more likely source for Krasner and Pollock's fascination with translating auto-

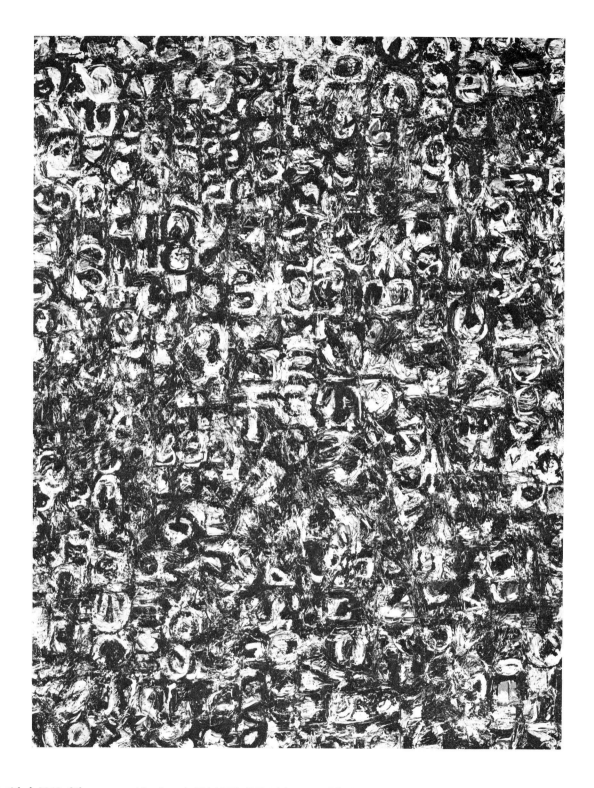

Fig. 51. Untitled. 1949. Oil on composition board. 48 × 37″ (121.9 × 94 cm). The Museum of Modern Art. New York. Gift of Alfonso A. Ossorio.

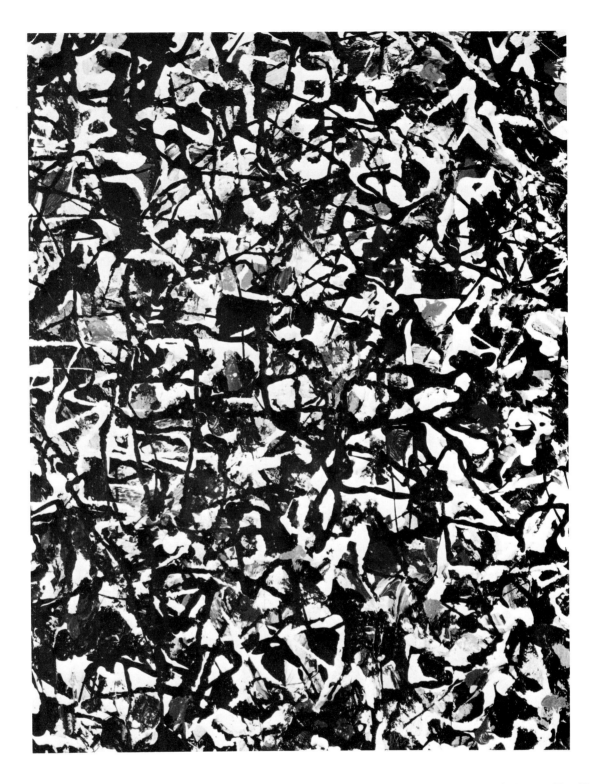

Fig. 52. *Continuum*. 1949. Oil and enamel on canvas. 54½ × 43⅞″ (138.4 × 111.4 cm). Collection Alfonso A. Ossorio, East Hampton.

matic drawing into paint in order to create a style as personal and subjective as handwriting. Indeed, Krasner and Pollock had begun to see Graham again in the late forties when he, too, moved to Southampton.

Krasner's dripped Little Image paintings are layered like Pollock's webs; however, because the dripping covers a smaller surface, there is little space or sense of layering (figs. 52, 55). Once again, the entire image, made up of densely woven strands and threads of paint, seems to be located on the picture plane. Infinity is hinted at in the sense that there is no beginning or end to Krasner's labyrinthine images, but they do not match the space of Pollock's big poured paintings, which has been referred to as "cosmic." There is a delicacy and filigree-like quality in the art of both artists in the late forties. The dense, resistant surface Krasner patiently builds up with her continuous overlays of patterning and dripping until they form an almost relief-like crust of impasto once again recalls Mondrian's late work.

The final series of Little Image paintings, based on hieroglyphics and ancient picture writing exhibit a new sense of authority and self-confidence that would permit her to begin painting in a far bolder and original way in the fifties (figs. 53, 54, 56).

Although Krasner's Little Image paintings are unquestionably nonobjective works, they hint at a dimension of metaphor. Krasner's metaphor is not at this point the human unconscious but the beauty of the structures of nature. The "webbed" series reminds one of stalactites and stalagmites. There is a quality of the crystalline about her Little Image paintings. Indeed, she has a collection of shells, crystals, and natural forms that have always interested her. Her experience in drawing *forminifera* should also be remembered in this context. It should be pointed out as well that the forties were a period when the New York School was much taken with D'Arcy Thompson's book *Growth and Form*, a discussion of the nature of organic growth in cells, tissues, and membranes. There is, for example, an entire chapter on spirals in *forminifera*. If we inspect Krasner's third series of Little Image paintings in which images are compartmentalized, we can detect such spirals. This series, like the flecked Neo-Impressionist and webbed series, had a fundamentally allover structure around a single dominant focus. This last series of Little

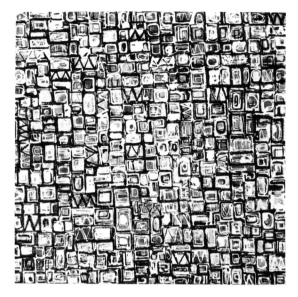

Fig. 53.
Untitled. c. 1949.
Oil on canvas.
32 × 33″ (82.1 × 84.7 cm).
Whereabouts unknown.

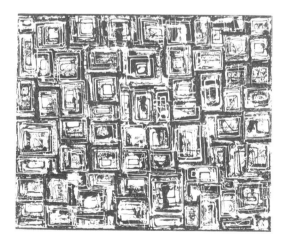

Fig. 54.
Black and White Squares #1. c. 1948.
Oil and enamel on linen.
24½ × 30″ (62.2 × 76.2 cm).
Collection Edward F. Dragon, East Hampton.

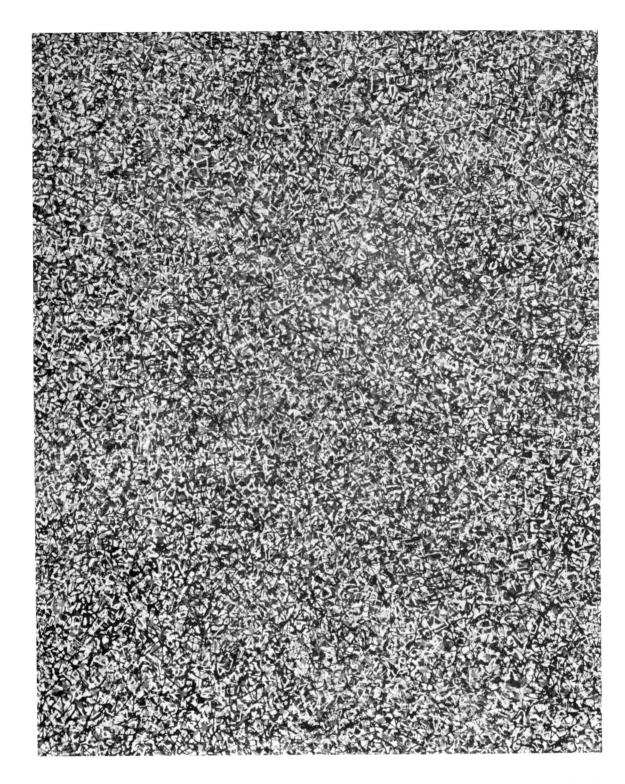

Fig. 55. *Continuum*. 1947–49. Oil and enamel on canvas. 53 × 42″ (134.6 × 106.7 cm). Collection Alfonso A. Ossorio, East Hampton.

Image paintings is characterized by a compartmentalized grid structure. Within her grid, she has inscribed hieroglyphic-like signs (figs. 53, 56), which reflect the picture writing of the Uruguayan painter Joaquín Torres-García, whose pictographs influenced Gottlieb's works of the forties. Whereas both Torres-García and Gottlieb include actual images like fish or eyes in their compartments, Krasner prefers a more ambiguous allusion to ancient script that can neither be confused with rebuses nor literally interpreted.

Apparently, the hieroglyphic Little Images, which once again strongly recall Mondrian's gridded compartments, evolved from Krasner's experience of making a mosaic table during the winter of 1947 (fig. 58). Because it was too cold to work in the bedroom, Pollock, who wished Krasner to keep working, suggested that she use the fragments of cut-up colored glass left over from his WPA mosaic and make a mosaic. This work could be done downstairs near the stove. They brought in two old wagon wheels they had found when the barn was cleaned out and moved from its position behind the house, where it had obscured the view of the marshes and pond. Using the wheels as armatures, Krasner made two mosaic tables, into which she set, along with tesserae, pieces of broken colored glass bottles she saved, old coins, jewelry, and personal memorabilia. The experiment of mixing mediums was a precedent for the collage paintings she would shortly undertake.

The process of setting the tesserae into plaster suggested the possibility for compartmentalizing color. After she had finished the tables, she used the masonite circle on which she had worked as a surface to paint on. The result was *Stop and Go*, the only tondo she ever painted. Apparently, it was also the first of the hieroglyphic Little Images (fig. 59). Krasner preferred a resistant surface on which to work; besides using masonite and pressed wood as supports for a number of her paintings of this period, she also continued to work on stretched canvases or canvas attached to the hard surface of the wall, as opposed to following Pollock's example of working on the floor. For this reason, even her biggest paintings have a specific orientation because they have been worked on from a vertical standing position.

As the Little Image paintings progressed, the black tracery, recalling the thick black drawing in her Cubist

Fig. 56.
Untitled. 1949.
Oil on canvas.
24 × 48″ (62 × 121.9 cm).
Private collection.

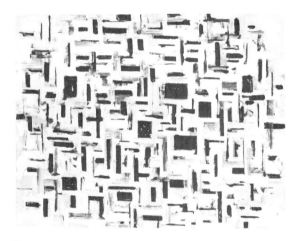

Fig. 57.
Untitled. 1948.
Gouache on paper.
22½ × 30″ (57.1 × 76.2 cm).
Collection the artist.

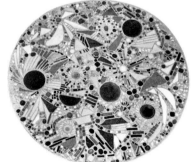

Fig. 58.
Mosaic Table. 1947.
Mosaic and mixed mediums.
48½″ (123.2 cm) diameter.
Collection the artist.

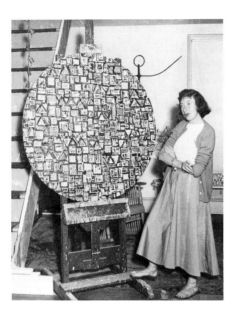

Fig. 59.
Lee Krasner with *Stop and Go*, c. 1949.

works, began to be equal in importance to what it contained. In one of the last, if not *the* last, of the Little Image paintings, the black drawing begins to take precedence over the white field (fig. 60). Gradually, the tracery is enlarged into angular gesture as in *Gothic Frieze* (fig. 61); it becomes looser and more gestural as in *Ochre Rhythm* (fig. 65). Both these works were probably started in 1950, a critical year for Krasner, during which she tried out and rejected a number of styles, destroying most of the work she produced.

The Little Image paintings are Krasner's closest approximation to a thoroughly nonobjective art. What is contained in each chambered compartment is as variable as the forms of nature; nevertheless, the ordering process seems to take precedence over spontaneity and accident, which are fully controlled. Krasner was only able to give up control, or to put it more bluntly, to be pushed to lose control by a real-life accident that shattered her life and left her with nothing but her art to live for.

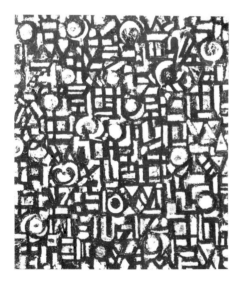

Fig. 60.
Untitled (Little Image). 1949.
Oil on linen.
38 × 38⅛″ (96.5 × 96.8 cm).
Collection the artist.

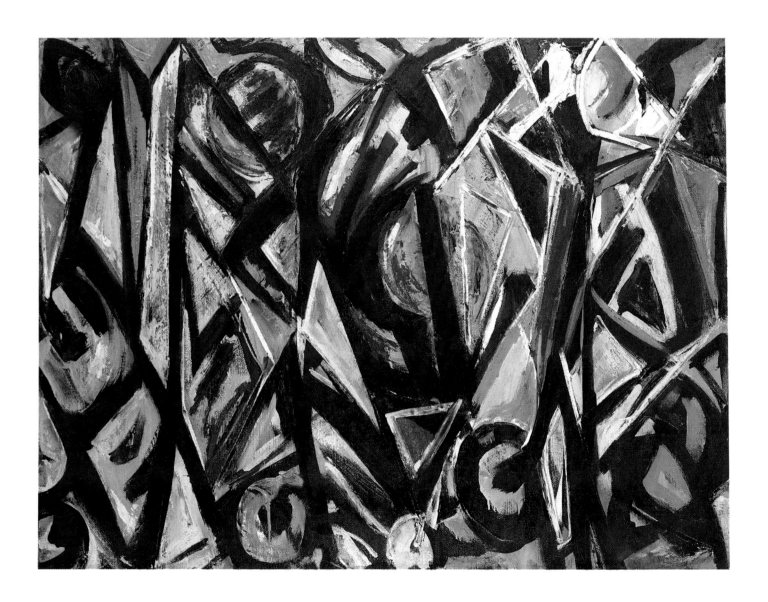

Fig. 61. *Gothic Frieze.* c. 1950. Oil on masonite. 36 × 48″ (91.4 × 121.9 cm). Collection Gordon F. Hampton, Los Angeles.

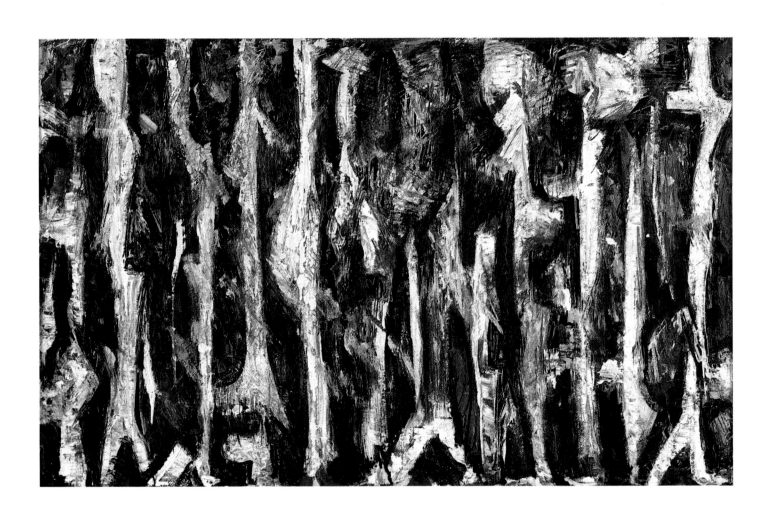

Fig. 62. *Promenade*. 1947. Oil on masonite. 30 × 48″ (76.2 × 121.9 cm). Courtesy Robert Miller Gallery, New York.

IV. Year of Decision: 1950

During the spring of 1947, Krasner and Pollock were taken by critic Clement Greenberg to see paintings by Joan Miró in a private collection in East Hampton. Pollock had been fascinated by Miró for some years, and had met him briefly at Stanley William Hayter's printmaking workshop Atelier 17.[39] Greenberg became so interested in Miró that he published a monograph on the Catalan artist later that year. Krasner does not consciously recall Miró as an influence on her work, but her willingness to use a variety of materials, including masonite and pressed wood, and her emphasis on the literal character of the support reflect a knowledge of Miró. Indeed, Krasner's 1954–55 collage paintings are hard to imagine without the precedent of Miró's experiments with unconventional support materials.

Krasner was highly conscious of the physical properties of both surface and support, and deliberately called attention to them. Many of the Little Image paintings were done on hard supports like masonite or pressed wood. There is an extreme spatial tension in these works, as if Krasner had stretched the image so tightly across that the surface was more like a wall than a canvas. The quality of this taut surface was in keeping with the acute degree of surface tension Krasner normally maintains even in her largest paintings. Her tough, tense surfaces communicate an active resistance that is intrinsic to her stance and expression as an artist.

Unquestionably, Miró affected Pollock's conception of the relationship of pigment to support at a decisive moment when he began pouring paint directly onto the canvas support, calling attention to the real identity of canvas as cloth. Krasner's awareness of the possibility of creating a new kind of optical illusionism by altering the relationship between the hard support and the liquid mediums or, in the case of her later collage paintings, the materials affixed to the support may also be traced to the influence of Miró. Sometime between 1947 and 1950, Krasner painted a unique painting unrelated to her abstract imagery, which also suggests she had Miró on her mind. *Promenade*, a horizontal frieze of interlocking *personnages*, is painted, like some of the hieroglyphic Little Image paintings, in oil on masonite (fig. 62). In *Promenade*, Krasner chose to emphasize the character of the support in a manner prefiguring her later work by painting on the rough, textured grainy side of the masonite as opposed to its smooth surface. The partial exposure of the ground also recalls Miró's paintings and the elongated stick-figure parade brings to mind Miró's gangly *personnages* of his *peintures sauvages* period.

Krasner had seen these paintings, both in the 1941 Miró retrospective as well as in Miró's regular exhibitions at the Pierre Matisse Gallery. Miró's considerable influence on the New York School was the antidote in many respects to the rigid structure and extremely shallow space of Mondrian. Miró's emphasis on the literal qualities of the support went far beyond Matisse's revelation of the canvas ground behind his transparent washes of color. Miró posed a deliberate conceptual challenge to Cubist space and offered the New York School an alternative to both Mondrian and Matisse.

The evolution of a post-Cubist space, which Pollock was the first to realize fully in his poured paintings, is the distinguishing stylistic characteristic of the first-generation Abstract Expressionists. This—not their presence in the 1951 photograph of the "Irascibles"—is what defines the group. The creation of this space and of a nonhierarchical structuring identifying the whole image with the entire pictorial field are the major innovations in painting since Cubism. This type of indeterminate "optical" space permitted a high degree of illusionism not related to the sculptural illusionism of representational art, which lingers on even in Cubism. Because her training in Cubism was the most thorough of that of any of the Abstract Expressionists outside of Reinhardt, Krasner's path to a post-Cubist style was particularly difficult. She understood Cubism too well to counter it with any naïve form of abstraction that rejected its conventions through ignorance of them. In this sense, her dilemma was once again related to Reinhardt's problem in opposing Cubism, although the two arrived at distinctly different solutions regarding a post-Cubist style.

Searching for a style more fully purged of Cubist elements than the Little Image paintings, Krasner found herself in 1950 torn by her dual allegiances to Mondrian and Matisse. Always a disciplined artist, she was now determined to give color a structure, not to use it arbitrarily, but as a means to create space and tension. She was also involved at the time in attempting to find a kind of imagery suitable for "action painting" that would relate to her own concerns with nature and the body, the two

subjects she had painted all her life. Nineteen-fifty was the year of decision for many other New York School painters as well: It was the year de Kooning, Kline, Philip Guston, and Jack Tworkov among others became abstract artists. There was a growing sense of power and urgency in the emerging avant-garde. Unquestionably, Krasner felt part of this urgency, if only on the periphery because of the lack of other women in the movement and because she was treated as an artist's wife as opposed to an artist. Yet Krasner had been a fully abstract painter since 1937 and a nonobjective artist since 1943. Her few surviving paintings of the mid-forties such as *Igor, Image Surfacing*, and *Blue Painting* employ automatic drawing. However, she was thinking of John Graham's conception of personal *écriture* and not of the type of automatism, or "doodling," as Robert Motherwell termed it, associated with Surrealist experiments. Indeed, Krasner was always far too conscious to doodle; on the other hand, she had always been fascinated, like Reinhardt who also disdained Surrealist automatism, with calligraphy.

We have seen how the last series of Little Image paintings, the so-called hieroglyphs, allude to ancient scripts that imply meaning, but are not necessarily decipherable. The phasing out of the atomized, compartmentalized Little Image was part of her search for a genuinely post-Cubist style. However, her problem was the opposite of that of the other members of the New York School. Abstraction, not representation, was her native tongue; now she wished to speak a more complex language that included psychological content. Her deep-rooted aversion to Surrealism, created both by Hofmann's training as well as by her own experience of Surrealist misogyny, was the major obstacle to her liberation from Cubism. By this time, she respected the unconscious as a source of psychological content, but she was not yet prepared to expose the contents of her psyche to public scrutiny. She did feel, though, that she had to take chances and break new ground, pushing herself to become more spontaneous and free, both in subject matter as well as form.

During the summer of 1950, while Pollock was still painting abstractly, Krasner experimented with automatic drawing in a quasi-figurative style. Ultimately, she rejected these works and opted once again for abstraction, aligning herself briefly in 1951 with the color-field paint-

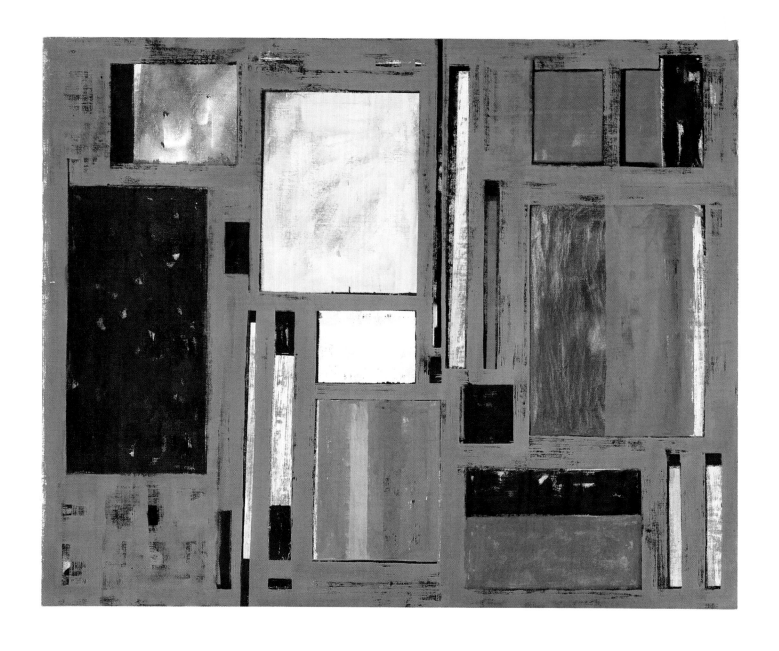

Fig. 63. *Equilibrium. c.* 1951–53. Oil on canvas. 46 × 58″ (116.8 × 147.3 cm). Courtesy Robert Miller Gallery, New York.

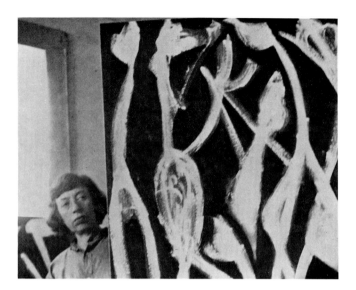

Fig. 64.
Lee Krasner in her studio in Springs, summer 1950.

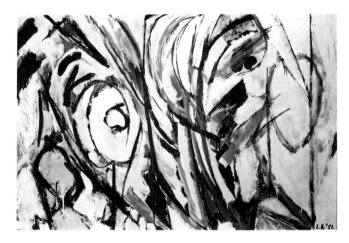

Fig. 65.
Ochre Rhythm. c. 1951.
Oil on canvas.
37½ × 58″ (95.2 × 147.3 cm).
Private collection.

ing of Newman and Rothko.

We can reconstruct some of the experiments Krasner was undertaking during the critical summer of 1950 from photographs made of her in her studio by Hans Namuth.[40] She is seen on a contact sheet with a number of works in progress, all of which she subsequently destroyed. The painting on the easel appears to be about six feet square; the image is of long-necked, long-legged *personnages* intertwined in a dancelike configuration brushed in freely in white on a black ground. Hybridized forms, they recall Picasso's rubbery stick figures of the late thirties as well as Miró's otherworldly vegetable humanoids of the *peintures sauvages* period (fig. 64). The shots Namuth recorded are interesting for several reasons: They show Krasner in her typical attitude of doubt, concern, and self-criticism, and they record the initial stages of a series she abandoned. By the summer of 1950 she had already reduced her palette to the stark dramatic opposition of black and white, whereas Pollock did not eliminate color from his poured paintings until 1951.

Through the few surviving works of this period and Namuth's photographs, we can pinpoint 1950 as the year Krasner began to work on a relatively large scale and to attempt fully automatic drawing directly in paint. Accident was permitted in the last two of the Little Image series, but in the allover webbed and grid hieroglyphic types, the dripping was so controlled that these works are automatic in only the broadest sense. In the series of destroyed *personnage* paintings of 1950, on the other hand, Krasner "switches gears," as she describes the abrupt stylistic ruptures that punctuate her career, which at first seem a deliberate negation of her preceding style. In the lost *personnage* paintings of 1950, instead of using geometry or the Cubist grid to lock forms into rigid compartments, she creates mysterious hybridized, somewhat monstrous creatures that are undeniably figurative. Typically, Krasner would permit an idea to germinate until she was prepared to deal with it fully. Six years after she abandoned these paintings, Krasner began a new cycle of figurative paintings.

The destroyed paintings of 1950 show how Krasner began drawing directly on canvas, freely improvising and altering as she progressed; they are her first automatic works alluding to figuration. The verticality still exhibits

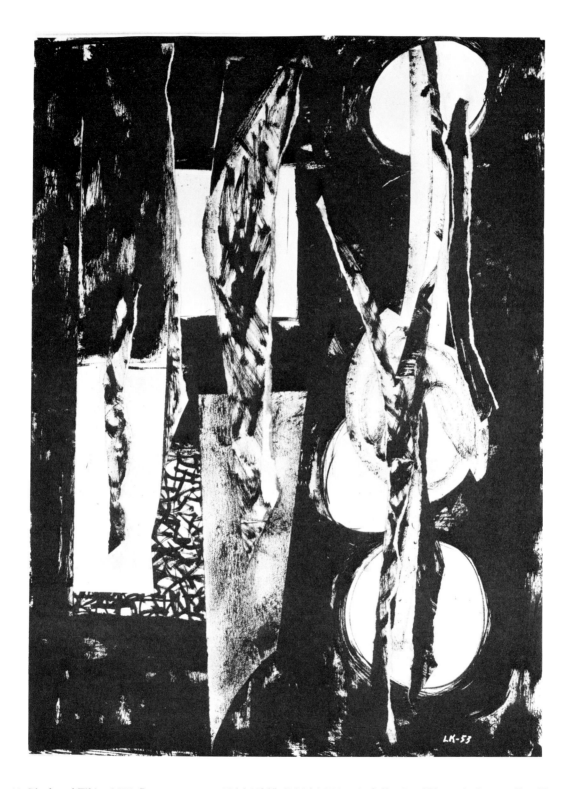

Fig. 66. *Black and White*. 1953. Paper on canvas. 30 × 22½″ (76.2 × 57.1 cm). Collection Alfonso A. Ossorio, East Hampton.

a strong need for the image to echo the framing edge, reinforcing the tight structure typical of Krasner's art. That they are painted on an easel reveals how faithful she was to her training as a painter within the easel tradition.

The paintings Namuth photographed in 1950 are clearly unfinished. Normally, after brushing in a preliminary composition, Krasner would continue working on a canvas until she was satisfied that it was sufficiently rich and developed and balanced out in terms of color, surface, and space. Thus her paintings are never flat or lacking a dynamic spatial tension. Often she considered a painting unfinished for years, changing it over a long period of time, until she felt she had expressed her intention fully.

We do not know what happened to the 1950 *personnage* paintings which were her first figurative automatic works. However, two significant paintings with hybrid figurative *personnages* related to these paintings exist. Both are small early collage paintings, which point forward to the great series of floral collage paintings Krasner would produce in 1955. *Black and White*, painted in 1953, was made by ripping up a brush drawing she had made and pasting the fragments together into three vertical *personnages* (fig. 66). Different textures—allover tracery, broad brushwork, and reserved areas of white paper—are combined for an effect of maximum complexity. Edges are torn: The effect is not of the clean mechanical straight-edge of Picasso's *Three Musicians*, but of the frangible, porous edge of forms in painterly Abstract Expressionism. Although this painting is a collage, it criticizes and subverts the conventions of Cubist collage in a number of significant ways which identifies it among the first post-Cubist collages. Foreground and background are co-valent, but they are not interchangeable. The lightly brushed aerated background cannot suddenly project forward to be read as a positive form because it is black, the most recessive color. Moreover, subsequent layers of collages sandwich shapes between foreground and background prohibiting such an easy interchange. The image remains strictly frontal; however, because it is so painterly and its edges so variable, it is difficult to read as separable planes. The painterly textured shapes do not lend themselves to the kind of graphic reading that was possible for the cutout shape in Cubist collage. *Black and White* is far more indeterminate, plastic, painterly, and metamorphic than Cubist

collage as well. Ambiguity—of image, of space, of subject—is for Krasner, as for the other members of the New York School, a vital tie to the tradition of Symbolism, which links painting more closely to poetry than to music.

The analogy between painting and poetry, the cornerstone of Surrealist thought, became an article of faith for the New York School painters in their debates on "subject matter." No matter how much Krasner held out against the Surrealist subjects, she was a great reader of modern French poetry. Before meeting Pollock she had come to admire Baudelaire, Rimbaud, and Verlaine. Indeed, on the wall of her studio, she had painted a quote from Rimbaud's poem *A Season in Hell*.[41] We have also seen that she had read both Graham on the importance of Jungian archetypes as well as Jung himself.

She did not use automatic drawing per se in figurative paintings until 1956. First, she experimented with color-field paintings that fused Mondrian's architectonic structure with Matisse's large expanses of transparent color. In 1951, Krasner showed a painting (as did Pollock) in the historic "Ninth Street Show," organized by the Abstract Expressionists as another challenge to the critics and by implication to the museums, which were not yet buying their works in great numbers. That spring, Pollock persuaded his dealer, Betty Parsons, to visit Springs to see Krasner's work. When Parsons arrived, Krasner was painting gestural abstractions. This visit occasioned Krasner's first solo exhibition in New York with Betty Parsons. Much to Parsons's surprise, if not displeasure, the works Krasner exhibited in the fall of 1951 had nothing in common with what Parsons had seen in Springs during her visit. According to Krasner, the work "broke," another way she describes a sudden change in styles, over the course of the summer. She had destroyed the paintings Parsons saw. We do not know what these paintings looked like, although judging from *Gothic Frieze* and *Ochre Rhythm*, they were probably improvisational "action paintings." On the other hand, the works she showed at the Betty Parsons Gallery were strictly formal chromatic abstractions that synthesized Matisse's color with Mondrian's structure. Only three paintings survive from this period. Two are large paintings, including Untitled, 1951 (fig. 68), a banded composition, bought later, in 1969, by The Museum of Modern Art; a composition with overlap-

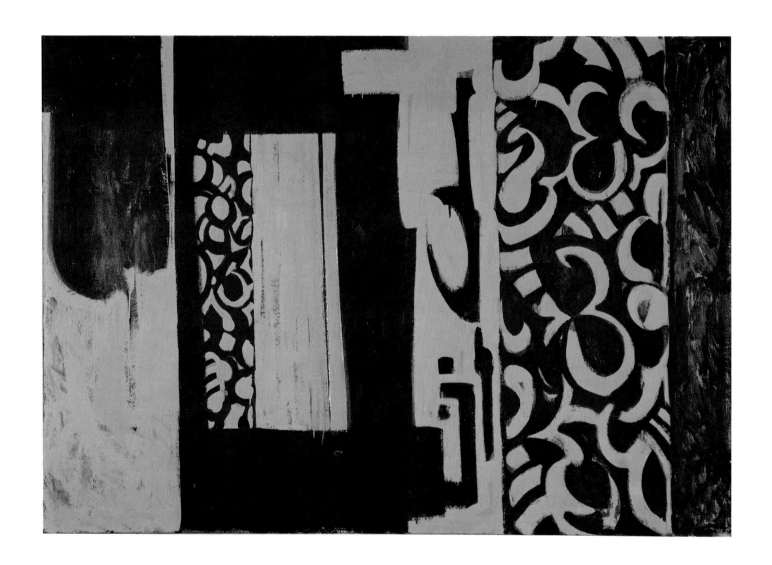

Fig. 67. *Blue and Black*. 1951–53. Oil on canvas. 58 × 82½″ (147.3 × 209.5 cm). The Museum of Fine Arts, Houston. Sarah Campbell Blaffer Fund.

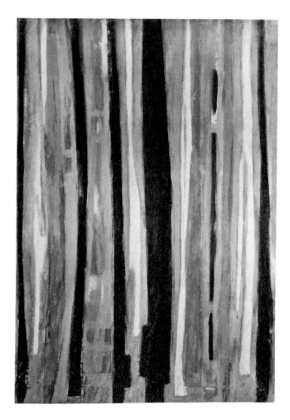

Fig. 68.
Untitled. 1951.
Oil on canvas.
82½ × 57⅞″ (209.5 × 147 cm).
The Museum of Modern Art, New York.
Mrs. Ruth Dunbar Cushing Fund.

ping rectangles; and *Equilibrium* (fig. 63), a smaller work that is striking in terms of the originality of its color contrasts of lavender with ochre. The works shown at the Betty Parsons Gallery were the first big pictures Krasner painted. With their implicit debt to Mondrian, they are clearly aligned more with the chromatic abstractions of Newman, Rothko, and Reinhardt rather than with "action painting." They are the logical outcome of her continuing dialogue with Mondrian.

The static iconic image was not natural for Krasner. It was impossible for her to continue to refine these paintings into an image that could be elaborated on as a series. Her style changed as often as Pollock's and in much the same way. Often she would work on paper, evolve imagery, translate it to canvas, and work as long as the subject continued to inspire her. She refused to force the process, since her idea of painting was as an experience that unfolds organically rather than as an a priori conceptual image. She turned on her color-field paintings with a vengeance, reworking all but the three pieces mentioned above. She later transformed these 1951 works into her collage paintings of 1955, reworking them and adding to them until they were unrecognizable.

The only surviving painting Krasner made between the Parsons show and the beginning of her collage paintings is a remarkable large painting titled *Blue and Black* in the collection of the Museum of Fine Arts, Houston. The painting has a bold simplicity in its two-color format (fig. 67). The repetition of the filigree motif at the left, in an enlarged version of itself at the right, sets up an original type of spatial tension. The suggestion is that the small filigree image is in the distance, when in fact it is as firmly anchored to the picture plane as its enlarged reflection. *Blue and Black* is a fully evolved color-field painting that successfully synthesizes Mondrian and Matisse and adds the new elements of spatial tension and dramatic impact.

The reductive, two-color palette, large format, and expanse of intense pure color align *Blue and Black* more closely with the chromatic abstraction of the New York School than with gestural or "action painting." The chromatic abstractionists, or color-field painters, concentrated on static, emblematic, frontal compositions expressing the iconic severity of stasis rather than the physicality of gestural abstraction. Krasner was especially impressed by Still's monumental and dramatic fields of interlocking flamelike patches of color. Still was not a typical color-field painter; he did not eliminate either detail or impasto like Newman and Rothko. His paintings, despite their consciousness of the framing edge, had a flickering, febrile quality, especially where ragged, irregular shapes met, a density of surface, and a defined edge, not as a hard boundary but as the irregular intersection of color with color.

In *Blue and Black*, Krasner comes closest to Still's conception of intricately interlocked shapes that avoid depicted contours or positive-negative reversals characteristic of late Cubist design. In Still's paintings, one cannot separate foreground from background because specific shapes are not depicted against a ground, but interlocked on the picture plane. This is also true of Krasner's *Blue and Black* so that we cannot really say whether the background is blue or black. The two colors are used in complex interplay and lock together on the plane of the picture. The repetition of the filigree element, which reminds one of the ornate pierced tracery of Moorish screens, appearing as a reduced doppelgänger, creates a challenging spatial ambiguity. Krasner's pigment is relatively diluted in this painting. Impasto is avoided, and a certain liquid transparency is sought, perhaps as an allusion to "sky" blue. However, subsequent layers of paint create a relatively opaque surface, which covers the entire canvas field from edge to edge. Varying the saturation of the blue field to create a color volume with a single hue recalls Matisse's *The Blue Window*. The black filigree pattern and black-and-blue combination bring to mind the music stand and spatial organization of Matisse's *Piano Lesson* as well as his later ornamental Moorish scenes. Krasner had studied both paintings in The Museum of Modern Art collection intently; they were important deposits in her permanent memory bank of images from which she drew inspiration throughout her life.

The spatial organization of *Blue and Black* and its uninterrupted color field identify the painting as a work that goes beyond Matisse to synthesize his conception of color as optical space with Mondrian's frontality and flatness. *Blue and Black* makes the entire image one with the total expanse of the pictorial field like the most advanced painting of the New York School in the early fifties. The tendency to echo the frame by the image, initially developed by Mondrian, was evident in the paintings Krasner exhibited at Betty Parsons in 1951, as we have seen. Her rejection of the banded and boxed geometry of Mondrian in favor of a freer and more painterly style was now firm. In this connection, it should be noted that of the American Abstract Artists, only Krasner broke with Mondrian completely to evolve a successful open, painterly style incorporating elements of baroque composition and drama and expunging the rigidity of geometry. Reinhardt's exquisite paintings of the early forties, which exhibit the influence of Chinese painting and Oriental calligraphy are, like his classical art in general, static and self-contained. When he opted for a monochrome palette, their iconic, contemplative, and deliberately anti–"action painting" aesthetic became even more pronounced, as he more and more rejected any element of the improvisatory. Krasner, on the other hand, finally managed to find an accommodation with both "action painting" and Surrealist automatism.

In many respects, *Blue and Black* represents a turning point; it marks both her liberation from Cubism and her acceptance of her own inclinations and sensibility. No longer torn between action and icon, between Mondrian and Matisse, between Hofmann and Pollock, she has found her own way at last as a painter of large-scale monumental canvases that synthesize an intellectual severity with an expressive tension, a dynamic improvisation with a structural clarity. *Blue and Black* emphatically declares her confidence that, from this point on, Lee Krasner will not swerve again in her course. She was over forty years old by the time *Blue and Black* was finished. Pollock had begun drinking again and was working less and less, but her own energies were just about to be fully tapped for the first time.

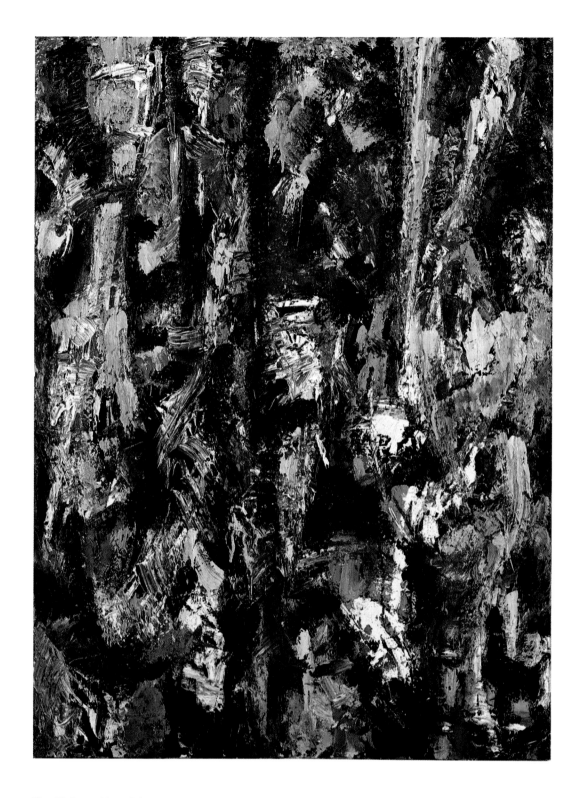

Fig. 69. *Lava*. 1949. Oil on masonite. 40 × 30″ (101.6 × 76.2 cm). Courtesy Robert Miller Gallery, New York.

V. The Shape of Color

Had Krasner's art followed a logical course of development, *Blue and Black* should have generated a series of "big pictures." As it stands, it is an exceptional prefiguration of works she would not feel free enough or sure enough to paint for a decade to come. Having destroyed the series of *personnage* paintings she was working on during the summer of 1950, with the exception of a few small paintings which she reworked, such as the richly impastoed, geyser-like *Lava* and *Vulcanic* (figs. 69, 73), Krasner turned to collage as a means of making a new kind of painting that would combine the energetic physicality and dynamism of "action painting" with the optical vibrancy of color-field painting. Perhaps unconsciously, she turned to collage, a technique she had used first on the WPA, to create an original style synthesizing Mondrian's rigorous flatness with Matisse's floral decorativeness and high color as well as Picasso's drama and monumentality. Collage, moreover, permitted Krasner to find a way out of an impass that had been troubling her for some years, a problem exacerbated by the division between color and line studies in the Hofmann School. That was the problem of how to create shapes without separating line from color, or simply using color to fill in contour in the manner of academic art. In post-Cubist art, shape was to be defined by edge rather than depicted by line.

The synthesis of drawing and painting was one of Pollock's major contributions to the New York School. Even Matisse and Léger—two of the most advanced School of Paris masters—continued to use line to depict shape in a conventional manner, and color to fill in the area between lines. Late in life, both tried, in different ways, to resolve this dichotomy. Léger used line and color as two different types of elements, autonomous of one another, and Matisse began cutting out shapes from papers he had painted in his last great series of découpages. Matisse's cutouts were first shown in New York in 1949 at the Pierre Matisse Gallery. Krasner admired them, but it was not until she became critical of color-field painting after her 1951 Parsons exhibition that Matisse's painted paper cutouts inspired her to a new kind of painting. She could eliminate the need to draw shapes by instead ripping them or cutting them out of different kinds of materials. The diversity of the materials she used contributed a rich texture that prevented these collage paintings from being literally flat. The way

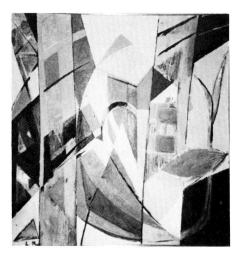

Fig. 70.
Offbeat. c. 1954–55.
Oil on canvas.
48½ × 47¾″ (123.2 × 121.3 cm).
Collection Mr. and Mrs. J. H. Dressler, Boston.

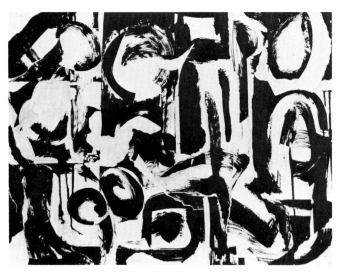

Fig. 71.
Black and White Collage. 1954.
Painted paper on canvas board.
22⅜ × 30″ (56.8 × 76.2 cm).
Collection Mr. and Mrs. Hans Namuth, New York.

Krasner arrived at these distinctively original collage paintings, which are related to both gestural and chromatic abstraction and yet are neither, is typical of her solution to a problem: Rather than verbally or psychologically denying her past, she literally incorporated it into her present works.

Reinhardt, Newman, and Rothko's paintings tended more and more toward static, iconic, and hieratic conceptual, disembodied images at the moment that Krasner was searching for a means to integrate what she knew and loved about Matisse and Mondrian with a more active, spontaneous, physical, and improvisational style. Her auto-critique took a particularly virulent form: She pasted torn and cut shapes over the large-scale geometric color-field paintings she had shown at the Betty Parsons Gallery. The applied shapes were often cut out of "left-overs," as she termed the many works she destroyed in her periodic bouts of artistic housecleaning. When asked why she saved these piles of used materials, she answered that, as a child of modest circumstances and a survivor of the Depression, she had learned to be thrifty. It was as a result of this thrifty attitude toward saving shards and fragments from the past that her next major series, the collage paintings of 1954–55, was born.

In addition to *Blue and Black*, Krasner painted one other large-scale color-field painting in the early fifties which she did not destroy. Later, she titled this unique painting *Offbeat* because it appeared unrelated to any of her other works of the period. In *Offbeat* (fig. 70), translucent planes of color are separated by fine lines into geometric segments. In its liberal interpretation of Matisse, it prefigures the color-field abstractions Richard Diebenkorn would paint twenty years later. Like *Blue and Black*, *Offbeat*, painted in 1954, was a painting that could easily have been extrapolated into a series of permutations. Once again, Krasner rejected the idea of serial imagery, although she did not reject the painting itself, and preserved the work intact instead of cannibalizing it for use in the collage paintings she was already making.

These two color-field paintings, plus a smaller variant of *Blue and Black*, continue Krasner's development as a color-field painter in the early fifties, which she would pick up again in the seventies. However, it was a development she was not prepared to pursue at the time for both

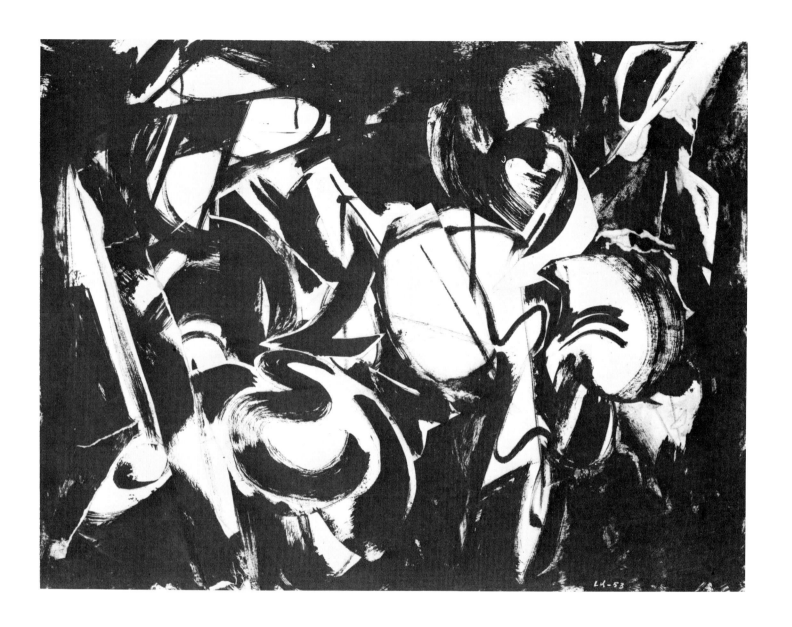

Fig. 72. Untitled Collage. 1953. Painted paper on canvas board. 22¼ × 30″ (56.5 × 76.2 cm). Collection the artist.

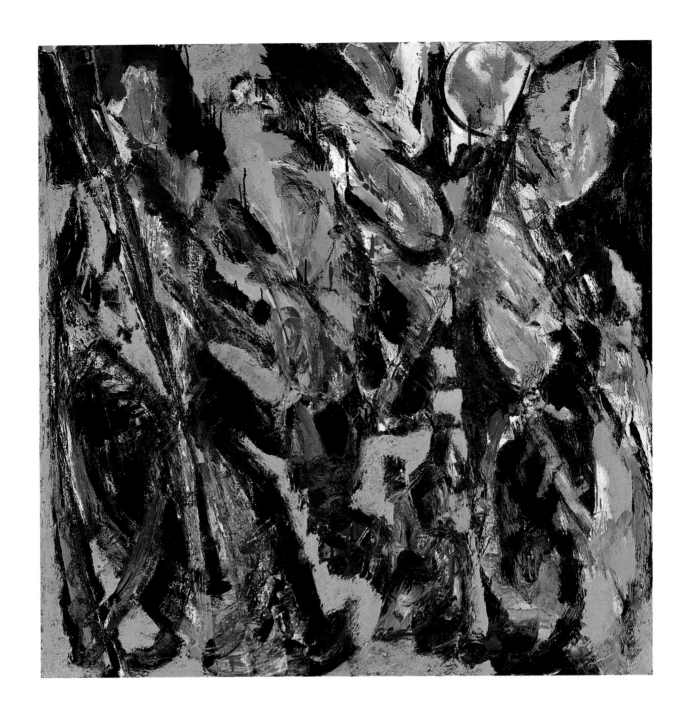

Fig. 73. *Vulcanic.* c. 1951–53. Oil on canvas. 48 × 48″ (121.9 × 121.9 cm). Courtesy Robert Miller Gallery, New York.

psychological as well as aesthetic reasons. She still had too much aggression and physical power to express to opt for the restful world of Matisse's *Luxe, calme et volupté*. The move toward collage painting evolved, as did many of her important stylistic innovations, from a period of working on paper. These black-and-white drawings of 1953–54 are Krasner's first fully "automatic" works, for, although the webbed Little Image paintings incorporated accident, they were very tightly controlled and generated texture rather than imagery. With brush and ink on paper, Krasner found a new fluidity and freedom to express herself in forms that were both gestural and at times figurative. It is important to note that these drawings, although they use a very different vocabulary of images, were done at the same time that Pollock was painting his black-and-white paintings, which were based on elaborations of his own early automatic drawings of the thirties, only known to Krasner at the time.

Between 1951 and 1953, the period she painted and repainted *Blue and Black*, Krasner made a series of painted paper collages, mainly in black and white. The original drawing, in black ink or wash, often in some way figurative, would be ripped and pasted back together (fig. 71). The results were in many cases dazzling. Extrapolating from her painted paper collages, Krasner began destroying the canvases which had come to represent, in her eyes at least, unsatisfactory paintings. Typically, she needed no critic to judge these works; she had the kind of rare objectivity toward her own work that made it possible for her to view it unsentimentally and to attack and destroy her own creations. She knew there was still too much Mondrian in the paintings shown at Parsons—too many rectangles and bands, too much architectonic severity, too little freedom and self-expression—for the work to be a full statement of what she had to say. Their stasis and relative symmetry were also at odds with anything she had done before, since all her other work bears the stamp of a dynamic, restless energy. The discipline of working on the small gridded compartments of the later Little Image series had come to seem a prison to her, a series of bars and grids she wanted to break out of. Tearing and ripping are violent acts; there is a new expression of aggression and powerful will, even in the first of the collages, the black-and-white series done on paper. As she became surer of herself, the

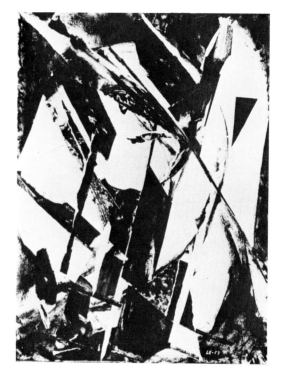

Fig. 74.
Black and White Collage. 1953.
Painted paper on canvas board.
29 × 23″ (73.6 × 58.4 cm).
Collection Mrs. Donald Braider, Sag Harbor.

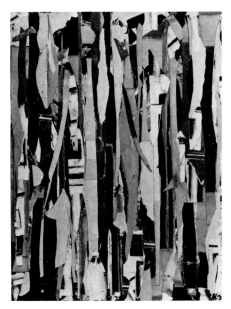

Fig. 75.
City Verticals. 1953.
Oil, paper, and canvas on masonite.
41¼ × 31⅛″ (104.8 × 79.1 cm).
Collection Richard and Gail Lippe, Great Neck.

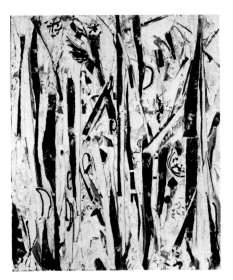

Fig. 76.
Untitled. c. 1953–54.
Oil, canvas, and paper on pressed wood.
56 × 48″ (142.2 × 121.9 cm).
Collection DeutschBank, A.G., New York Branch.

other part of Krasner's sensibility—the delicacy and finesse, the patience that creates the refined detail—returned in later large-scale works.

We have seen how, by 1950, linear drawing was expunged from Krasner's work as an element separable from painterly patching. Thus, *Lava, Vulcanic,* and the collage paintings do not treat shape as a flat plane with discrete contours depicted against a passive background. The activation of the background, which one sees in Kline's works of the period as well, became a principal focus of her activity, especially at the stage when she began to revise compositions. For even if Krasner had begun to accept automatic drawing as a way of creating images, she was too much the student of Cézanne and Matisse to accept the given without further critical re-evaluation and revision. It is, indeed, this process of revision that created the works of the early fifties. Many of the black-and-white brush drawings of this period were cut up and turned into collages by shifting the image (and consequently the space) in the manner Hofmann had taught his students to do (fig. 72). These black-and-white paper collages of 1953 (fig. 74) have a great deal of rhythmic energy as well as painterly surface; edges are soft rather than hard, and geometry, if it is recalled at all, is but the dimmest memory. Soon, Krasner began to use collage in a far more complex and pictorial manner. After pasting painted paper on paper, Krasner pasted painted paper on masonite later in 1953 in paintings such as *City Verticals* and Untitled (figs. 75, 76). She had already pasted shreds of paper painted with oil onto masonite grounds in paintings like *The City,* in which diagonal tentacles of elongated paper shreds create an explosive energy. *The City,* a vertical painting roughly four by three feet, is related to *Promenade* and the collage paintings that suggest *personnages.*

Krasner's destruction of her earlier drawings and paintings resulted in a remarkable series of small collage paintings in 1953–54 composed of their fragments. These first collage paintings manifested their pictorial qualities and their distance from both drawing and collage immediately. Her extreme patience and innate inclination toward precision permitted her to work and rework these paintings, slicing and chopping materials from different sources, carefully gluing them to masonite or canvas grounds until a richly variegated, tactile surface was built up. No ma-

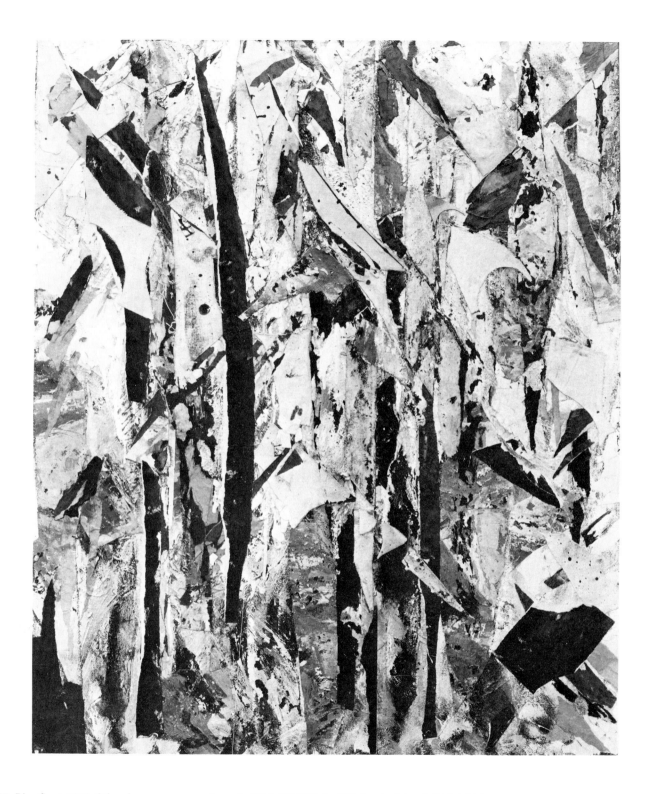

Fig. 77. *Blue Spot*. 1954. Oil and paper on pressed wood. 48 × 40″ (121.9 x 101.6 cm). Atlantic Richfield Corporation Art Collection, Los Angeles.

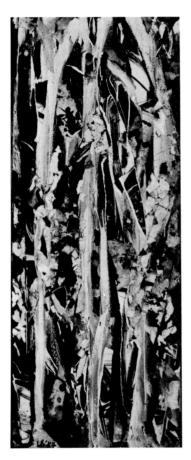

Fig. 78.
Forest No. 1. 1954.
Oil and paper on pressed wood.
60 × 24″ (152.4 × 61 cm).
Private collection.

terial ever projected beyond the plane of the surface, and the integration of form into interlocking form once again had the jigsaw-puzzle-like cohesiveness of the interlocking figure-field of *Blue and Black* and *Offbeat*. Mondrian's frontality and flatness had not been forgotten, but a far freer kind of form, broken, painterly, and sometimes accidentally arrived at, was now Krasner's to play with. The first series of collage paintings seems to follow directly on the heels of the *personnages* of *Promenade*, turning verticals into tree- and forest-like configurations. Two paintings that also seem to issue from the destroyed black-and-white *personnages* series are *Vulcanic* and *Lava*, whose gray, red, and blue palette is related to *Promenade*, and geyser-like eruptions once again refer to natural phenomena. They seem to burst and overflow before our eyes. Technically, they are interesting because they show Krasner again reworking a pre-existing image, going back into the painting and brushing color around forms, leaving some exposed, covering over others, and in general permitting what should normally be interpreted as background to invade foreground. Perhaps her awareness of Mondrian's method of reworking his paintings led her to this way of revising paintings, bringing the background forward to interlock ultimately with the surface brushwork.

In paintings like *Blue Spot, Forest No. 1*, and *Forest No. 2* (figs. 77, 78, 79), Krasner gives the impression that the paper is imbedded in the masonite support. She applies a crust of oil over the pasted paper, enriching the surface, adding detail and a restrained but dramatic note of color into the otherwise monochrome works. Tall verticals—trees or treelike personae—appear in some; others recall the verticality of skyscrapers. The strength of the repeated vertical elements reinforces the boundary of the framing edge in compositions of an uncompromising architectonic monumentality. The severity of the vertical shafts is softened by the multiplication of small mosaic-like patches of pasted paper or applied color. In works like *Porcelain* and *Shattered Light*, canvas pieces are introduced along with paper (figs. 80, 81). Diverse textures and materials are integrated into a unified whole by the application of oil brushwork where the artist deems it necessary. These delicate but forceful paintings combine the fragility of the finest artisanship of the great enamels, ivories, and mosaics of earlier ages into a harmonious unified texture and a coherent pictorial space. They succeed in being ornamental in the highest sense. The artist's patience, sensibility, restraint, and reticence are noticeably at work in these painstakingly detailed collage paintings on masonite. Krasner's sense of what to take out and what to leave in seems infallible, especially in these densely packed, richly textured images.

During the summer of 1954, Carol and Donald Braider, neighbors in Springs, gave Krasner an exhibition in The House of Books and Music, the bookstore-gallery they operated on Main Street in East Hampton. Installation shots show both early collage paintings as well as late Little Image paintings, which had not been previously exhibited (fig. 84). The collage paintings represent a definite turn away from nonobjective abstraction toward a more metaphorical and content-laden art, with allusions to both figure and landscape. The following year, Krasner continued her collage paintings, becoming increasingly adept at the process of mixing mediums and integrating materials taken from a variety of sources into a cohesive composition by working over the whole composition with oil once she had pasted down the cutout portions. It seems likely that the earliest collage paintings of 1955 are *Burning Candles* and *Color Totem* because their splintered and slivered allover imagery refers back to the previous collage and Little Image paintings. Krasner was now working on a larger scale (roughly five feet high), and varying the material of her supports. *Color Totem*, for example, has swirls of oil-painted paper cut into diced or torn fragments no bigger than mosaic chips—which, indeed, they recall— pasted onto a rough cotton duck ground (fig. 82). *Burning Candles* (fig. 83), which recalls the diagonal branching out toward the corners of *The City*, is another fragile and delicate work of scraps of oil-painted paper and canvas glued to a linen support. These paintings are related to the exquisite allover mosaic-like horizontal collage paintings of 1954, *Shattered Light* and *Porcelain*, as well as to *Broken Gray* of early 1955.

The relationship between Krasner's collage paintings and her experience in making the mosaic tables in 1947 seems relatively clear: At least part of the preparation of the collage paintings required her to work on the painting looking down on it, as she glued the pieces into place. Her procedure in executing the collage paintings was usually

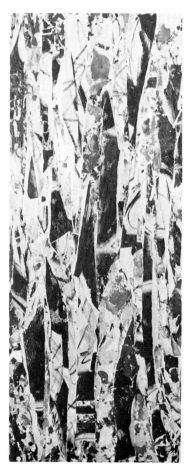

Fig. 79.
Forest No. 2. 1954.
Collage and oil on panel.
59⅞ × 24″ (152.1 × 61 cm).
Collection Mrs. Edward L. Gersing, Miami.

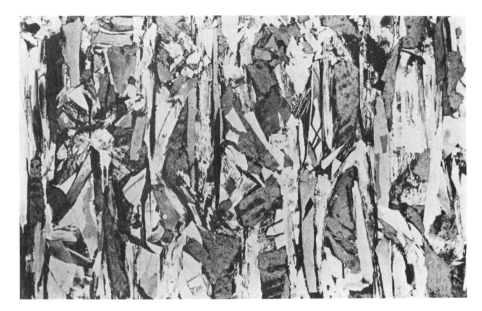

Fig. 80. *Porcelain.* c. 1954. Oil and paper on pressed wood. 30 × 48½″ (76.2 × 123.2 cm). Private collection.

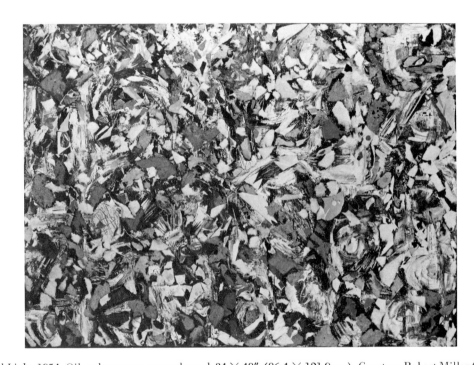

Fig. 81. *Shattered Light.* 1954. Oil and paper on pressed wood. 34 × 48″ (86.4 × 121.9 cm). Courtesy Robert Miller Gallery, New York.

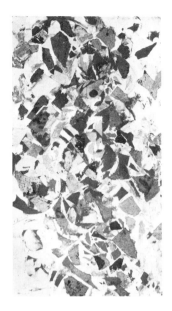

Fig. 82.
Color Totem. 1955.
Oil and paper on cotton duck.
57½ × 31⅞″ (146 × 96.2 cm).
Estate of Betty Parsons.

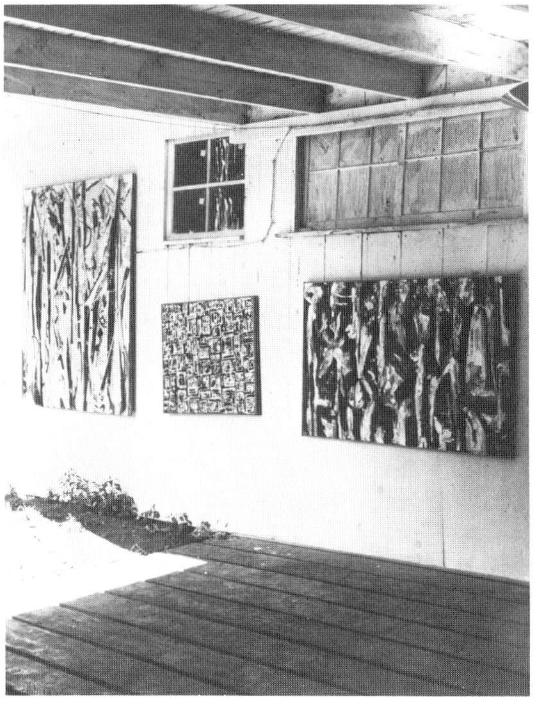

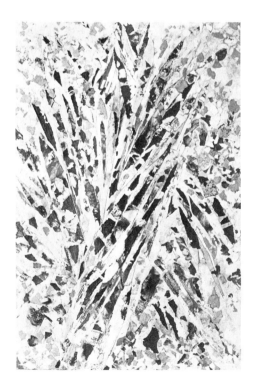

Fig. 84.
Exhibition installation at House of Books and Music, 1954.

Fig. 83.
Burning Candles. 1955.
Oil, paper, and canvas on linen.
58 × 39″ (147.3 × 99 cm).
Neuberger Museum, S.U.N.Y. College at Purchase.
Gift of Roy E. Neuberger.

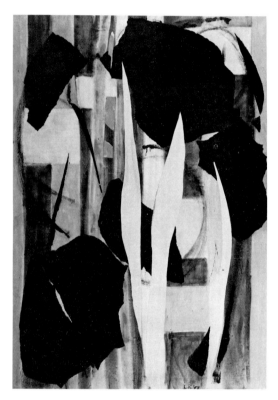

Fig. 85.
Milkweed. 1955.
Oil, paper, and canvas collage on canvas.
82⅜ × 57¾″ (209.2 × 146.7 cm).
Albright-Knox Art Gallery, Buffalo, New York.
Gift of Seymour H. Knox.

to take a painting she had rejected and start pinning onto this surface pieces of painted paper or canvas she had cannibalized from still other works. At this point her training with Hofmann in judging spatial relations once more came into play. As Cézanne would adjust the balances in his works by looking at his canvases from different points of view, Krasner would step back and evaluate the overall effect of a collage painting while the material was still pinned to the surface, modifying the work over a period of time as it stood on the easel or against the wall. Once satisfied, she would put the canvas on a table and glue the pieces down. She might then add color with a brush to further unify the elements and imbed the pieces between the brushed surface and the support in a process resembling lamination. The result was a totally original use of collage as a means of creating, not graphically decorative works, but painterly paintings in which shape is not drawn or depicted but literally cut out. The irregularity of her edges, the emphasis on canvas as painted cloth, the play on canvas as both support and applied surface, all contribute to making paintings like *Milkweed, Bird Talk,* and *Bald Eagle* remarkably advanced works whose implications are only now being understood (figs. 85, 86, 87).

We have discussed the reaction of first-generation New York School artists to Cubist drawing. They did not wish to depict shapes against a field in the manner of Cubist design, with its inevitable reference to the conventions of figurative representation, but to synthesize drawing with painting. In her collage paintings Krasner hit on a way of creating shapes without drawing them. Arranging and pasting cutout pieces was a means of structuring textured fabric that an artist like Sam Gilliam would understand how to use in the eighties. To achieve the detail and scale of shape, without wishing to turn back to academic methods of depiction, was an innovation of no small consequence, not thoroughly understood until recently, and then by artists much younger than those of Krasner's generation.

Two of the 1955 collage paintings, *Bald Eagle* and *Bird Talk,* have a more whirling and allover pattern than the more architecturally structured works in which shapes are strictly aligned with the vertical framing edge. The spattered fragments in *Bald Eagle* were apparently cut out of a canvas Pollock had splattered paint on and thrown away. The reserved areas of linen support in *Bird Talk,*

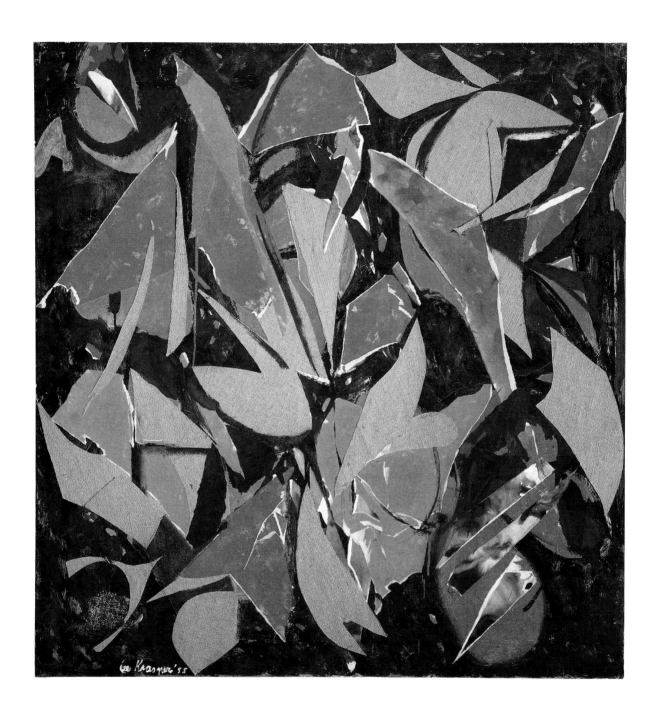

Fig. 86. *Bird Talk*. 1955. Oil, paper, and canvas on cotton duck. 58⅛ × 56″ (147.6 × 142.2 cm). Collection the artist.

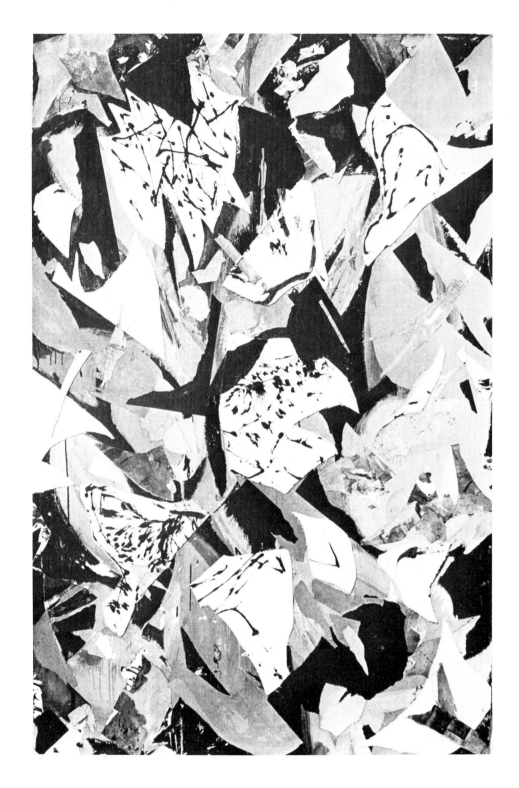

Fig. 87. *Bald Eagle*. 1955. Oil, paper, and canvas on linen. 77 × 51½″ (195.6 × 130.8 cm). Collection Mr. and Mrs. Aron B. Katz, Boulder.

a roughly five-foot-square painting, are treated as pale ochres contrasting with the predominantly intense orange and magenta palette of the work.

It is perhaps significant that the first time Krasner signs her full name in script is on two of these collage paintings: *Bird Talk* and *Shooting Gold* (fig. 89). Previously, her signature had been only the initials L.K. in block letters.[42] The acceptance of her handwriting as a signature corresponds to her escape from what she had come to see as the prison of the Cubist grid. The use of the raw linen reserved ground as a shape is related to Pollock's attempt to create a new kind of figure-ground in *Out of the Web* and *Cut-Out*. However, Krasner has solved the problem of the reserved shapes—which can no longer be read as negative or left-over shapes in the background—by locking them into the complex interplay of pasted paper petal-like shapes by filling in around both applied and reserved freeform shapes with brushed paint, applied in several carefully considered layers. *Bird Talk* is a tour de force, a format that might have once more led to a series of paintings in the same mode. As usual, Krasner abruptly changed direction.

Shooting Gold, a large vertical painting appears to be the last of the series because it introduces a new element of freehand drawing in addition to painted paper and cloth. The elements are glued to a banded ground that must originally have been a painting resembling the 1951 untitled abstraction in The Museum of Modern Art collection. Once more, Krasner's capacity to create space while asserting the flatness of the picture plane is exhibited with masterful authority. The specific qualities of materials are particularly emphasized here, with threads of the torn linen "stalks" deliberately dangling to create a hairy painterly edge. These collage paintings represent a high point in Krasner's career, a thoroughly original creation melding Matisse's sense of the decorative and his airy, translucent painterliness with Mondrian's structure and the big bold black forms of a Picassoid drama. Improvised drawing is constrained by a pictorial intelligence few, if any, of her contemporaries could match at the time.

Pollock seemed the artist most excited by these paintings, which were shown in fall, 1955, by Eleanor Ward at the Stable Gallery. Most of the paintings were large-scale verticals, over six feet high. Among these highly

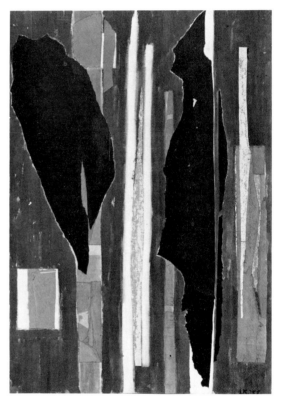

Fig. 88.
Lame Shadow. 1955.
Oil and collage on canvas.
82 × 58″ (208.3 × 147.3 cm).
Courtesy Robert Miller Gallery, New York.

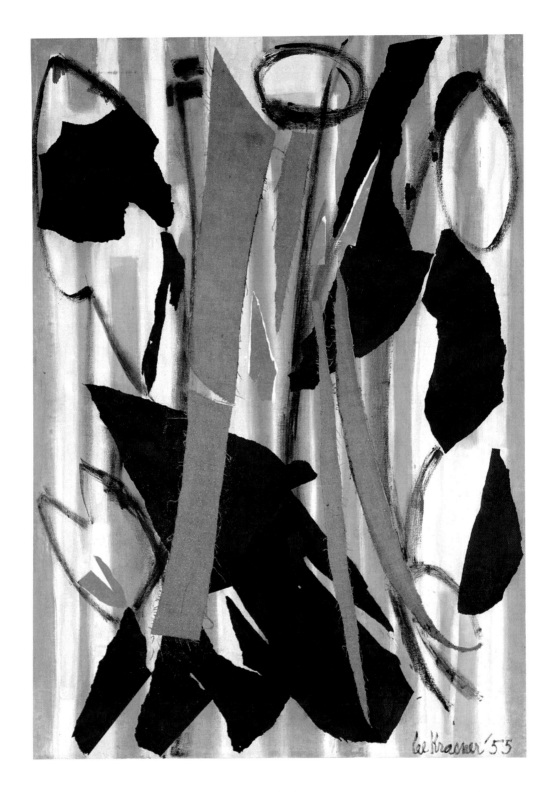

Fig. 89. *Shooting Gold*. 1955. Oil, paper, and canvas on cotton duck. 82½ × 58⅜″ (209.5 × 148.3 cm). Collection the artist.

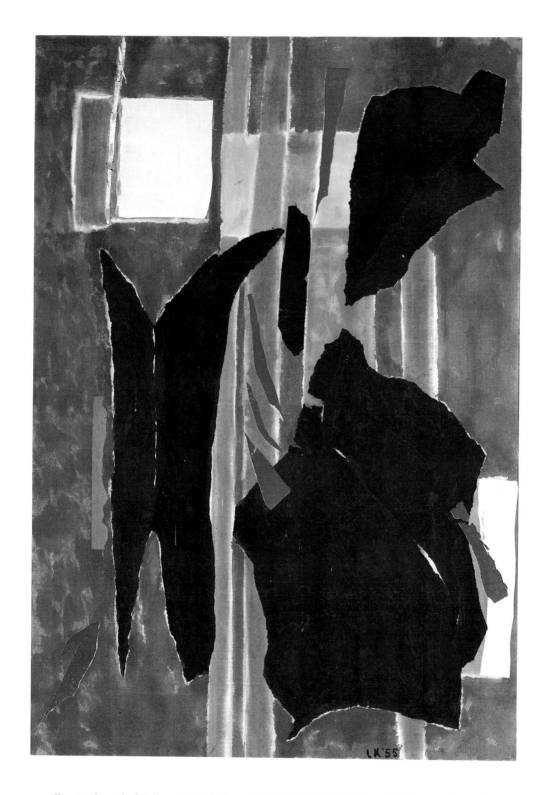

Fig. 90. *Stretched Yellow*. 1955. Collage. 83 × 59″ (210.8 × 149.8 cm). Collection the artist.

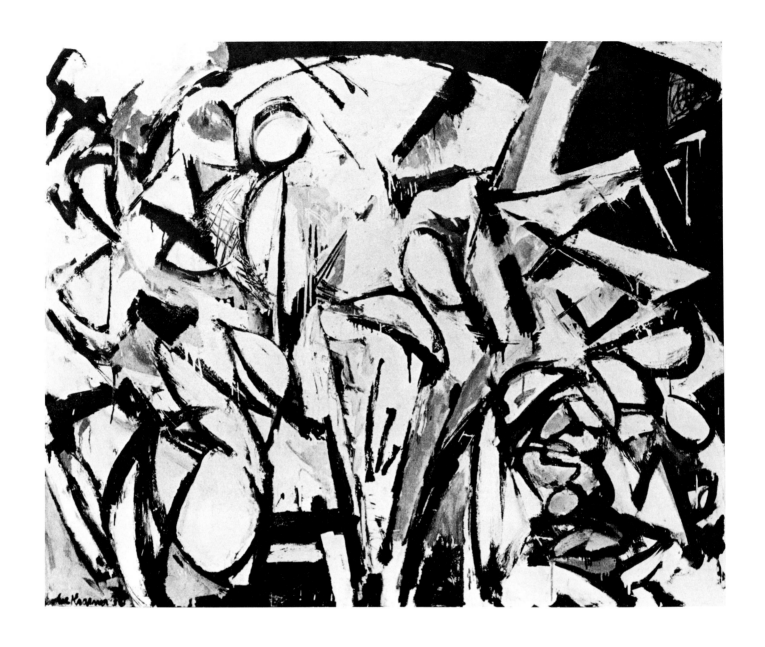

Fig. 91. *Easter Lilies*. 1956. Oil on cotton duck. 48¼ × 60⅛″ **(122.5 × 152.7 cm)**. Courtesy Robert Miller Gallery, New York.

original works are *Lame Shadow, Stretched Yellow* (figs. 88, 90), and *Shooting Gold.* The cutout forms now are larger and more irregular. They recall plant or organic motifs but are neither biomorphic nor geometric. Edges are often torn to create more painterly effects; white space is sometimes left around the cutout shapes to accentuate the buoyant quality of the works, in which forms seem to ascend with a new sense of liberation. Color is used with extraordinary sophistication to create space as well as drama.

Fairfield Porter reviewed Krasner's Stable Gallery collage show in the November, 1955, issue of *Art News.* He described them as "abstractions, in oil and oil-plus-collage" larger in scale than formerly. "Some of the largest with huge forms including black patches with torn edges, and with titles like *Stretched Yellow, Milkweed,* and *Blue Level* . . . are like nature photographs magnified. The irregular shapes and simple colors of the former paintings. as well as the bumpily irregular surface of *Broken Gray,* like a messed up beach of pebbles—all these things 'slow the pictures up.' When nature is photographed in detail, its orderliness appears: Krasner's art, which seems to be about nature, instead of making the spectator aware of a grand design, makes him aware of a subtle disorder greater than what one otherwise might have thought possible."

Once again, Krasner had produced a brilliant series of works that were remote from Pollock's concerns and very much her own statement, and which had no public acclaim. She continued to work at an intense pitch, but she now turned more to the automatic drawing hinted at in *Shooting Gold. Easter Lilies* (fig. 91), signed with her full signature and dated 1956, appears to have been painted in the spring following her Stable Gallery show. Its churning imagery relates to that of *Vulcanic* and *Lava.* It seems to have little of the joyousness of a bouquet about it. Black is used as automatic drawing, but in a way that ties it to Krasner's cloisonné Cubist works, only now the drawing is free, broken, and nonobjective as opposed to hard-edged, linear, and descriptive. Areas are scratched out vehemently, paint is left to drip in the "action-painting" mode. The opposition of dark and light is used for maximum drama, with white drips and strokes in black areas and vice versa. The palette is generally restrained, predominantly ochre and brown. It is probable that the untitled

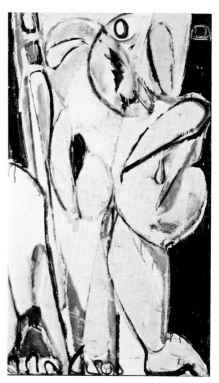

Fig. 92.
Prophecy. 1956.
Oil on cotton duck.
58⅛ × 34″ (147.6 × 86.4 cm).
Collection Alfonso A. Ossorio, East Hampton.

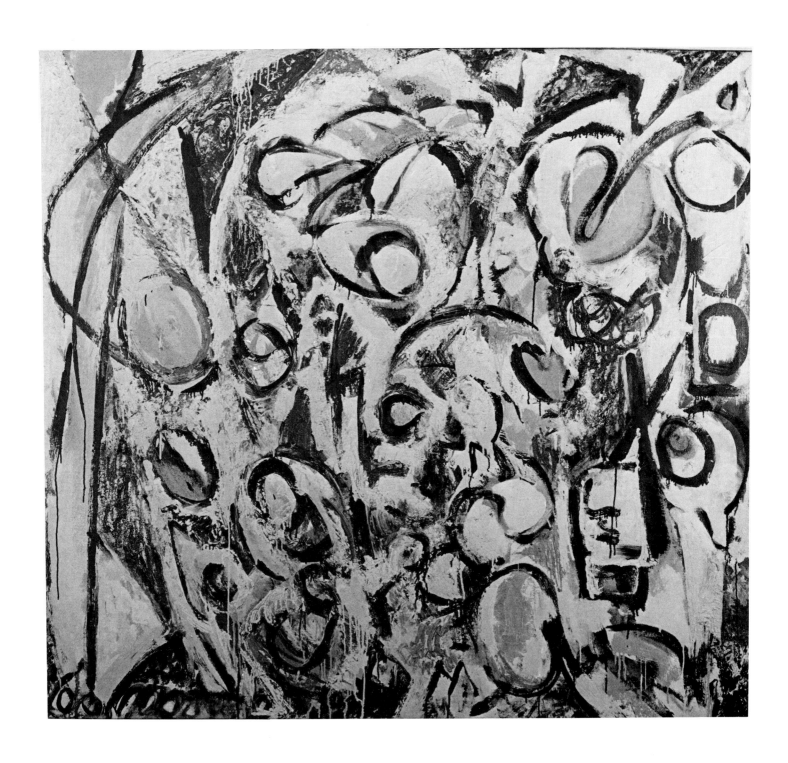

Fig. 93. Untitled. 1956. Oil on canvas. 58¾ × 66″ (149.2 × 167.6 cm). Collection Mr. and Mrs. Charles Glickman, Palm Beach.

painting (fig. 93), which is full of anatomical fragments, follows *Easter Lilies*.

By late spring 1956, when this agitated "action painting" was executed, Krasner decided to travel to Europe for the summer, to visit museums and pay a call on Peggy Guggenheim in Venice. Pollock had been drinking heavily. "I wanted to get away," she recalls, "from the complexity of everything." Before she left, she painted her first genuinely figurative automatic painting—a hybridized, three-legged standing figure, merging male and female anatomical parts. Far more grotesque and disturbing than anything Krasner had ever done, the painting was on her easel when she left for Europe. She had scratched an eye into the black area in the upper righthand corner, which Pollock urged her to remove. She decided to let it remain. Alfonso Ossorio, who bought the painting, suggested it should be titled *Prophecy* (fig. 92). The "third eye" Krasner had scratched in may have been an unconscious reference to her knowledge that her grandmother was known as a psychic.

She sailed for Europe in July on the *Queen Elizabeth*. It was her first trip abroad. She was anxious to know if the New York School had missed a great deal by being out of touch with Europe. On July 21, 1956, she wrote a concerned and affectionate letter to Pollock, mentioning her enjoyment at seeing Paris with John Graham:

Dear Jackson—
I'm staying at the Hotel Quai Voltaire, Quai Voltaire, Paris, until Sat the 28 and then going to the South of France to visit with the Gimpels and I hope to get to Venice about the early part of August—It all seems like a dream. . . . Thursday nite ended up in a Latin quarter dive, with Betty Parsons, David, who was at Sidney's, Helen Frankenthaler, the Jenkins, Sidney Geist & I don't remember who else, all dancing like mad. Went to the flea market with John Graham yesterday—saw all the left-bank galleries, met Drouin and several other dealers (Tapié, Stadler, etc.) Am going to do the right-bank galleries next week. I entered the Louvre which is just across the Seine outside my balcony which opens on it. . . . It is overwhelming—beyond belief. I miss you and wish you were sharing this with me. . . . The painting here is unbelievably bad. (How are you Jackson?) [43]

Krasner went from Paris to Menerbes in the south of France with the art dealer Charles Gimpel and his family and friends. Because Peggy Guggenheim would not receive her in Venice, she returned to Paris to stay with Paul Jenkins and his wife, Esther. It was there that she received a phone call from Clement Greenberg on August 12 informing her that Pollock had died in an auto accident the preceding evening. She returned immediately to East Hampton to arrange for the funeral and deal with the affairs of the Pollock estate. She signed the death certificate as she had signed her wedding certificate: "Lenore Krassner," and arranged to have Pollock buried at the Green River Cemetery in Springs on August 15.

It was the first time in fourteen years she and Pollock had been separated. "I had to realize that things would have happened in the same way even if I had been sitting right here in my living room," she later said.

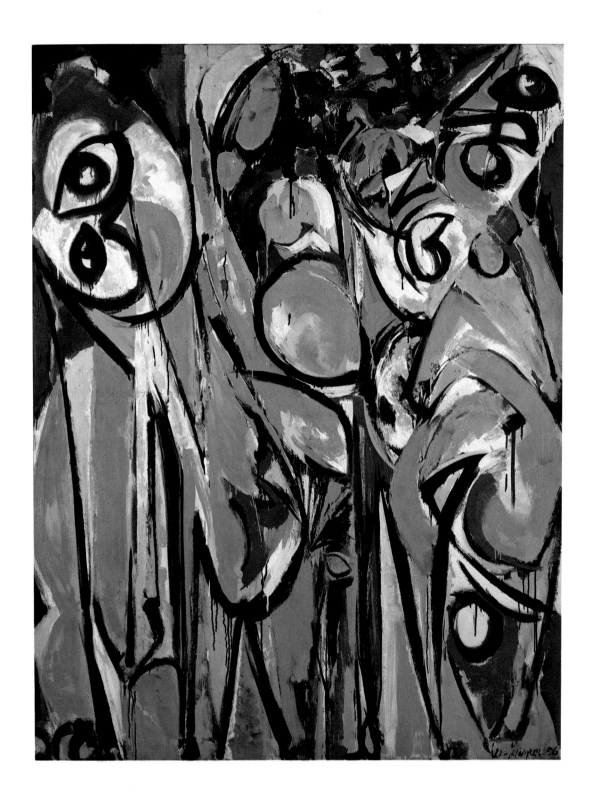

Fig. 94. *Three in Two*. 1956. Oil on cotton duck. 78 × 58″ (190.5 × 147.3 cm). Courtesy Robert Miller Gallery, New York.

VI. A Season in Hell

To whom shall I hire myself out? What beast must one adore? What holy image attacked? What hearts shall I break? What lie must I maintain? In what blood must I walk?

ARTHUR RIMBAUD, *A Season in Hell*
(Inscription on the wall of Lee Krasner's studio on Ninth Street, 1941.)

Prophecy was still on her easel, its scratched-out "third eye" like an allusion to Tiresias's psychic gifts, staring at her when Krasner returned to her studio. It became the point of departure for a group of the most moving and disturbing works by an Abstract Expressionist artist. These figurative paintings were totally at odds with the prevailing aesthetic of the New York School, which by the mid-fifties was virtually entirely abstract. Krasner's paintings done immediately after her husband's sudden, violent, accidental death were an exorcism of her feelings of rage, guilt, pain, and loss: the stormy emotions she could no longer suppress in the face of a catastrophe for which she was in no way prepared. Until the critical year of 1956, both her life and her work had been ruled by her own need for discipline and order, a need intensified by her role as the rock of stability to which Pollock anchored his own sense of reality.

Writing of Pollock, Clement Greenberg maintained that it was Pollock's great achievement to wrest order from chaos. We can see in retrospect that Krasner's natural inclination to orderliness, reinforced by her academic training and her admiration for Mondrian, the master of a transcendent order, had slowed her development as the major artist she became with her collage paintings, which were her first fully realized series of large-scale works. Ironically, her ultimate conversion to a completely post-Cubist style after 1956 was the result of a real-life accident that shook her to a point that changed her art into a direct expression of her feelings, receptive to aesthetic accident.

Krasner has always maintained that her work is autobiographical, and that the events of her life are the content of her art. Nowhere is this clearer than in the change of style, content, and technique that took place in her work beginning in 1956. No longer could she hold back the anger that is and always had been a dominant characteristic of hers; nor could she keep at bay the demons that disturbed her sleep, finally bringing down the walls of the iron discipline that had confined her will to self-expression. Lee Krasner never chose to be liberated, as a woman or an artist: It was a fate imposed on her by chance. She had been consciously seeking greater liberty and spontaneity in her work throughout her life. The evolution of her art from academic realism to Cubism to Abstract Expressionism reveals a steady progress toward an art more and more

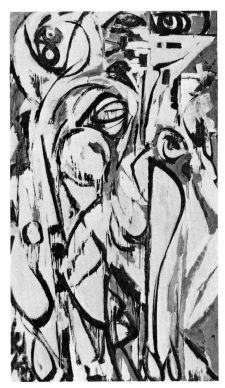

Fig. 95.
Birth. 1956.
Oil on cotton duck.
82½ × 48″ (209.5 × 121.9 cm).
Courtesy Robert Miller Gallery, New York.

free of the restraints of convention and of any a priori concepts, an art more specifically based on the unknown quantities of freely associated images uncensored by inhibition. Krasner was always independent and original, but she was not a "bohemian"; and the combination of her upbringing and schooling worked against her drive toward total emotional expression. As long as Pollock was alive, Krasner could not afford to enter the world of trancelike "otherness" in which he operated when he painted. *Her* feet, at least, had to be securely planted on the ground. This earthiness is reflected in the strict horizontal and vertical orientation of her paintings which, although they do not refer to a horizon line, have a single specific orientation which parallels that of the earthbound viewer. They are securely anchored. The disorienting quality of Pollock's churning, swirling imagery, especially after he began to work on the floor, approaching the painting from all four sides, is not found in Krasner's art. No matter how turbulent or agitated her imagery becomes, her images are always securely anchored to the top and bottom edges of her canvas, the explosive movement contained within the frame.

Lee Krasner lived with Jackson Pollock for less than fourteen years of her career as an artist, which now spans a half century. To be sure, the years they spent together were decisive for both. Krasner recalls a dream which is perhaps a metaphor of Pollock's influence on her art, as well as her life: "Jackson and I were standing on top of the world. The earth was a sphere with a pole going through the center, I was holding the pole with my right hand, and I was holding Jackson's hand with my left hand. Suddenly I let go of the pole, but I kept holding onto Jackson, and we both went floating off into outer space. We were not earthbound." While Pollock lived, Krasner could not afford to float away into outer space because she, like her mother before her, took on the responsibility of dealing with the practical matters of daily life. That she continued to work and to grow as an artist during her years with Pollock is indisputable, as is the fact that by 1950 her work was very different from his as both began to look for inspiration in the work they had produced in the thirties. Without doubt, Pollock influenced Krasner as much as he did the rest of the New York School. On the other hand, Krasner put him in touch with the aesthetics of

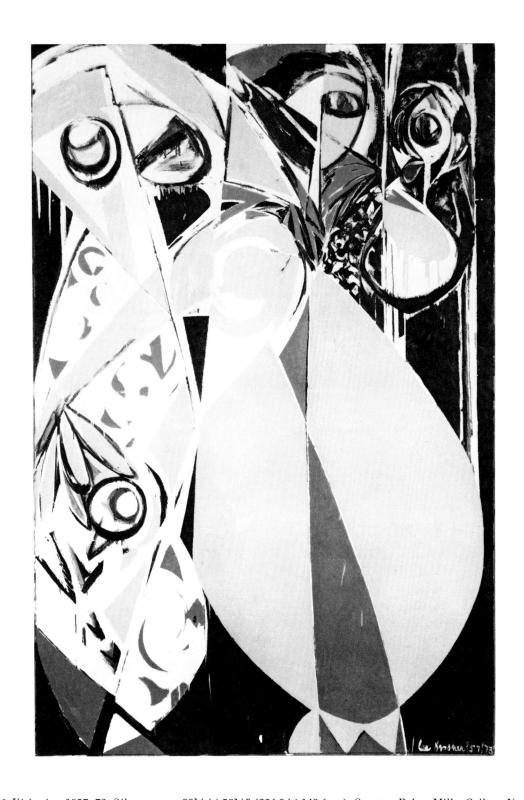

Fig. 96. *Visitation.* 1957–73. Oil on canvas. 88½ × 58½″ (224.8 × 148.6 cm). Courtesy Robert Miller Gallery, New York.

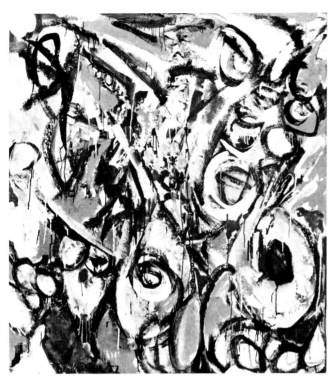

Fig. 97.
Four. 1957.
Oil on cotton duck.
58½ × 53¾″ (148.6 × 136.5 cm).
Collection Alfonso A. Ossorio, East Hampton.

modernism and a more international, sophisticated view of art than Benton's narrow provincialism. Pollock's "break-through" to a larger scale, an allover composition with no single focus, identifying the whole image with the entire canvas field, and his use of automatic drawing to generate psychologically charged imagery affected the other advanced artists of his generation. The chromatic abstractionists, led by Newman and Rothko, rejected gesture, emphasizing color as content. Reinhardt, consciously in opposition to Pollock, eliminated not only detail and internal relationships within the field because they recalled Cubist "rhyming" of a form with an analogous form, but ultimately rejected color and contrast as well in his "black" paintings.

We have seen how in 1950–53, Krasner swung back

and forth between "action painting" gesture and color-field reductiveness, resolving the dichotomy between the two in her brilliant series of collage paintings. These paintings also in many respects resolved issues Pollock himself was grappling with at the time. The visual evidence reveals that Krasner began as a stronger, more confident, and more conventionally talented artist, with a far more thoroughgoing understanding of modernism than Pollock. Once she started pouring her energy and ideas back into her own work in the early fifties, the artistic symbiosis that appears to have been the core of their relationship was ruptured. Apparently a major cause of this rupture was their common dissatisfaction at a certain point with the interdependence that united them. This symbiosis was illustrated by Krasner in the merging of male and female into a single androgynous *personnage* in *Prophecy*. In 1953, Pollock, who had been analyzed in the thirties by a Jungian, re-entered psychoanalysis. This time, however, he was seeing a Sullivanian therapist who counseled enjoying his success in the world rather than turning his attention back into himself and the dream imagery and archetypes that reappear in his 1951–52 figurative black-and-white paintings. At about the same time, Krasner entered analysis for the first time, in an attempt to cope with crises in both life and art. As their union began to dissolve, the two returned to what each had been as a young artist: Krasner regained her autonomy and confidence, and Pollock became more overwhelmed and alcoholic. As Pollock became more and more involved with the social life of the New York art scene, which centered around bars and drinking parties, Krasner withdrew into her own work. She refused to go with him to the Cedar Bar or the Artists Club. However, she and Pollock continued their artistic dialogue: Until his death he remained her greatest—virtually only—supporter, always encouraging her work and praising it to others.

Despite the tragic circumstances in which they were created, it would be erroneous to infer that Krasner's figurative paintings of the late fifties, which are large-scale Expressionist "action paintings," employing the technique of automatic drawing in paint, were simply the result of her reaction to Pollock's death. She had in fact begun the cycle of flesh-colored *personnage* paintings while he was still alive. *Prophecy* became the prototype for the series of

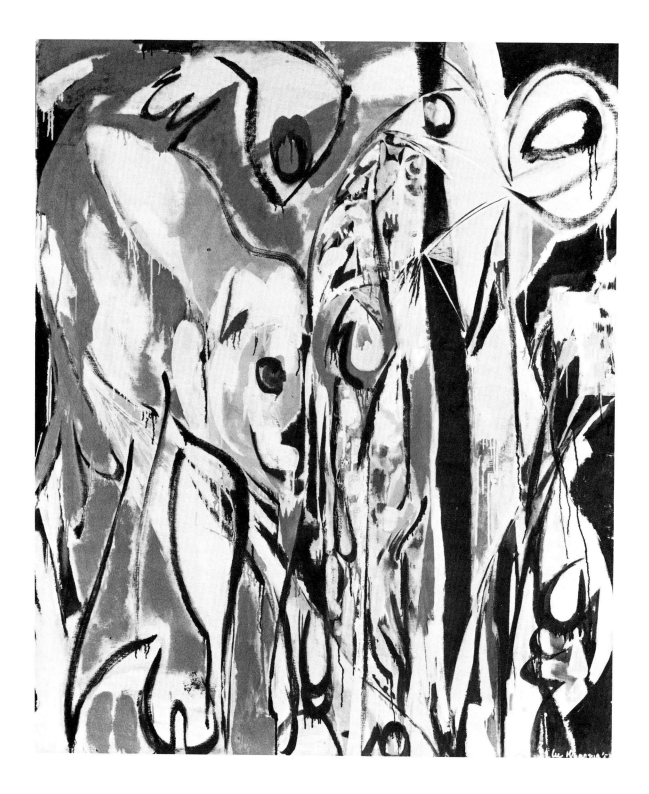

Fig. 98. *April.* 1957. Oil on canvas. 68½ × 50¼″ (174 × 127.6 cm). Sarah Campbell Blaffer Foundation, Houston.

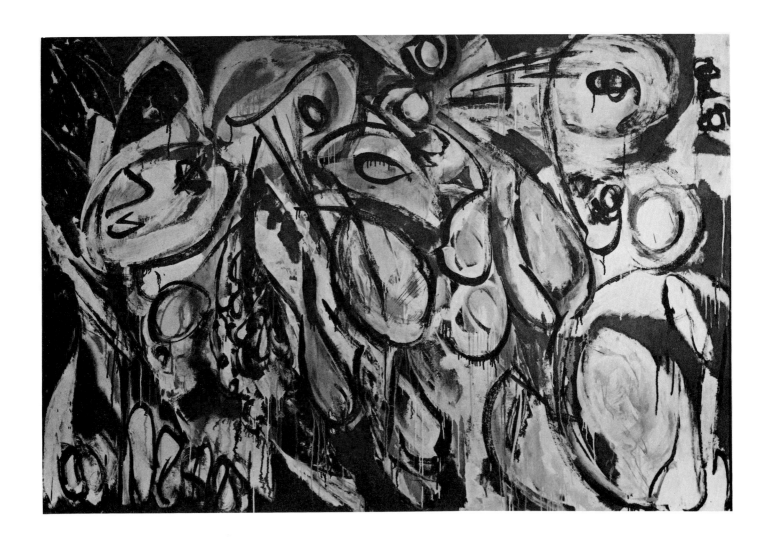

Fig. 99. *Upstream.* 1957. Oil on canvas. 58 × 88″ (147.3 × 223.5 cm). Private collection.

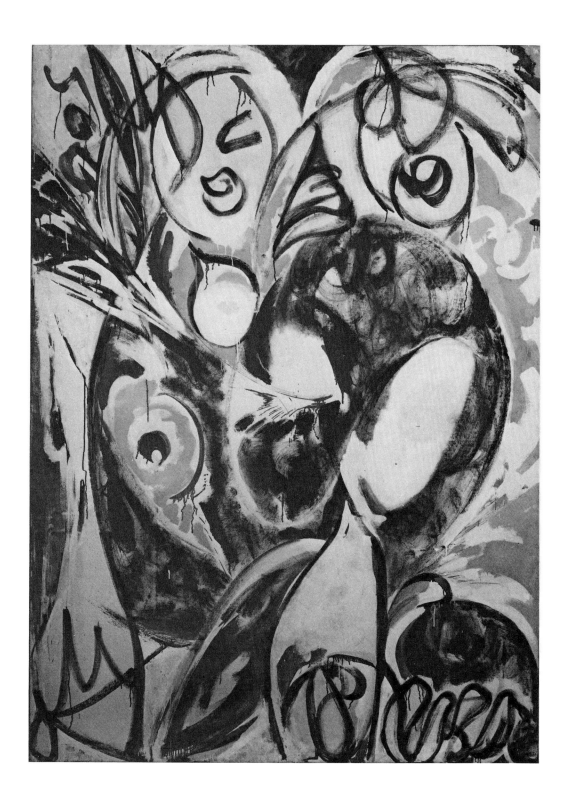

Fig. 100. *Sun Woman I*. 1957. Oil on canvas. 97¼ × 70¼″ (247 × 178.4 cm). Collection Donald B. Marron, New York.

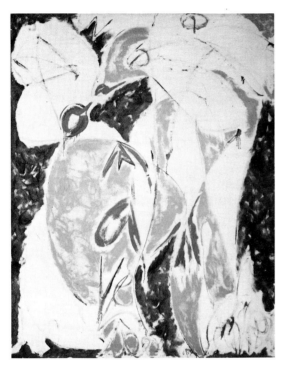

Fig. 101.
Earth Green. 1957.
Oil on cotton duck.
95⅛ × 75⅛″ (241.6 × 190.8 cm).
Collection Bryan Robertson, London.

hybridized figures that, like Gorky's paintings, mix natural and anatomical motifs, synthesizing the landscape with the human figure. Krasner's *personnages*, are as inclusive of polarities and as fully hybridized as possible: Neither demonic nor angelic, neither male nor female, they subsume organic and natural forms in an essentially anthropomorphic image of interpenetrating *personnages*. Drips are permitted to run in rivulets, merging form with form and connoting a spontaneous urgency. However, as usual, Krasner displays her sense of architectonic monumentality by emphasizing the horizontal and vertical axes of the framing edge, thus insuring that structure dominates any Expressionist tendencies (fig. 94).

Krasner's choice of flesh tones as the dominant color and of blood-red accents in the 1956 paintings, such as *Birth*, is deliberate (fig. 95). Once again, we are reminded of Gorky's tragic late paintings, with their references to wounds and pain. However, she never gives one the sense that inner organs are exposed as in an autopsy; figures may "bleed," but they remain intact and upright, on guard like wounded soldiers. Her Expressionist paintings of the late fifties are as clear a record of profound pain as Gorky's anguished works of the late forties. Only Pollock's early drawings of martyrdom and crucifixion express such a degree of subjective, personal suffering. It is significant that Krasner was at this time the only artist (outside of his brother Sanford) who knew Pollock's early drawings based on an amalgam of sources ranging from tribal images to Old Master and Mexican mural art. The last and strongest of the drawings is inspired by Picasso's *Guernica* style. Pollock had recourse to these drawings in the imagery he evolved in his 1951–52 black-and-white paintings. Krasner's figurative Expressionist style of the late fifties, although richly colored, marks a return to her own interest in Picasso, which was eclipsed during her life with Pollock, when Mondrian and Matisse were uppermost in her mind. *Visitation* (fig. 96), for example, specifically recalls Picasso's double image of the *Girl before a Mirror* in The Museum of Modern Art. Krasner had not studied the painting for years, but it remained part of her bank of images, to be retrieved at a later date.

Other paintings in the figurative Expressionist style of 1956–57 include *Four, April,* and *Upstream* (figs. 97, 98, 99). Their tone is predominantly flesh-colored, which

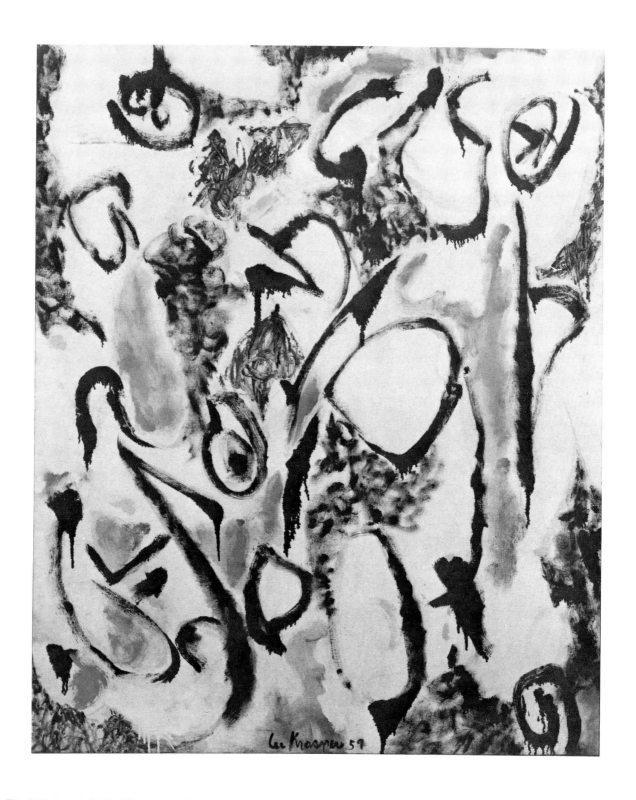

Fig. 102. *Breath*. 1959. Oil on cotton duck. 60 × 49½″ (152.4 × 125.7 cm). Collection Mrs. Peter Roussel Norman, New Orleans.

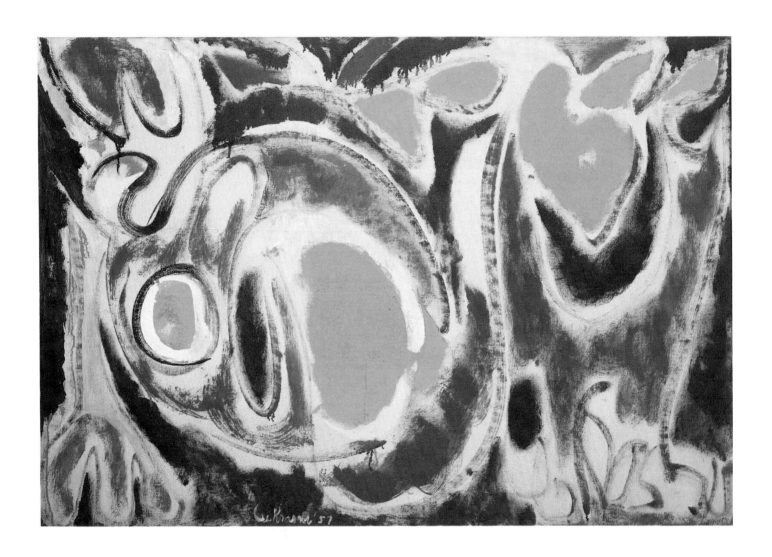

Fig. 103. *Cat Image*. 1957. Oil on cotton duck. 39⅛ × 58⅛″ (99.4 × 147.6 cm). Courtesy Robert Miller Gallery, New York.

furthers the allusion to the body evoked by anatomical fragments suggestive of bulging breasts, bellies, and buttocks. Paint runs, drips, spreads, invading adjacent forms, indicating a speed of execution and a willingness to relinquish absolute control new in Krasner's work. For if Pollock's problem was to wrest order from chaos, Krasner's was to learn that she could use her rage without losing control.

The last paintings Pollock did had huge staring eyes, and eyes stare, too, from the jumble of bursting forms created by the swerving and looping black brushstrokes of Krasner's paintings of this period. However, the disembodied eye was hardly unique to their work. Surrealists from René Magritte to Man Ray had used disembodied eyes. The eye is one of the commonest hieroglyphic symbols, and Krasner was familiar with the connotations of the eye as a symbol of psychic insight from John Graham's use of the eye as a sign of clairvoyance. The disembodied, all-seeing eye of *Guernica* may also have been in Krasner's mind at the time. She felt that she was particularly vulnerable to the many hostile eyes watching and reporting on her every move, for while she was painting these disturbing works, she was harrassed by journalists, collectors, dealers, and others eager to profit from Pollock's death. It was an extremely difficult period for her, yet she managed to deal with matters beyond her control and to accept a certain degree of loss of control in her art at the same time.

The works of 1956–57 appear full to overflowing, in both an expressive and a formal sense. They are crowded, densely packed with bursting and bulging forms. Gene Baro, who organized a show of Krasner's works at the Corcoran Gallery in 1975, wrote perceptively of "the muscularity of her dense textures that seem almost to grow upon the surface . . . the vivid and darting shapes of the splashed or thrown paint" and of her images that "express flux or mirror rippleness."[44] Baro observed: "There is almost too much and yet somehow the pictorial energies are disciplined . . . by a precise sense of scale. Nothing spills over. There is intensification of effect without dissipation."

The memory of Pollock's early friezelike paintings such as *There Were Seven in Eight* is recalled in Krasner's *Three in Two*, one of the series of flesh-colored paintings of interpenetrating figures in which black is used as ges-

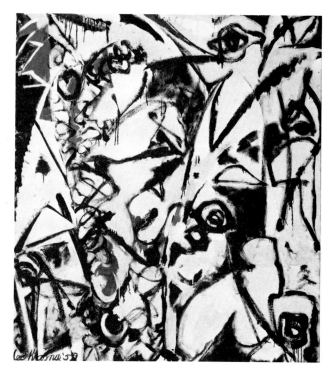

Fig. 104.
Fledgling. 1959.
Oil on cotton duck.
64 × 58″ (162.6 × 147.3 cm).
Courtesy Robert Miller Gallery, New York.

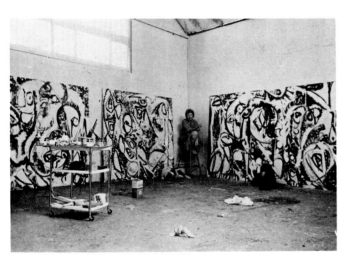

Fig. 105.
Lee Krasner with *Siblings*, 1959.

tural drawing (fig. 94). Gray and white are used sparingly and are painted into the flesh-colored, painfully contorted limbs and scattered intermingled anatomical fragments. Black, which Pollock had warned her to use with care, is the color of the gestural drawing used to "correct" and multiply contour in a manner revealing Krasner's understanding of Cézanne's technique. Gray and white impinge on flesh-colored surface mass to integrate paint surface and the cursory, continuous automatic drawing that insures no hard-edge forms are depicted through the use of line. The limbs of these *personnages* are stalk-like; in later paintings like *Sun Woman I*, heads and arms suggest flowers in an even further hybridization of form (fig. 100). These limb-stalks tend to line up vertically with the framing edge. Writing about Pollock, William Rubin has called attention to the way that Pollock consciously turned his baroque compositions inward at the corners toward the center, not permitting his looping arcs to break the frame. Krasner respected the frame perhaps more scrupulously than Pollock, never, as Baro noted, allowing the contents of the painting to "spill over."

Toward the end of 1957, the densely compacted forms which seem about to burst from fullness of feeling, give way to an airier, more transparent painting style that uses brighter colors and a lighter touch. The thick, heavy black strokes of automatic drawings are replaced in 1957 paintings like *Earth Green, Cat Image,* and *Listen* (figs. 101, 103, 106) by a more sparing use of line, which is now brushed on in a transparent, diluted brownish-black. As usual, Krasner confines her palette to two or three colors plus white. She also leaves part of the background of these paintings exposed, so that one has a sense of openness of the images, spreading, "breathing." This lightness and airiness contrasts with the claustrophobic crowdedness of the works during the year after Pollock's death when Krasner first began to paint in the barn beside the house in Springs, where she remained until 1966. Drawing still suggests figuration, but the metaphor now seems floral rather than anatomical. Color is bright and fresh rather than dull and gray, and forms seem buoyant rather than heavy and lumbering. The new palette is high-key and intense in contrast: In *Cat Image*, brilliant yellow is opposed to crimson and magenta. *Sun Woman I* pairs viridian green with an intense sunny yellow, magenta, and white.

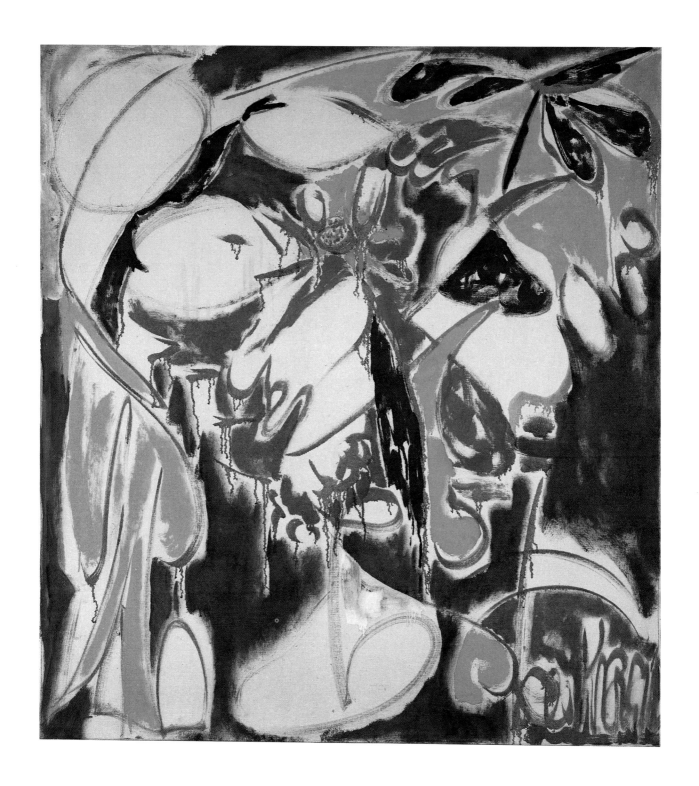

Fig. 106. *Listen*. 1957. Oil on cotton duck. 63½ × 58⅜″ (161.3 × 148.3 cm). Private collection.

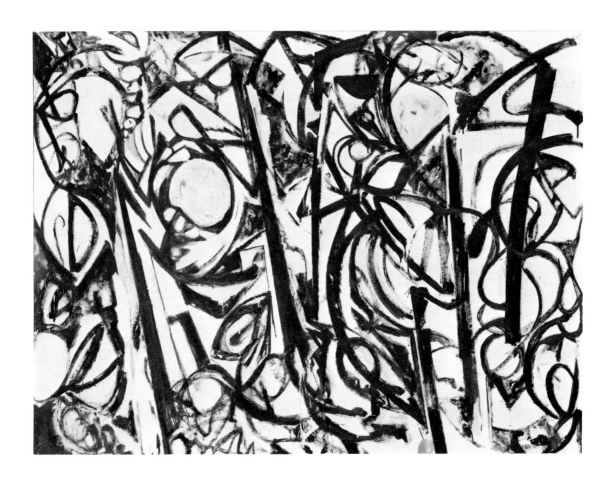

Fig. 107. *Gothic Landscape*. 1961. Oil on canvas. 69⅝ × 93⅝″ (176.8 × 237.8 cm). The Trustees of the Tate Gallery, London.

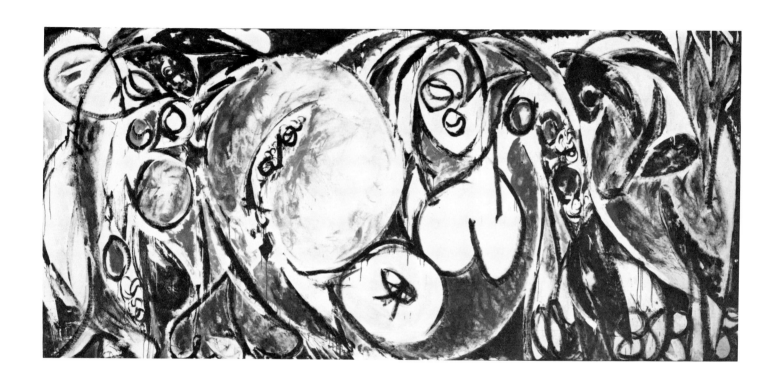

Fig. 108. *The Seasons.* 1957. Oil on cotton duck. 92⅞ × 203¾″ (235.9 × 517.5 cm). Courtesy Robert Miller Gallery, New York.

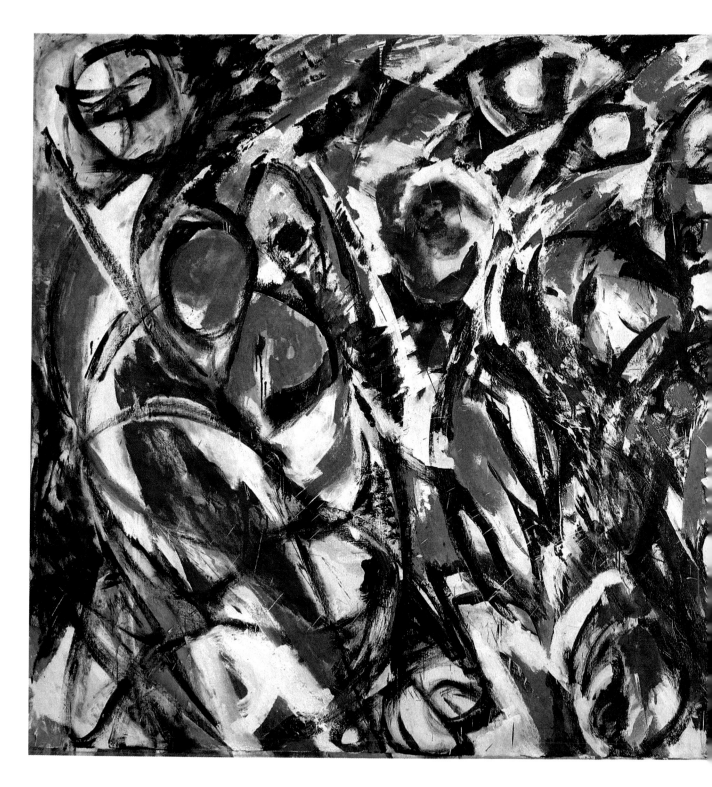

Fig. 109. *Celebration*. 1959–60. Oil on canvas. 92¼ × 184½″ (234.3 × 468.6 cm). Private collection.

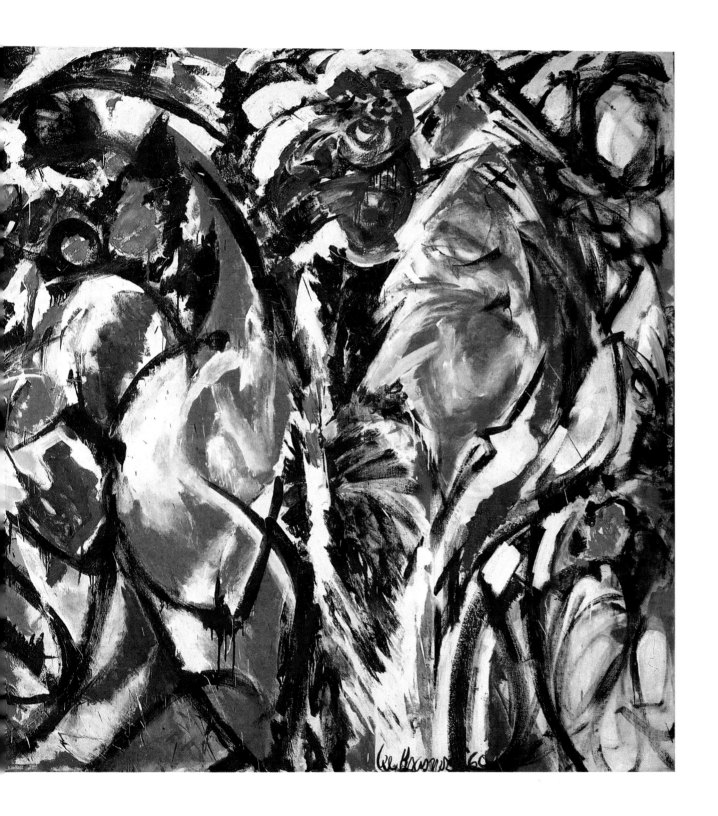

Listen, perhaps the most brilliant and bouquet-like of the series, combines cobalt violet and viridian green with rose red. Exposed canvas acts as a foil for transparent color, creating an atmospheric openness not seen in Krasner's previous works. Openness and transparency are also characteristic of a brilliant series of paintings that use both automatic drawing and original, unconventional color combinations such as the umber-orange-alizarin triad of *The Bull* (fig. 114) and the yellow ochre, earth green, and cadmium red mixed with white of *Cornucopia*, whose forms seem to overflow with the lush ripeness of the traditional harvest symbol. Some of these combinations are seen first in Krasner's oil-and-paper still-life abstractions of the late thirties. Twenty years later, the full range of her physical energy is the animating force in compositions that are integrated by a gyrating rhythmic linear arabesque. In *Breath* and *Spring Memory*, flesh tones reappear, but they are lighter and patched rather than solid and opaque; the drawing also is less figurative, and areas of white, raw canvas and thinly brushed, dappled paint give the effect of both a greater openness and a more abstract feeling (fig. 102). The image of the mortification of the flesh has been replaced by a less specific allusion to skin and hair. None of these paintings is very large, but they express a potent sense of drama because of the variation of line and rhythm and the intense color contrasts Krasner uses. The new fluidity Krasner achieves appears related to her return to drawing in 1958, when she made a series of impressive black-and-white figurative brush drawings, incorporating the white page as an active element into their elegant curving contours. Ink is brushed with great fluidity, or at times a relatively dry brush is passed across the surface. These drawings seem an immediate precedent for the way she handles the brush now, painting with a new ease, applying pigment more sparingly, diluting it more than in the past or using a drier brush. This fluidity and transparency add to the airiness and expansiveness of such works as *Fledgling*, *Siblings*, and *Gothic Landscape* (figs. 104, 105, 107).

In 1957, Krasner painted *The Seasons*, the largest work she had executed to date (fig. 108). Nearly seventeen feet long, *The Seasons* combines automatic drawing with intense color. In 1960, she completed the fifteen-foot-long *Celebration* (fig. 109), which was originally begun

in 1957 and titled *Upstream II*. The frontal, friezelike arrangement of this canvas mural is once again reminiscent of the interwined figures and dancelike procession Pollock depicted in his first "big picture": the 19¾-foot-long mural Peggy Guggenheim commissioned in 1943. Krasner helped Pollock create the wall on which this portable mural was actually painted; the experience may have suggested working on such a large scale by tacking a long roll of canvas onto the studio wall.

Between 1959 and 1960, Krasner revised and finished the monumental *Celebration*. Late in that year, she began painting in black or umber and white figurative works like *Messenger* and *Siblings*, based on her brush drawings of 1958. These were roughly six-foot-square works that used drawing in an increasingly painterly way, opening contours, feathering lines with a dry brush. Although figurative, these works pointed to a new kind of abstract style that combined the densely impacted forms, horizontal format, and large scale of *Celebration* with automatic drawing and a virtually monochromatic palette. These linear works, such as the elaborately ornate *Uncaged*, were the beginning of a new series of umber mural-size paintings whose horizontal formats appear an implicit reference to landscape.

In 1957–58, the cycle of automatically generated *personnage* imagery is complete, and floral allusions displace the monsters of *Prophecy*. In a certain sense, the process of exorcism has ended, only to give way to an even more explosive and thunderous expression of a rage so overpowering it can only be pictured in a distanced form as abstraction. At the end of 1959 Krasner's style "broke" again. Late in that year, Krasner began *The Gate* (fig. 110), the first in a series of abstract mural-size paintings which combined an aggressive, highly charged imagery with a technique that appeared a vehement attack on the canvas with the loaded brush. The palette, predominantly shades of earthy umber and white, is not the palette of high drama, but in Krasner's hands it became the color of earthquake, shipwreck, and scenes of catastrophe so devastating one felt she was expressing not only her own rage, but the wrath of God.

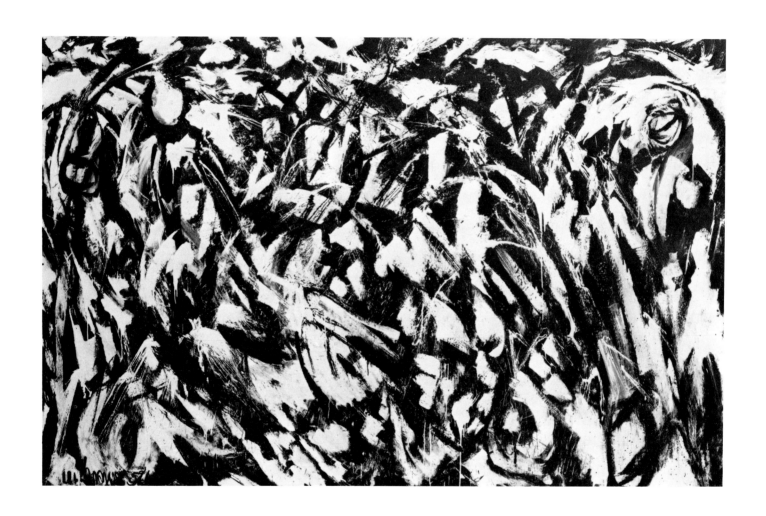

Fig. 110. *The Gate*. 1959–60. Oil on canvas. 92¾ × 144½″ (235.6 × 367 cm). Courtesy Robert Miller Gallery, New York.

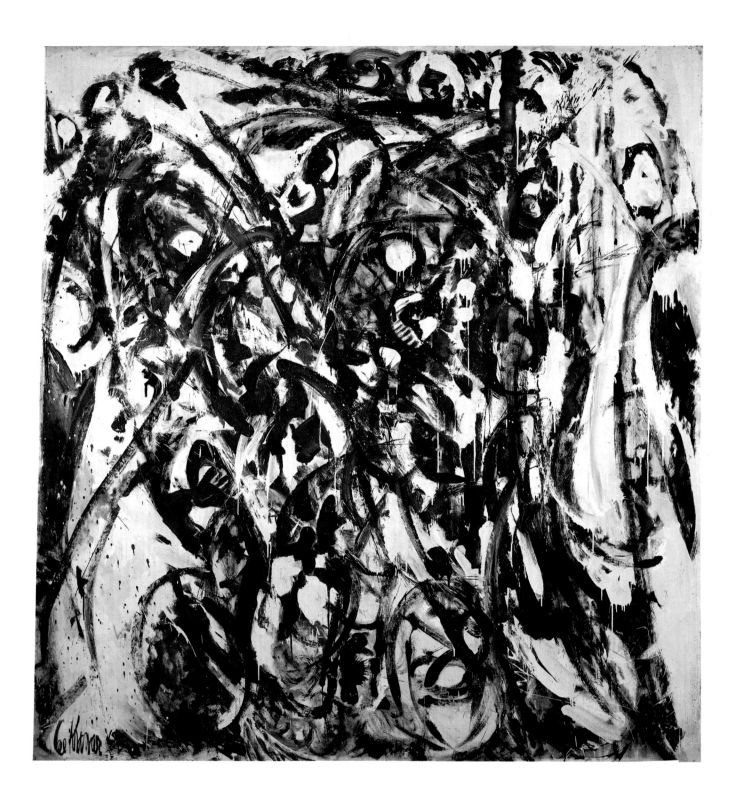

Fig. 111. *Uncaged*. 1960. Oil on cotton duck. 96⅞ × 93½″ (246.1 × 237.5 cm). Collection Jeanette Leroy, Paris.

VII. Big Pictures

Executing an abstract mural, whose purpose was to embellish architecture, was, as we have noted, Krasner's ambition when she worked on the WPA. This cherished dream came true in 1958 when B. H. Friedman, an executive of Uris Brothers, commissioned her to create two mosaic panels for their new office building at 2 Broadway. At the time, the idea of public art and architectural decoration, the essence of the WPA, had been virtually forgotten. There were two spaces to be filled: a square area about fifteen by fifteen feet over the Broad Street entrance of the thirty-story building (fig. 112), and an eighty-six-foot-long, narrow, horizontal frieze over the main entrance. It was the second time Krasner had had to translate an image into a mosaic mural, but at least this time it was her own abstract design she was working on. Certainly the full-scale drawing on paper she executed to guide the artisans setting the mosaic focused her on the edge where shape meets shape (fig. 113).

The final mosaics, still in situ, were a collaboration between Krasner and her nephew, Ronald Stein. It was a difficult and time-consuming challenge. Working on the collage maquettes provided Krasner with a means of translating her winged, floral, and organic forms into monumental abstractions on a public scale. The cutout painted paper collage-on-canvas maquette for the square mosaic connects Krasner's 1955 collage paintings to the series of color-field murals on canvas she painted in the seventies. The collage maquette for the long thin frieze, on the other hand, because of its odd format, forced her to find a means of carrying the eye across the whole of the extended surface. It became the inspiration for the series of big pictures she began in the late fifties. According to Friedman: "There were four major color groups in the collage studies Krasner prepared for the mural—eight earth greens, six ultramarines, four alizarin crimsons, and three blacks, ranging from a deep warm umber tone to a fairly cool gray-black similar to that used on the spandrels of the building itself. Finally a small amount of golden yellow was selected for accents."[45]

The colors Krasner used in the 2 Broadway mosaics were her basic palette, once she became an original colorist and dropped Mondrian's Neo-Plastic palette of primary colors, which she had adopted in the late thirties and early forties. A reduced number of colors is typical of the color-field painters among the Abstract Expressionists, who tend to limit themselves to a few colors, usually found in nature, as opposed to the sizzling and psychedelic colors later found in Pop and Op art. Their choice has more in common with Nicolas Poussin's attitude toward the necessity for restricting the palette in classical art than it does with the riot of artificial colors, often arbitrarily mixed and combined to create novel effects, of the next generation of abstract artists, who were as much influenced by commercial color as Pop artists were influenced by commercial images. For Krasner's generation, color was a serious tool to be used expressively, but with reticence and a sense of decorum.

Color in Krasner's art is a subject in itself. Her training with Hofmann in color theory provided her with the knowledge of how adjacent contrasting colors would interact to produce maximum brilliance. In *Blue and Black* and *Offbeat*, she used relatively large areas of local color. Beginning in 1971, she would paint works that employed a single unbroken color as a luminous glowing field. Before she could settle down to such relatively tranquil concerns, however, she seemed to need to release more of the explosive physical energy and aggression that had been pent up inside her for so many years.

The bridge to a dramatic new style that was both abstract and Expressionist was, as we have seen, the collage maquette for the mosaic commissioned to decorate the horizontal facade of 2 Broadway. The long, narrow format forced her to slice shapes into smaller units and spread them out in a rhythmic, dancing pattern, sufficiently dynamic to carry the eye across the field. Thus, this friezelike collage maquette prefigures her Abstract Expressionist style of 1960–62. Dark and light elements interpenetrate, leap, and dance, creating a sense of constant movement and animation. The basic unit is an oval that is twisted, turned, and dispersed across the entire horizontal surface. No doubt we have come a long way from the WPA mural of the *History of Navigation* here; however, the knowledge of how to fill a wall with detail and use scale elements to create a larger-than-life monumentality served Krasner well when she began to paint mural-size pictures.

Krasner's mural-size big pictures are typical of the New York School. Academic art frequently produced very large paintings to decorate public spaces. However, once

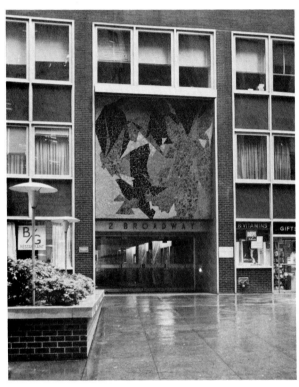

Fig. 112.
Untitled. 1958–59.
Mosaic mural.
180 × 180″ (457.2 × 457.2 cm).
Uris Building, 2 Broadway, New York.

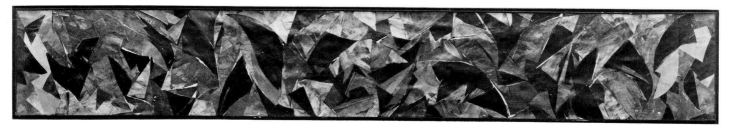

Fig. 113.
Study for mosaic at 2 Broadway, New York. 1958–59.
Paper on cotton duck.
Whereabouts unknown.

patronage became private and artists no longer worked on commissions, the scale of paintings was reduced. There were, of course, exceptions, such as Picasso's *Guernica* and Miró's 1947 Cincinnati mural, both designed for public spaces, but for the most part it was the experience of the WPA that apparently gave the New York School an appetite for large-scale works. The idea that such works were de facto only appropriate for public spaces appealed to the social conscience of New York School artists, many of whom, like Krasner, were involved with Marxism in the thirties.

According to E. C. Goossen, the "big canvas" first appears in New York School art in 1949.[46] The argument of who did what and when is still raging, but it becomes irrelevant once we recall that Pollock painted a portable mural on canvas in 1943. Krasner did not realize her own initial impulse to paint mural-size canvases until the late fifties, another reason she has only recently been properly seen as a first-generation Abstract Expressionist. We have noted that an intrinsic monumentality is a key quality in Krasner's work from an early date as a result of her attraction to Mondrian's architectonic formats. At first she achieved monumentality without working on a literally large scale. The expansion of power, indeed, explicitly physical power, is already characteristic of her first attempts to draw the nude in Job Goodman's classes at Greenwich House in the thirties. As we have seen, her

drawings of both male and female nudes show well-developed, muscular bodies. These firmly rounded, heroic nudes also reflected the classical ideal taught at the National Academy. Krasner's knowledge of Renaissance and Baroque epic styles, which antedated her training in Cubism with Hofmann, remained part of her total consciousness, to be called on when she painted her complex, detailed big pictures. In fact, it is the complexity and detail of her mature style as a colorist that differentiates her work from the reductive forms of color-field painting.

Clearly, Krasner had aspired to the heroic sweep and epic drama of the big picture since the thirties, when she painted murals for the WPA. Like all the artists of the New York School, Krasner had been deeply impressed by the size, impact, and drama of Picasso's *Guernica*, a memory that stayed with her throughout her life, perhaps even helping inspire her switch to a somber monochrome palette in 1959–60.

When Marcia Tucker first assembled a group of Krasner's large mural-size paintings in an exhibition at the Whitney Museum of American Art in 1973, she defined them as frontal, reductive in color, and consistent in their improvisatory technique. It is true even of the hard-edge works of the seventies that the images evolve during the painting process rather than being copied or adapted from a pre-existing drawing. The strong rhythmic component in these basically horizontal images is another consistent

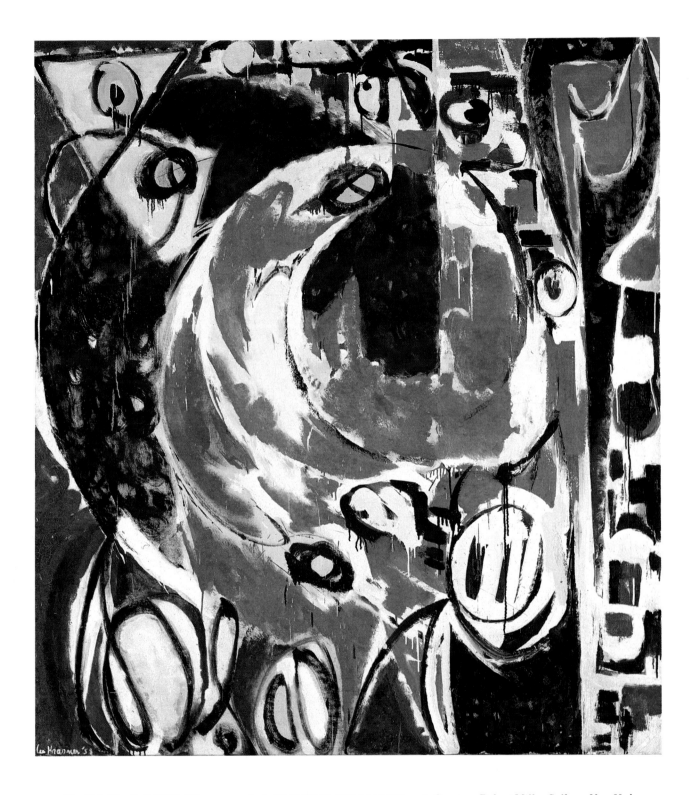

Fig. 114. *The Bull*. 1958. Oil on cotton duck. 77 × 70⅛″ (195.6 × 178.1 cm). Courtesy Robert Miller Gallery, New York.

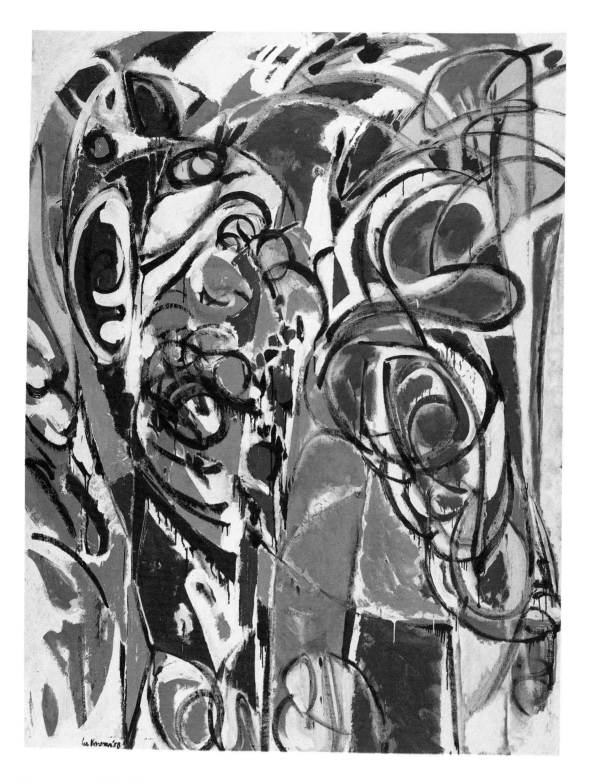

Fig. 115. *Cornucopia*. 1958. Oil on cotton duck. 90⅝ × 70″ (230.2 × 177.8 cm). Collection Gordon F. Hampton, Los Angeles.

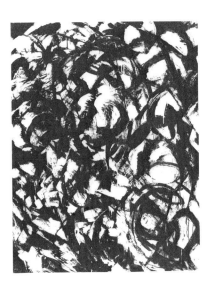

Fig. 116.
What Beast Must I Adore? 1961.
Oil on cotton duck.
75 × 57⅞″ (190.5 × 147 cm).
Courtesy Robert Miller Gallery, New York.

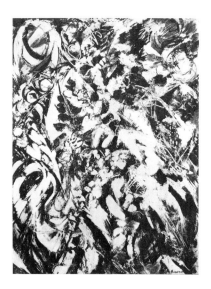

Fig. 117.
Primeval Resurgence. 1961.
Oil on cotton duck.
77 × 57¼″ (195.6 × 145.4 cm).
Collection Gordon F. Hampton, Los Angeles.

element in Krasner's style, which we have remarked on in all her work from her earliest Cubist drawings to her current paintings.

The allover patterning of the maquette for the frieze-like mosaic, although it was executed during a period when Krasner was painting bright-colored automatically drawn figurative paintings, is entirely abstract. Linear drawing does not depict shape; rather, the edge of a cut-out shape is its own contour. At the end of 1959, around the time the mosaics were actually executed and put in place (only to be burned and damaged), Krasner painted those two remarkable "action paintings," *Uncaged* and *The Gate.* In the delicate, complex arabesques of paintings like *The Bull* and *Cornucopia,* colors were presented as transparent screens (figs. 114, 115). In subsequent paintings like *Uncaged,* linear patterns are brought to a rich textured complexity through the application of additional white and ochre paint. *The Gate,* begun in 1959 and finished in 1960, is a far less lyrical and more ferocious painting than *Uncaged* (fig. 111). Dark and light are severely contrasted, as if to create a deliberate Manichaean opposition. Indeed, the vehement attack of brush on canvas suggests a battle scene.

The Gate was the beginning of one of Krasner's most striking series of "action paintings"—the huge, mural-size compositions she showed at the Howard Wise Gallery in 1960 and 1962. Once more, she had "switched gears." No linear tracery of automatic drawing describes organic forms. No grid of compartments confines the raging energies that animate the brush loaded with thick paint, now slapped or dragged across the canvas, leaving a trail of flaring drips and sputtering comet-like flashes of paint. The allover images and glazed transparencies of these works suggest wind-whipped storms or glacial events. The furious migrations of heaving ice-age behemoths are alluded to in the title of one of these paintings, *Polar Stampede* (fig. 118). Although these paintings appear to have been executed in a moment of frenzy, one sees that every gesture is counter-balanced by a gesture curving in toward the other side. Despite this antiphonal movement, the eye cannot focus on a dominant form or shape that permits it to rest its attention. We are condemned, like the artist, to be buffeted by the storm from which, as long as we remain with the painting, there is no shelter.

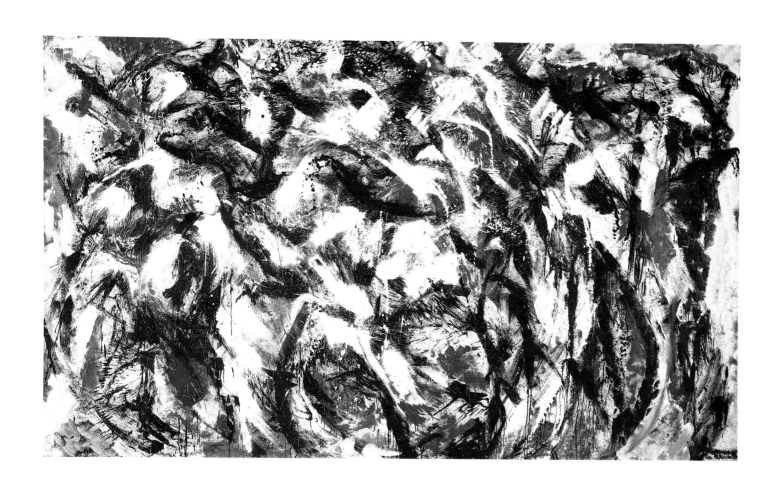

Fig. 118. *Polar Stampede*. 1960. Oil on cotton duck. 93⅝ × 159¾″ (237.8 × 405.8 cm). Courtesy Robert Miller Gallery, New York.

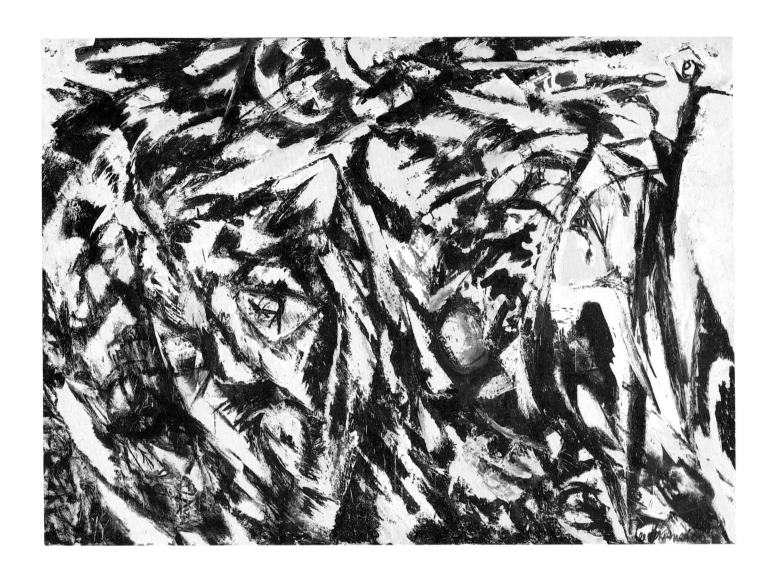

Fig. 119. *Charred Landscape*. 1960. Oil on cotton duck. 70⅛ × 95⅝″ (178.1 × 250.5 cm). Courtesy Robert Miller Gallery, New York.

Because of their size, these paintings, like the largest of Pollock, Newman, and Still's horizontal paintings, cannot be seen entirely from one point of view, even with peripheral vision. They encompass the viewer. One is "in" them as one is "in" Claude Monet's huge pools of *Water Lilies*, paintings both Krasner and Pollock admired. When a painting becomes an environment, however, we are more fully and intimately exposed to the psychic state of the artist. There is no way in or out of a painting like *The Eye Is the First Circle*, a nearly sixteen-foot-long oil on canvas. The painting has become a place rather than an object. There is no overt figuration in this monumental painting, named after Emerson's celebrated essay, or in related pictures, such as *Charred Landscape*; however, one has an almost subliminal sense of a primeval landscape, torn and rent by natural catastrophe, of the movements of polar caps, the slide of glaciers , the eruption of lava.

Krasner's eschatological vision is once again totally at odds with the tenor of the times in which the painting was made, the "swinging sixties." The ambiguous imagery brings to mind the veiled images of Pollock's black-and-white paintings. Those were enigmatic, powerful paintings that provoked us to read images into them, but these images of Krasner's are as mysteriously buried as the strange configurations Pollock admired in the pulsating surface of her thickly textured Little Image painting *Continuum*.

Like all Krasner's paintings, the Umber series, as these huge canvas murals have been called because of their predominantly umber tone, are constructed with the care of medieval stonemasonry. No forms break the frame even in these, her most baroque paintings, in which the central metaphor is either a storm or a geological upheaval. They are landscapes, but landscapes of a primeval moment of creation that also portends violence.

Despite their tempestuous imagery, there is a deliberateness constantly at work disciplining spontaneity into coherent pictorial structures. Indeed, we may trace the source of the flickering, pulsating, allover imagery of Krasner's 1960–62 big pictures to the first series of allover Little Image paintings. Now, however, instead of the regularity and predictability of brushstrokes of more or less equal size and density placed next to one another, we have the explosion of big patches of white, shades of the

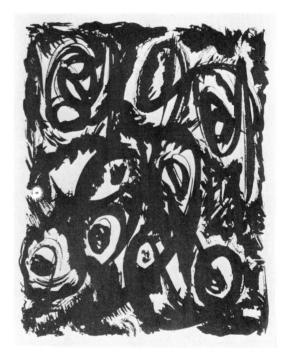

Fig. 120.
Untitled. 1958.
Ink on drawing paper.
11¾ × 9½″ (29.8 × 24.1 cm).
Courtesy Robert Miller Gallery, New York.

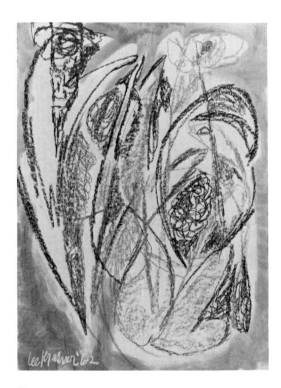

Fig. 121.
Untitled. 1962.
Watercolor and crayon on paper.
30 × 22″ (76.2 × 55.9 cm).
Collection the artist.

earth tones, umber, and sienna applied with varying degrees of saturation (figs. 116, 117). In some spots canvas shows through; in others, as in *Charred Landscape*, opaque build-up of paint obscures the support entirely (fig. 119).

These mural-size paintings are in many respects intensified, enriched, and enlarged painterly equivalents of Krasner's black-and-white figure drawings. Figurative elements are more obvious, and the dramatic opposition of dark and light, invading one another's territory, is posited for the first time (fig. 120). Krasner has explained her switch from bright colors to a tonal monochromatic palette as the result of painting with artificial light instead of daylight during this period, when she suffered from chronic insomnia. As she expressed it to her friend, poet Richard Howard, "I realized that if I was going to work at night, I would have to knock color out altogether, because I couldn't deal with color except in daylight."

When Krasner began painting very large horizontal paintings, she could no longer use an easel, so, wanting a hard surface to paint on, she tacked unstretched canvas to the wall. If Krasner had been Pollock's follower like those who, introduced to Pollock's manner of working, painted on the ground on unstretched, unprimed canvas, she would certainly have changed her technique, since she had more opportunity to study his art than anyone. However, in her typically contrary fashion, she took the path directly opposed to Pollock's and continued to work on the wall, sizing her canvas with Rivet, a transparent glue that sealed the surface so that paint would not permeate the cloth. For this reason, it is not surprising that the looseness and openness she developed came out of her works on paper, where she could draw freely with the brush, in the fashion of the Oriental and Islamic calligraphy both she and Pollock admired, without risking drips running down an upright canvas.

In 1963, Krasner painted a big picture that is a coda to this Expressionist series. Entitled *Another Storm*, its structure is like the allover gestural splashes of the Umber paintings, but its dominant tonality is a brilliant alizarin crimson. Like the Umber paintings, *Another Storm*, too, is a painting that must be seen at a distance to be taken in entirely (fig. 122). Signaling a return to bright colors, which she had not used since 1957–58, *Another Storm* is both a brilliant finale and an auspicious renewal.

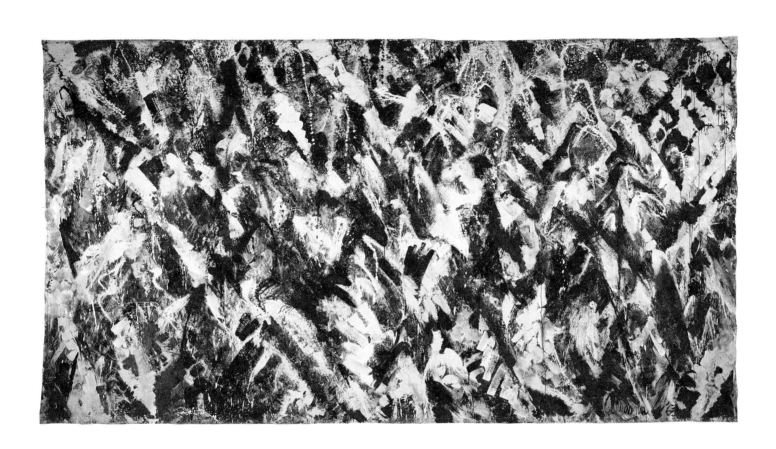

Fig. 122. *Another Storm*. 1963. Oil on cotton duck. 93⅝ × 175⅝″ (237.8 × 446.1 cm). Courtesy Robert Miller Gallery, New York.

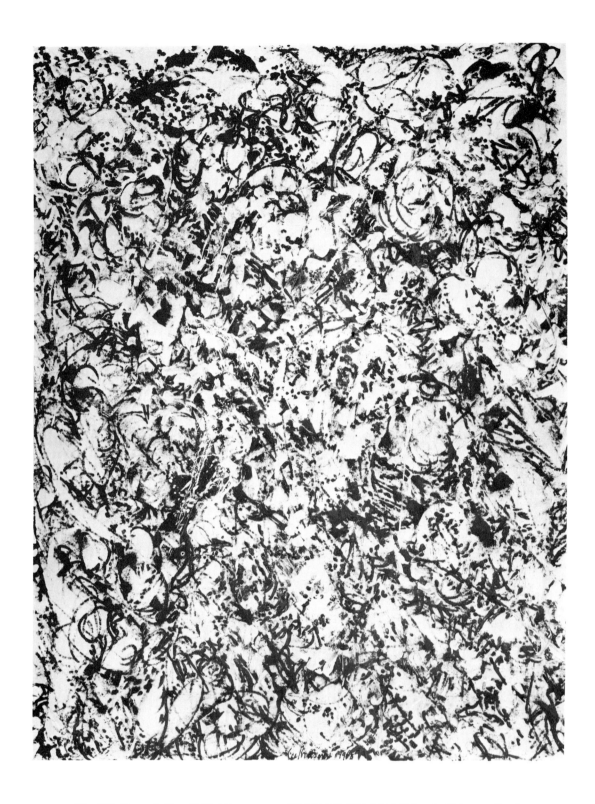

Fig. 123. *Through Blue*. 1963. Oil on canvas. 75½ × 58″ (191.8 × 147.3 cm). Private collection.

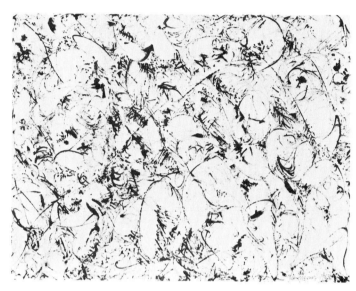

Fig. 124.
Happy Lady. 1963.
Oil on cotton duck.
58⅛ × 75¾″ (147.6 × 192.4 cm).
Flint Institute of Arts, Flint, Michigan.
Purchased with funds provided by
the National Endowment for the Arts
Museum Purchase Grant and from
the Samuel and Alma Catsman
Foundation.

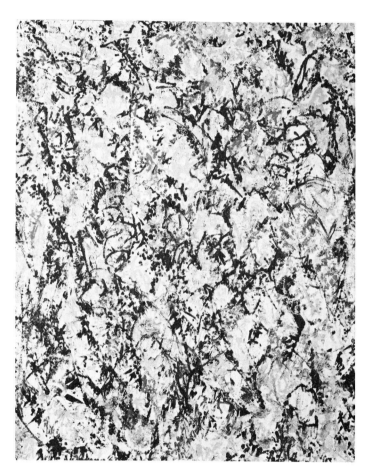

Fig. 125.
Flowering Limb. 1963.
Oil on canvas.
58 × 46″ (147.3 × 116.8 cm).
Whereabouts unknown.

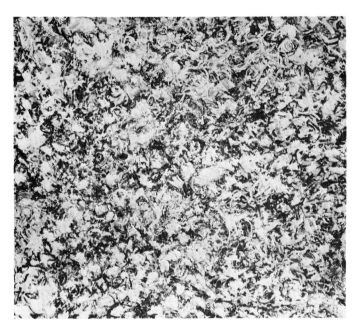

Fig. 126.
August Petals. 1963.
Oil on canvas.
55 × 48″ (139.7 × 121.9 cm).
Courtesy Robert Miller Gallery, New York.

Reviewing a show of Krasner's large-scale paintings of the late fifties and sixties, Hilton Kramer wrote in the February 9, 1979, *New York Times:*

These were, I believe, Miss Krasner's first really large-scale paintings. It was to be expected that they would reflect Pollock's influence in their scale, their method and their imagery—Miss Krasner has never denied that Pollock was an important influence on her work—they do. That they encompass this influence with a confident authority of their own is also true.

This is Abstract Expressionist painting of the "classic" type—all energy and struggle and outsize gesture finally resolved in a pattern of hard-won coherence. Painted in the immediate aftermath of Pollock's death, these paintings also have a certain elegiac quality, and a certain fury, too.

The first hint of a new style of floral imagery and a return to intensely contrasted color is announced in a series of watercolors and crayon-on-paper works executed in 1962. The new style retains the freedom gained through suffering, using that freedom now to celebrate the vital rhythms of life (fig. 121). The return to bright color announces a new direction in her art, which becomes increasingly abstract once more.

In *Through Blue,* an elegant monochromatic painting of 1963, the nightmares and chimeras that appear to have evoked the imagery of the 1960–62 big paintings begin to subside; there is less sense that the splatters and bursts conceal subliminal apocalyptic imagery (fig. 123). The storm is over. It is as if anguish has been exorcised and rage disciplined to the point that Krasner is free to return to another aspect of her sensibility: her love of the richly textured and the ornamental, of color and nature in its more benign and less threatening moments.

Her own life, however, continued to have its difficult moments, but her response now was less anger than a calm resolve to overcome obstacles. For example, in 1963, Krasner was walking down Main Street in East Hampton when she slipped, breaking her right arm. Her right hand and thus her painting arm were out of commission; as usual she courageously fought back against circumstance, and painted with her left hand. Three important paintings were

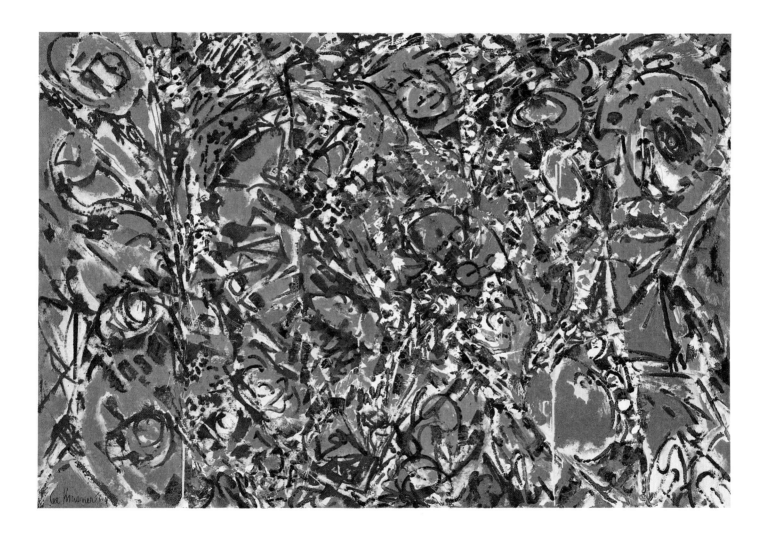

Fig. 127. *Icarus*. 1964. Oil on cotton duck. 46 × 69″ (116.8 × 175.3 cm). Courtesy Robert Miller Gallery, New York.

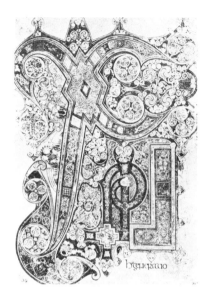

Fig. 128.
Illustration from The Book of Kells.

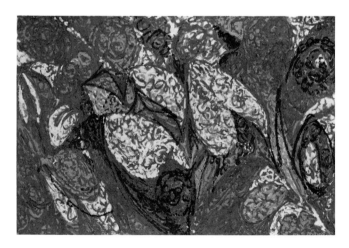

Fig. 129.
Untitled. 1965.
Gouache on paper.
26¾ × 40″ (67.9 × 101.6 cm).
Private collection.

done by holding the paint tube in her left hand directly next to the canvas and moving her left hand around with her right, which was in a cast. In *Happy Lady*, much of the canvas is left exposed (fig. 124). *Flowering Limb* and *August Petals*, in contrast, are thick with impasto of paint squeezed liberally from the tube and worked around into curlicues that repeat an allover patterning (figs. 125, 126). Out of necessity, gesture was reduced and overt physicality restrained.

During the winter months, Krasner was living in Manhattan, doing mainly small paper works, since she did not have a proper studio to execute large paintings. Automatic drawings with vaguely figurative overtones were executed in watercolor applied in feathered scrawls. Later, watercolor was added to unify the design. Her colors were rich and bright, but not garish. Sometimes the classic ultramarine and vermillion were paired for maximum brightness.

When Krasner recovered from the fracture and regained health and stamina after a serious illness in 1964, she brought to her painting a new lightness, transparency, and more decorative, less aggressive style of allover patterning. The imagery is related once more to calligraphy and ornament rather than to physical struggle or emotional upheaval.

The filigreed calligraphic allover paintings of 1963, like *Blue*, announce a new period of monochromatic paintings. However, now, the dominant color is a brilliant, fully saturated hue. *Sunspots*, for example, is, as its title indicates, a sunny yellow painting. The foliate imagery of 1963 continues to dominate the paintings of 1964 like *Icarus*, a brilliant rose red and orange painting, in which the entire surface is covered, edge to edge, with a rich allover decorative patterning suggesting lush tropical vegetation (fig. 127).

Here a word should be said regarding Krasner's use of "allover." When Bryan Robertson organized her first retrospective exhibition at the Whitechapel Gallery in London in 1965, Lord Kenneth Clark, who admired the show, singling out *Polar Stampede* as his favorite work, invited Krasner to dinner. She, in turn, as an admirer of the writing of the eminent English art historian, suggested that he turn his eye to modern art. Lord Clark had used the word "decorative" to describe modern art. Krasner

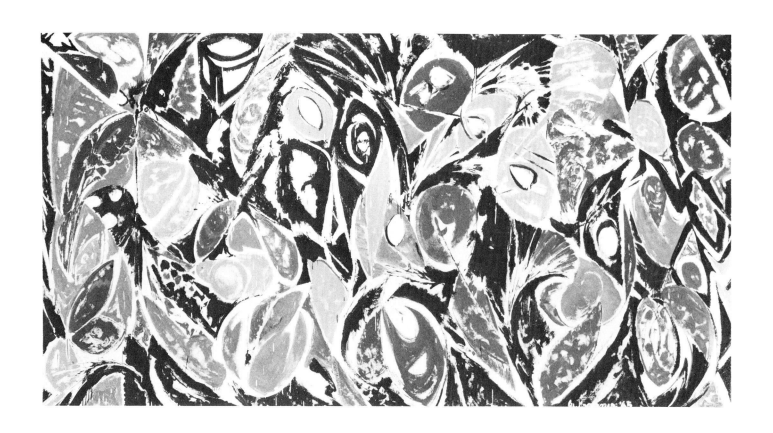

Fig. 130. *Right Bird Left*. 1965. Oil on canvas. 70 × 135″ (177.8 × 342.9 cm). Private collection.

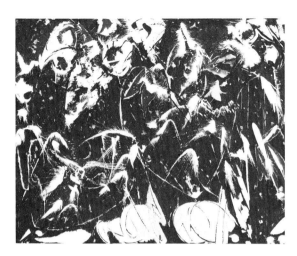

Fig. 131.
Uncial. 1967.
Oil on canvas.
68 × 85″ (172.7 × 215.9 cm).
Collection Dr. Jerome Hirschman, Winnetka.

attempted to explain to him the distinction between the decorative as a pejorative and the expressively decorative content of an artist like Matisse. Like Pollock, Krasner also had turned to earlier sources than modern art for inspiration. She was particularly interested in Celtic illumination and Islamic art, which had fascinated Matisse. The calligraphic ornamentation of the initial page in the Book of Kells, for example, was very much on her mind as part of her conception of the "decorative" (fig. 128), which had nothing to do with the idea of decorating with repeated images. She was not interested in flatness—the hallmark of decorative styles—but in the textured and richly embellished surfaces and the rhythmic movement that is common to Celtic illumination and Islamic art. Krasner's allover patterning is not uniform or literally repetitive. It is linked to the forms found in nature which are similar but not identical, altering when they repeat, rather than to the repeating motifs of textile, wallpaper, and pattern painting. The latter, however beautiful, have a domesticated way of being decorative in content as well as in design, which Krasner's art never is.

In 1965, Krasner produced a large number of high-key color gouaches on paper. Once again her style changed as a result of working on paper (fig. 129). Two large

paintings, *Icarus* and *Right Bird Left* (fig. 130), continue her preoccupation with mural-size horizontal painting of essentially floral motifs. In *Uncial* (fig. 131), white spaces are left around the brightly colored dancing leafy forms. Forms change, mutate, dissolve, appearing to somersault into one another. These interlocking floral shapes connect the whole of the image, with its many details and its variable brushwork, into a single consistent surface pattern implying the growth preceding flowering. *Combat* (fig. 132), a title that may refer to two of the strong colors, alizarin crimson and orange, which fight each other for attention, is a powerfully impressive image, once again suggestive of the lush and unchecked growth of a tropical rainforest. In a sense *Combat* and related paintings of the mid-sixties like *Gaea* (fig. 133), *Uncial, Pollination,* and *Courtship* (fig. 134), represent the tropical antithesis of the icy polar landscapes suggested by the Umber series of 1960–62. Both series have a quality of the primeval world that existed before man conquered nature. By the late sixties, the glaciers are gone, replaced by jungles, the turbulence of catastrophe given way to dancing, leaping, and flowering imagery.

Describing her method of filling a surface with intricately detailed, fine scrolling calligraphy Krasner has stated:

Painting, for me, when it really "happens" is as miraculous as any natural phenomenon—as, say, a lettuce leaf. By "happens," I mean the painting in which the inner aspect of man and his outer aspects interlock. One could go on forever as to whether the paint should be thick or thin, whether to paint the woman or the square, hard-edge or soft, but after a while such questions become a bore. They are merely problems in aesthetics, having only to do with the outer man. But the painting I have in mind, painting in which inner and outer are inseparable, transcends technique, transcends subject and moves into the realm of the inevitable—then you have the lettuce leaf.

In this concordance of macrocosmic and microcosmic imagery, Krasner has finally found the means to express the spiritual conversion, which was one of the great bonds she shared with Pollock, that "man was part of nature, not separate from it."

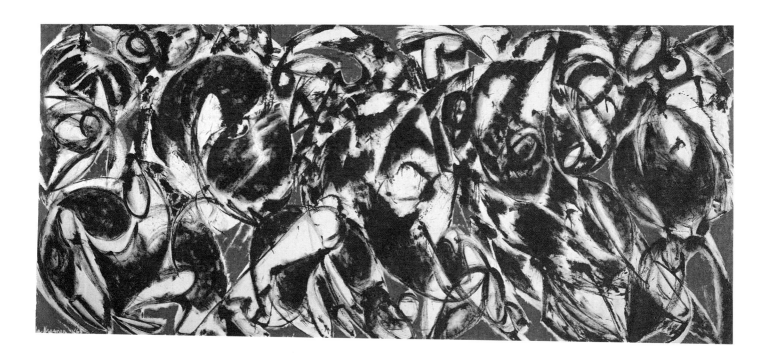

Fig. 132. *Combat*. 1965. Oil on canvas. 70½ × 161″ (179.1 × 408.9 cm). Courtesy Robert Miller Gallery, New York.

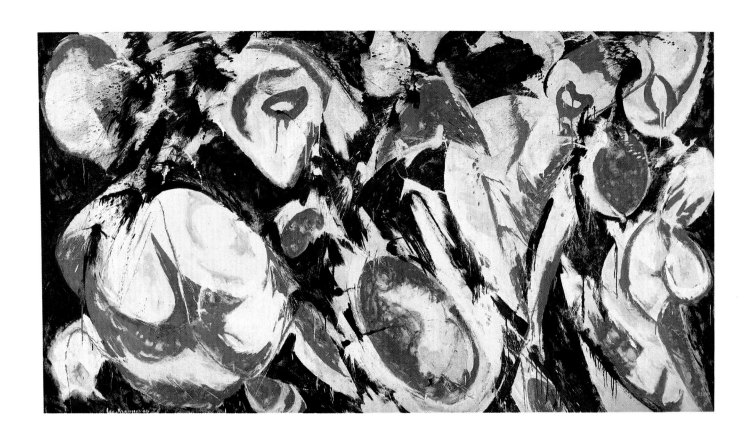

Fig. 133. *Gaea*. 1966. Oil on canvas. 69 × 149½″ (175.3 × 379.7 cm). The Museum of Modern Art, New York. Kay Sage Tanguy Fund.

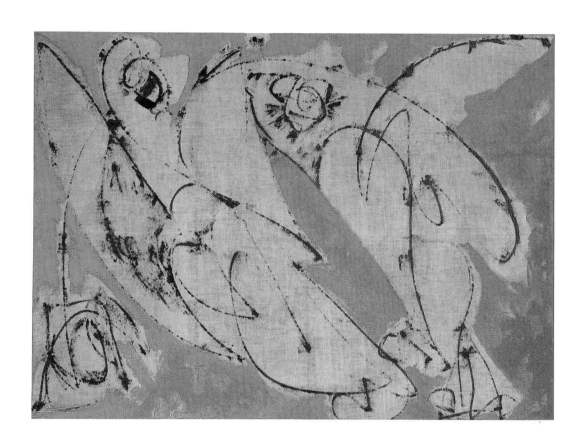

Fig. 134. *Courtship.* 1966. Oil on canvas. 51 × 71″ (129.5 × 180.3 cm). Courtesy Robert Miller Gallery, New York.

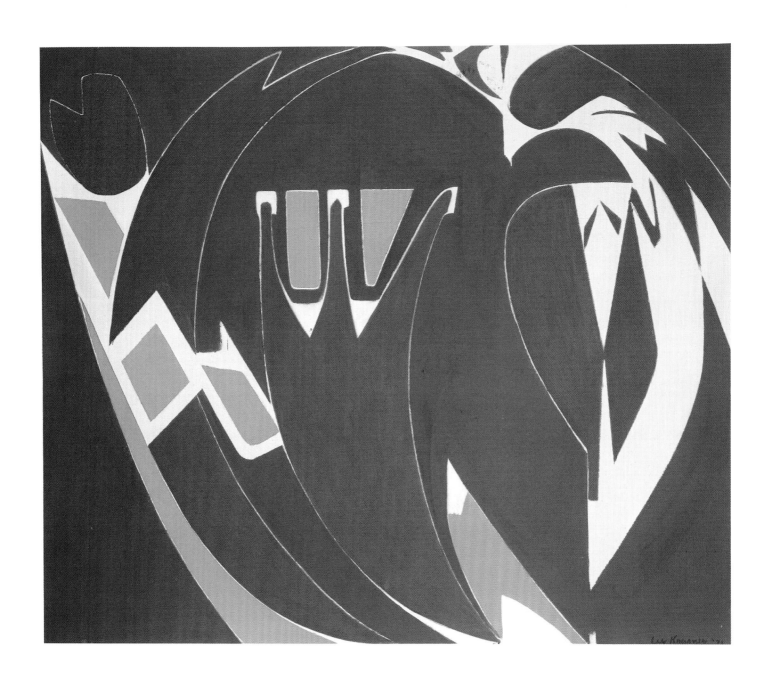

Fig. 135. *Majuscule*. 1971. Oil on cotton duck. 69 × 82″ (175.3 × 208.3 cm). Collection FMC Corporation, Chicago.

VIII. The Pendulum Swings Back

My own image of my work is that I no sooner settle into something than a break occurs. These breaks are always painful and depressing but despite them I see that there's a consistency that holds out, but is hard to define. All my work keeps going like a pendulum; it seems to swing back to something I was involved with earlier, or it moves between horizontality and verticality, circularity, or a composite of them. For me, I suppose that change is the only constant.

LEE KRASNER, in Whitney
Museum of American Art catalogue, 1973

After a decade of producing very large paintings, Krasner concentrated on small works on paper almost exclusively in 1969. She completed four extensive series of gouaches painted on coarse-grained, highly absorbent textured paper hand-made by a local artist named Douglas Howell. The four series recall previous preoccupations: Three are involved with the forces of nature, the fourth with mysterious sacred writing. The titles of two of the series, *Earth* and *Water*, refer to the elements; *Seed*, germination; and *Hieroglyphs*, picture writing. Together, the titles sum up the content and imagery of her mature paintings, indicating as well the means by which they were created: pigment (earth) dissolved in liquid (water) coaxed to flower from initial marks (seeds) that often grew into calligraphic figurations (hieroglyphs) (figs. 136, 137, 138, 139, 140). She had treated all these themes in previous paintings. Now she was entering a period of critical revision.

From 1970 until the present, Krasner has, in a sense, been looking back and creating her own retrospective version of her career, bringing the issues that have preoccupied her since she was an art student fifty years ago up to date in the present. In the masterful series of gouache paintings on paper, which are no less paintings for being on paper, she challenges the spontaneity, economy, and ability to control accident of the Japanese *sumi-e* painters who appear her most direct inspiration in these works.

To create a style that subsumed the history of Oriental as well as Occidental art—a truly international style—had always been one of her ambitions, as it had been one of Pollock's. Krasner's internationalism was part of her European background; she detested provincialism of any kind, and there is no hint of it in her work from the moment she sees her first School of Paris paintings. Indeed, the last two decades of her life have been spent creating post-Cubist revisions of the art of her revered masters Matisse, Picasso, and Mondrian, and freeing herself of any residual influence of Hofmann and Pollock, the titans who set the tone of the New York School. They had made their statement, she had reflected on it critically, and now she was fully prepared to reply on her own terms.

Krasner has never written anything about art. Any quotation from the artist is taken from a verbal interview. However, it is clear that she has been participating in the dialogue all along, answering the critical issues in her own

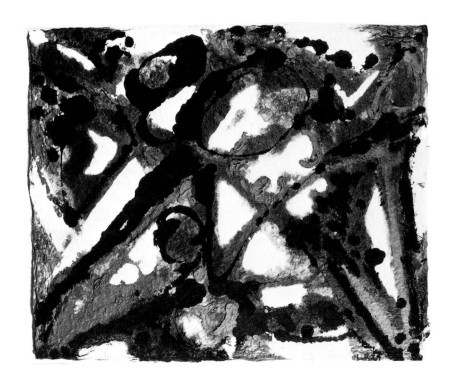

Fig. 136. *Earth #1*. 1969. Gouache on paper. 18¼ × 22½″ (46 × 57.1 cm). Collection Spencer A. Samuels & Company, Ltd., New York.

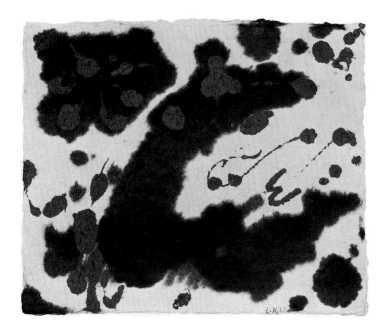

Fig. 137. *Water #4*. 1969. Gouache on paper. 18 × 22½″ (45.7 × 57.1 cm). Collection Mr. and Mrs. John Marin, Jr., New York.

Fig. 138. *Earth #9*. 1969. Gouache on paper. 19 × 14½″ (48.3 × 36.8 cm). Whereabouts unknown.

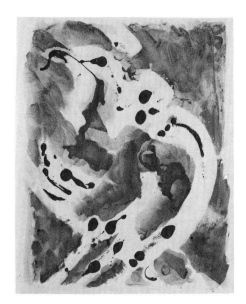

Fig. 139.
Seed #1. 1969.
Gouache on paper.
24 × 19¾″ (60.9 × 50.2 cm).
Collection Ella M. Foshay, New York.

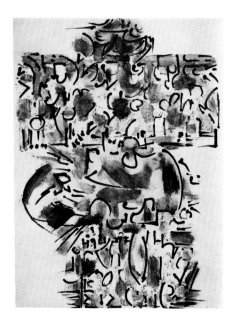

Fig. 140.
Hieroglyphs #4. 1969.
Gouache on paper.
29½ × 22″ (74.9 × 55.9 cm).
Collection the artist.

work. The gouache on paper paintings of 1969, for example, can be seen as her correction of Greenberg's theory, of post-painterly abstraction, and his espousal of artists who copied Pollock's working methods: using automatic techniques to allow pigment to sink directly into raw canvas.[47] Pollock had used enamel or aluminum paint, which could not be fully absorbed into the ground, whereas the painters of "stained" color canvases who came after him, like Morris Louis and Kenneth Noland, deliberately sank the diluted pigment directly into unprotected cloth to merge surface and image. This procedure, which exposed the threaded weave of the cloth, permitted them, in Greenberg's view, to create an exclusively optical illusionism, more advanced than previous types of pictorial illusion because it was more abstract and addressed to eyesight alone. In Krasner's view, stain painting was technically unsound. She left large areas of canvas exposed and unprimed in a number of airy, atmospheric paintings. However, she sealed the surface with Rivet glue. Often she painted transparently, in thin coats, but she knew too much about technique to wish the image to be absorbed by the canvas support, because of the problems of deterioration. She stressed both surface and support and their relationship in accommodating an exclusively optical illusion, but she refused to risk the physical deterioration and fading that were the seemingly inevitable fate of staining paint into untreated cloth, which would continue to absorb pigment.

The novelty of stained paintings is that they take the technique of watercolor and blow it up to monumental proportion in paintings on canvas, in which the canvas acts like the page in watercolor, absorbing color into it at a varying rate. As much as she has been an unconventional experimenter, Krasner has always detested novelty for its own sake. Her answer to the stained color painting Greenberg was calling the new avant-garde was to paint a series of gouaches in which flooding, spilling, and virtual liquidity were intrinsic to the technique. The paint is *in* the paper when it dries, the illusion of infinity opening up behind the image more convincing than its counterpart in stained painting. Once again, Krasner kept pace with developments in contemporary art, but she did it her way.

The last of the brilliantly colored gouaches, in which spontaneity and control are balanced in a new equilibrium,

Fig. 141. *Comet.* 1970. Oil on canvas. 70 × 86″ (177.8 × 218.4 cm). Whereabouts unknown.

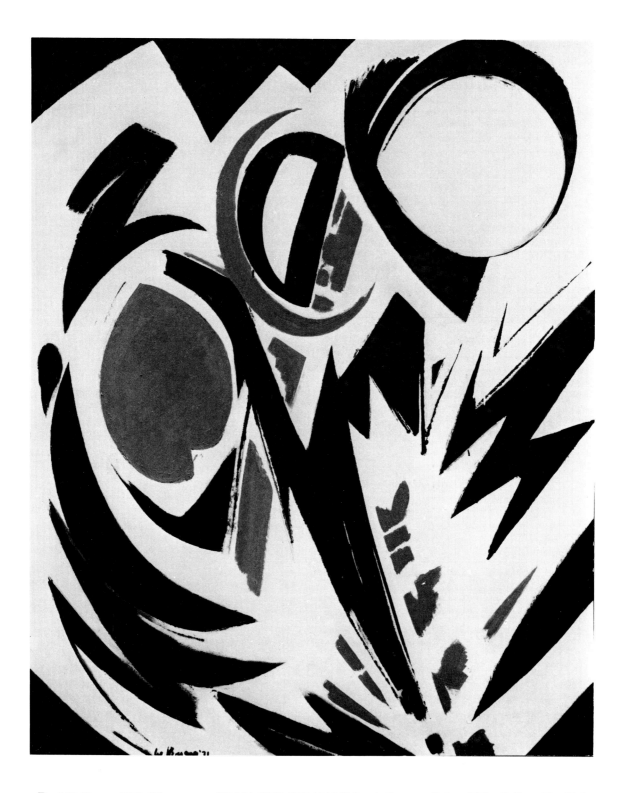

Fig. 142. *Meteor*. 1971. Oil on canvas. 81¼ × 66¼″ (206.4 × 168.3 cm). Courtesy Robert Miller Gallery, New York.

was painted in 1970 (fig. 143). It is complex spatially and technically in the way edges tremble and bleed away, in the number of types of marking, in the way the brush drawing has become literally painting. It indicates yet another about face in Krasner's career, the germination of a style of mural-size color-field paintings; these slowly evolve out of the Rorschach-like imagery of the gouaches. *Comet* (fig. 141), a large oil painted on the heels of the gouaches, has a residue of "action painting" spurts and splashes that Krasner disciplines into a more formal order of jagged shapes in *Meteor* (fig. 142). *Comet* launches a new series of color-field paintings that lasts until 1973. These include large horizontal paintings like the predominantly red and green *Palingenesis* (fig. 144), the two greens and sapphire blue of *Majuscule* (fig. 135), the intense blue and green of *Lotus* (fig. 146), the Indian motifs painted in gray, white, burnt sienna, and crimson of *Mysteries* (fig. 145). Although they have closed rather than open spaces, these paintings cannot really be classed as hard-edge—the prevailing geometric style of the moment: Their forms are too irregular and improvised with closer reference to natural and organic forms than to geometry. They are lush without being agitated, combining the static, strictly frontal, iconic quality of the enlarged hieroglyph with the unexpected high-contrast color combinations that are Krasner's forte. They are, without doubt, the work of a master painter, completely in control of her art. In *Rising Green* (fig. 150), a major portion of the canvas is left exposed. Leafy green forms invade the "clearing" in the center, and the purple and green mountainous grouping in the lower left rises like the magenta shape which is reminiscent of Egyptian architectural ornament. Indeed, there is something of the gravity of Egyptian architectural ornament in a painting like *Lotus*, which reminds one of the capitals of the columns of the Temple of Luxor, in the way the palette and ornament of *Mysteries* brings to mind the austere art images of Northwest Coast Indian art.

The last painting in this series, *Looking Glass* (fig. 147), is more electric in its frozen gesture, less contained and architectonic in its springing movements, which uncharacteristically for Krasner do break the frame. *Looking Glass*, painted in 1973, is 75 inches high by 58¼ inches wide. *Abstract Human Figure* (fig. 148), a 1938 oil-on-paper collage, is 22 by 20 inches, i.e., roughly a third its

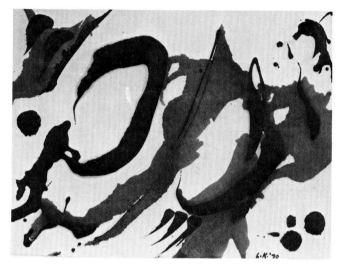

Fig. 143.
Untitled. 1970.
Oil and gouache on paper.
22¼ × 30¾" (56.5 × 78.1 cm).
Private collection.

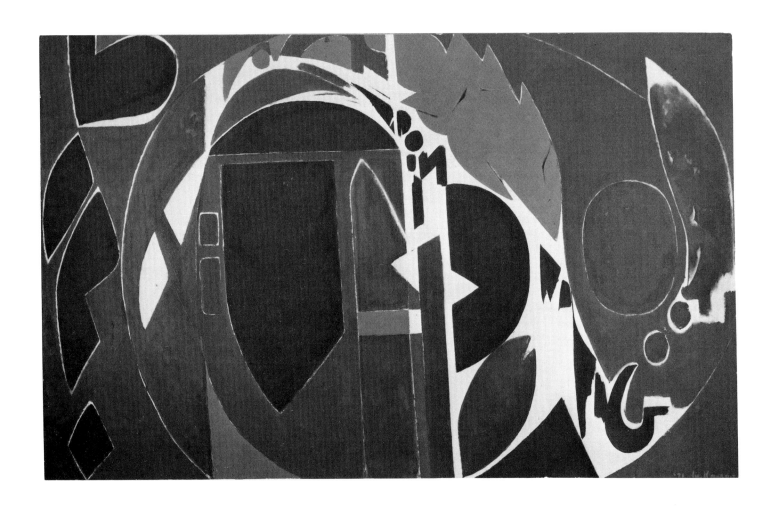

Fig. 144. *Palingenesis*. 1971. Oil on cotton duck. 82 × 134″ (208.3 × 340.4 cm). Courtesy Robert Miller Gallery, New York.

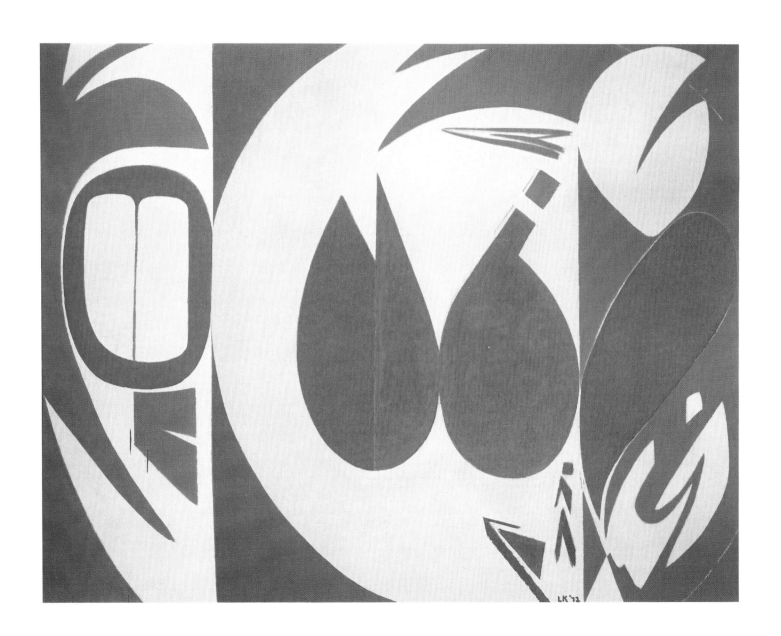

Fig. 145. *Mysteries.* 1972. Oil on cotton duck. 69 × 90″ (175.3 × 228.6 cm). Brooklyn Museum, Brooklyn, New York. Dick S. Ramsay Fund.

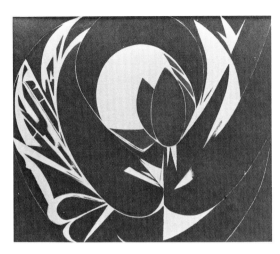

Fig. 146.
Lotus. 1972.
Oil on canvas.
69 × 82″ (175.3 × 208.3 cm).
Collection First City Bancorporation of Texas, Houston.

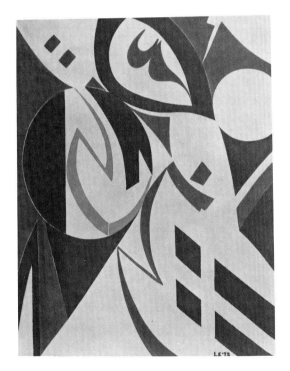

Fig. 147.
Looking Glass. 1973.
Oil on cotton duck.
75 × 58¼″ (190.5 × 147.9 cm).
Private collection.

size. To compare these two works, however, is to see the continuity and consistency of Krasner's concerns—the pendulum swings back and forth from the abstract to the figurative, the geometric to the organic. Her early attempts at defining drawing as edge rather than contour or as an autonomous rhythmic element are finally realized in her mature paintings.

No series perhaps more clearly illustrates Krasner's method of subsuming her past in a thoroughgoing synthesis in the present than the second major series of collage paintings she embarked on in 1976. *Abstract Human Figure* is probably Krasner's first collage painting. It was made by cutting up overpainted color corrections of the many oil-on-paper paintings she had executed during the late thirties and pasting the cutout shapes back into a coherent pattern. It was one of her first efforts at creating color-shapes without depicting contours in the conventional academic manner.

Krasner had put away her drawings and oils on paper done in the late thirties in portfolios and had not looked at them for twenty-five years. On one of his visits to the studio, Bryan Robertson asked to see the contents of the portfolios. Later, Krasner went through them herself, setting some aside as finished, separating others to be sacrificed to her knife or scissors. Unconsciously Krasner had made the decisive act of self-criticism: What was vital and salvageable of the past was to be retained and incorporated into the present.

Because the materials were mainly the grisaille charcoal drawings of figure studies and still lifes, which were constructed with Cubist *passage,* the effect of turning them into flat shapes counterposed to exposed areas of canvas, created a new kind of spatial tension that synthesized the sculptural space of Cubism and the flatness of Matisse and Mondrian. The paintings had the excitement of "action painting," only now gesture was with scissors, not brush. "Yes," Krasner explained, not without irony, "this is action. Action for the nervous system."[48]

Like the 1955 collage paintings, which were a complex painterly response to Matisse's découpages, the present series of collage paintings incorporates pieces of old works, in this case, the charcoal drawings and oil-on-paper studies executed in 1937–40 that Krasner for one reason or another rejected—either because she was unhappy with

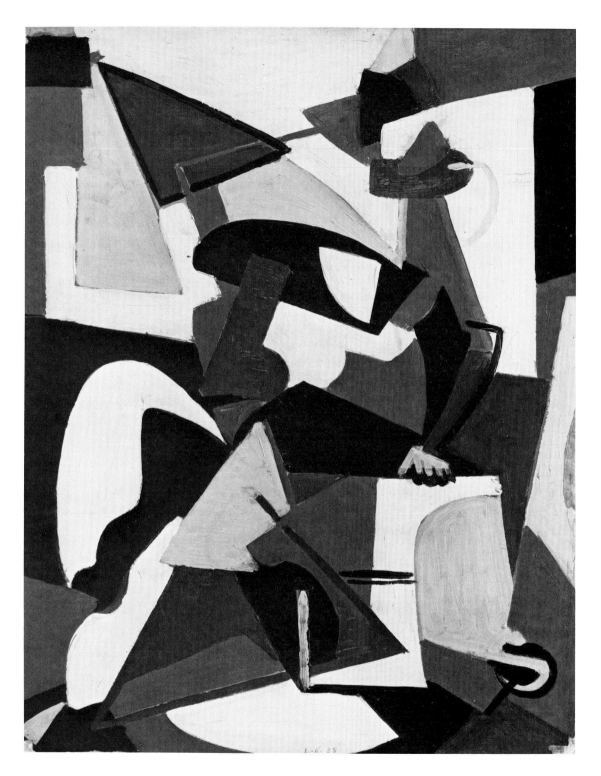

Fig. 148. *Abstract Human Figure*. 1938. Oil-on-paper collage. 22 × 20″ (55.9 × 50.8 cm). Private collection.

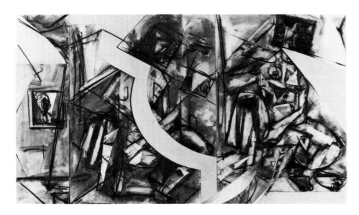

Fig. 149.
Past Conditional. 1976.
Collage on canvas.
27 × 49″ (68.6 × 124.5 cm).
Private collection.

them or because, as a result of not having been protected with fixative, the charcoal had rubbed off on the sheet above. In the latter case, a "ghost" impression that is like a pale mirror image of the original drawing has resulted. In several of the current works, Krasner juxtaposes the original drawing with its printed reflection, establishing a conceptual relationship between the original image and its reversed impression. In a sense, these paintings reformulate in contemporary terms Krasner's earlier concern with Picasso and Matisse, who by this time are merely background memories as ghostly as the spectral rubbings of drawings done forty years before in Hofmann's studio.

As opposed to the rough, torn, painterly edges of the brilliantly colored 1953–55 collage paintings that recall tropical forests, Krasner's new works are made up of hard-edged shapes cut out of the old drawings, alternated with reserved areas of sized but unpainted canvas and passages of muted color that result from paint bleeding through the colored sheets she reversed to use as collage elements now. She further dramatized the generally austere quality of these paintings with the dark grays of the blurred charcoal drawings that have been sliced, slivered, and reconstituted into large geometric curvilinear shapes reminiscent of the floral and Indian patterns in the large-scale paintings that Krasner executed in 1971–73.

The use of drawings made during the artist's youth is an act of self-retrieval of heroic dimensions. Retrieved as well in a contemporary context is Krasner's experience as a mural painter on the WPA, which impelled her initially to work on large-scale horizontal formats in 1951. In *Diptych* (fig. 151), a horizontal work composed essentially of two interrelated easel paintings, the flatness and decorative effects of mural painting are evoked through the rhythmic curves of the big cutout shapes, only to be contradicted by the painterly modulations and shadings covering the sheets of paper out of which these shapes are made. Texture, always a concern of Krasner's since her early, heavily impastoed Picassoid works, is evoked both by the literal contrast of smooth paper with rough canvas as well as by the chalky and oily tactility of the pasted passages.

The late collage paintings (fig. 149) are a brilliant tour de force of balancing out antithetical elements to arrive at a believable and consistent whole that is not only more than its parts, but also, because of its internal co-

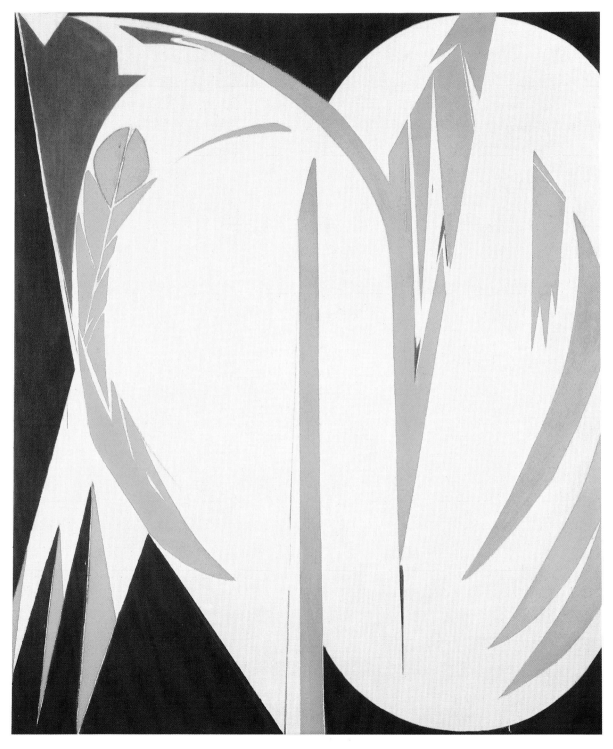

Fig. 150. *Rising Green*. 1972. Oil on cotton duck. 82 × 69″ (208.3 × 175.3 cm).
The Metropolitan Museum of Art, New York. Gift of Mr. and Mrs. Eugene V. Thaw.

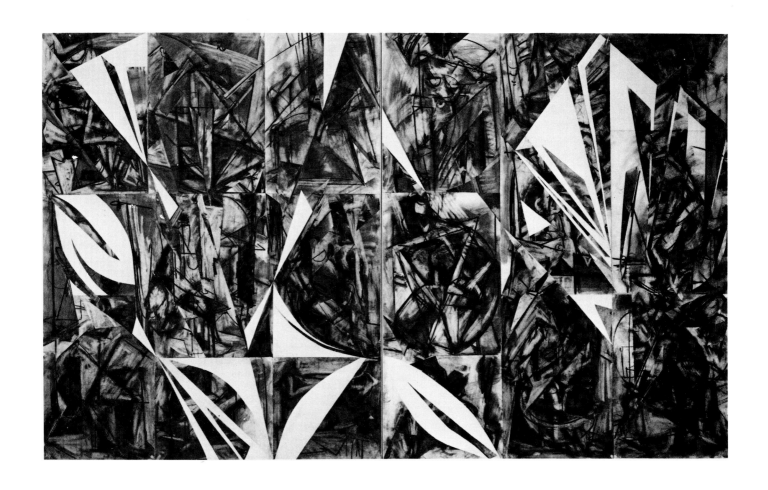

Fig. 151. *Diptych.* 1977–78. Collage on canvas. 66 × 114″ (167.6 × 289.6 cm). Courtesy Robert Miller Gallery, New York.

herence, is understood as a single, complex image. The impact of the sixties is preserved but now it is countered by the detail of traditional art; the architectonic qualities of mural painting are never permitted to degenerate into mere decorative flatness—the flaw of much hard-edge or geometric abstraction. Instead, the ambiguous space of easel painting is simultaneously evoked and canceled in a precarious balance between the conventions of mural painting and easel painting that is one of the crucial and most original features of Abstract Expressionism. The paintings also deal with pictorial irony in a contemporary manner. Value contrast functions to suggest illusionistic depth; however, because the drawings are constantly interrupted —at times with a kind of violent thrusting intrusion—by intercalations from other drawings, contradictory passages of shading nullify the suggestion of illusion. The result is that the conscious *mind* rather than simply the *eye* is awakened to the cognizance of flatness as a conception not irreconcilably antagonistic to illusion.

Hofmann's Cubist lessons demanded that the eye be convinced of the integrity of the picture plane. But nearly forty years have elapsed since the moment these drawings were made. Their current resurrection as elements within a fresh pictorial synthesis, which departs as much from "action painting" as "action painting" departed from Cubism, is a moment of summing up the history of art of the last forty years. The paintings contain allusions to Fauvism, Cubism, Futurism, and Constructivism as well as to Abstract Expressionism. Their subject is not only the biography of the artist, but also the history of modern art, not as clever commentary, but as content. It is as if Krasner had turned Cubist collage inside out, mocking its depiction of flatness with chiaroscuro contradicted by being cut up and consequently disjointed. To the initial Cubist fragmentation of reality, she has added the fragmentation of representations of those very fragments! Normally one would expect that the act of fragmenting the fragmented would result in total chaos, but she makes it work as order.

These works are not illustrations of philosophical propositions. They are thought made concrete. A brilliant balance is achieved: Richly elaborated passages full of detail and nuance, vitalized by the energy of youth, collaged into bold forms, are locked into negative shapes of bare reserved areas, securely structured as only the stability and maturity of age could conceive. The dual use of sizing to affix the paper to the surface as well as to accentuate the cloth texture of canvas as nothing other than a piece of woven material is Krasner's way of bringing her work into line with the latest developments in painting, which draw attention to not only the flatness of the support, but also to its actual identity as a piece of cloth. By turning back to reconsider where she began on her own, Krasner has come out ahead again. This time, however, she is capable of realizing what she intuitively knows. Her ability to embody concepts within a concrete work of art exposes the cowardice of disembodied idea art as much as it criticizes the vacuity of current abstraction, devoid of mental content. Ignored by the canonizers of the pantheon of Abstract Expressionism, Krasner emerges as a survivor, with history now on her side.

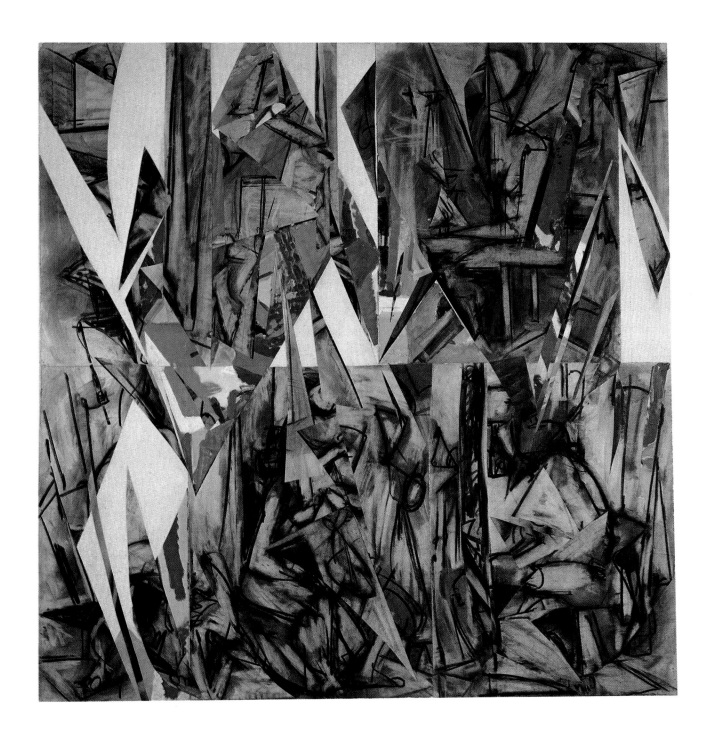

Fig. 152. *Imperative.* 1976. Collage on canvas. 50 × 50″ (127 × 127 cm). Collection Mr. and Mrs. Eugene V. Thaw, New York.

Epilogue:
The Artist as Critic

I make the first gesture, then other gestures, then observation. Something in the abstract movement suggests a form . . . . I'm often astonished at what I'm confronted with when the major part comes through. Then I just go along with it; it's either organic in content, or quite abstract, but there's no forced decision.

LEE KRASNER, interview with Marcia Tucker in Whitney Museum of American Art catalogue, 1973

The titles of the collage paintings of the late seventies are all forms of the verb "to be." In *Imperative* (fig. 152), one of the most beautifully integrated of these paintings, the somberness of charcoal gray is enlivened by additional brushstrokes of bright red and green, applied in judicious places over the surface of the collage. One of the largest of this series is entitled *Present Indicative*. This is the tense Krasner characteristically uses in speaking. Indeed, one of the oddities of her conversation is that she appears not to distinguish between past, present, and future. She still relates incidents that occurred even fifty years ago in the present tense. At first, this is jarring. Then one realizes the nature of her experience is that everything, including all world art she has seen, co-exists in the present. Sometimes, she may focus on one or another aspect of her past experience, but it is all available to her in a synchronic rather than a sequential sense. This peculiarity is reflected in her art. Thus, it seems appropriate to conclude this study of Krasner's career, as she would, in the present tense:

For years, I am puzzled by the disjunction between the quality I perceive in Krasner's art whenever I encounter it and the fact that her work is not seen as first-generation Abstract Expressionism, is not judged on its merit, indeed, is virtually ignored. I am introduced to Krasner by John Bernard Myers, and I begin to visit her studios in Manhattan in the winter and Springs in the summer. In the summer of 1978, I go to Springs to see her. She invites me to observe the yearly housecleaning process that takes place at the end of the summer, when she is ready to pack up after Labor Day and return to the city. She pulls the canvases out of the racks in the studio by herself, refusing to let me help unless a very large picture needs moving. She must do it all herself, which accounts for why she has no servants or assistants.

As she struggles to pull out pictures, she tells me of Clement Greenberg's visit to her studio in 1959. He had just been made director of French & Company and offered her a show. However, her work had changed, and he does not like the paintings he sees. "We had words," she says, "and he exited." I imagine the words and the exit. I also realize it was her last chance to become part of the official avant-garde and that she deliberately refuses to

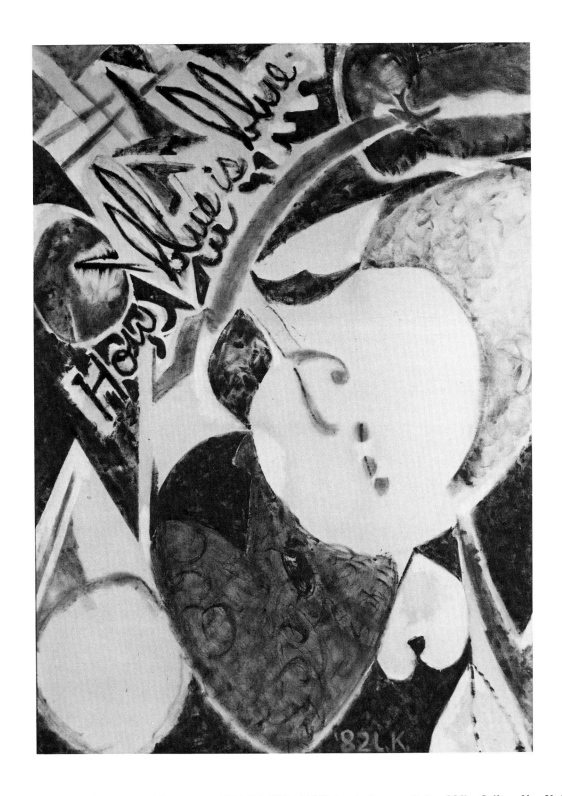

Fig. 153. *Morning Glory*. 1982. Oil on canvas. 84 × 60″ (213.4 × 152.4 cm). Courtesy Robert Miller Gallery, New York.

conform. She will get where she is going her own way, in her own good time. Nobody rushes Lee Krasner. As for criticism, it can be argued that hers is the greatest critical eye of her generation, and that her insights shaped the taste of both Greenberg and Pollock at a crucial time.

Now she is surveying her paintings again as she reviews them at the end of every year. She makes up her mind whether to sign a work, which means she accepts it as finished, to cut it up into pieces to re-use as painted textures in future collage paintings, or, as she puts it, to "re-enter" the work. To re-enter for Krasner is to correct or revise, according to her own critical perspective, works she holds onto but considers problematic. She picks a series of paintings to have shipped back to Manhattan. Eventually, these will be reworked, some elaborately with additional paint and collage, such as the brilliant *Vernal Yellow* of 1980 (fig. 154) and the "re-entered" 1981 *Between Two Appearances* (fig. 155). Others are to be torn off their stretchers and slashed. Another group waits to be reconsidered yet again next year. This constant process of revision and auto-criticism has always preoccupied Krasner. There are few lesser works left in her oeuvre, because she has acted as her own critic.

I marvel at her ability to use white to give more power and coherence in works that need some small revision. She overpaints sparingly, preserving freshness by knowing just when to stop, leaving the original drips or spatters intact and integrated into the new surface.

She scrutinizes her works with the same sense of critical distance and objectivity one perceives in the photos Namuth took of her in 1950. Her eyes narrow, she crosses her arms, she decides. "All right," she says. "Now I know what I'm going to do. Let's go back to the house and I'll make tea."

We walk across the lawn to the house where she has lived for more than thirty years now. She says: "You know, Jackson used to grab me by the arm, shaking, and show me what he was working on and ask, 'Is this a painting?' Not a good or a bad painting—just was it a painting at all." She pauses, "Sometimes I feel that way, too."

Some of the paintings of the eighties represent self-critical revisionism; others, like *Morning Glory* (fig. 153), are painted from scratch. *Morning Glory* is one of Krasner's several homages to poets. She was asked to do a painting for a show of painters and poets at Guild Hall, the East Hampton art gallery. Poet Howard Moss asked her to work with him. She inscribed the line from his poem *Morning Glory*, "How blue is blue," on the painting the way she had once written lines from Rimbaud on the wall of her studio. Throughout her life, her association with poetry and poets like Frank O'Hara and Richard Howard has been important, keeping her in touch with the lyric attitude of painting that is akin to poetry.

She is making tea—no, I am not to help with anything, just to sit and look at the huge ferns and plants, the shell and rock collections, the incredible richness of natural forms that she collects to correspond to a life lived richly, organically, authentically, and bravely, expressed in an art one could describe in the same manner. The pieces of the puzzle begin to fit together. The mosaic, the patchwork, the emotional cycles that interrupt one style and gave birth to another, start looking like a coherent pattern I can reconstruct from shards and fragments, interviews and archives.

"Let me help with the tea," I offer.

"Absolutely not." She is both imperious and generous, unequivocal and inflexible; but most of all, she is absolutely *there*, totally involved in what she is doing in the present.

"I don't need any help, and that's a good thing. I like to do it my own way, thank you."

She calls the truck to pick up the paintings singled out for resurrection. Tomorrow we go back to the city, where she will continue to do things her way.

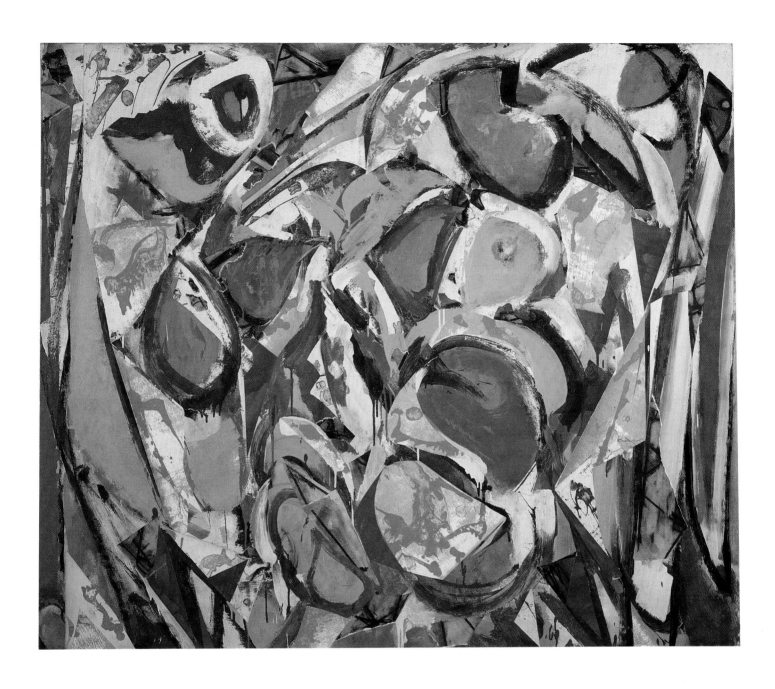

Fig. 154. *Vernal Yellow*. 1980. Oil and collage on canvas. 59 × 70″ (149.8 × 177.8 cm). Ludwig Museum, Cologne. The Ludwig Collection.

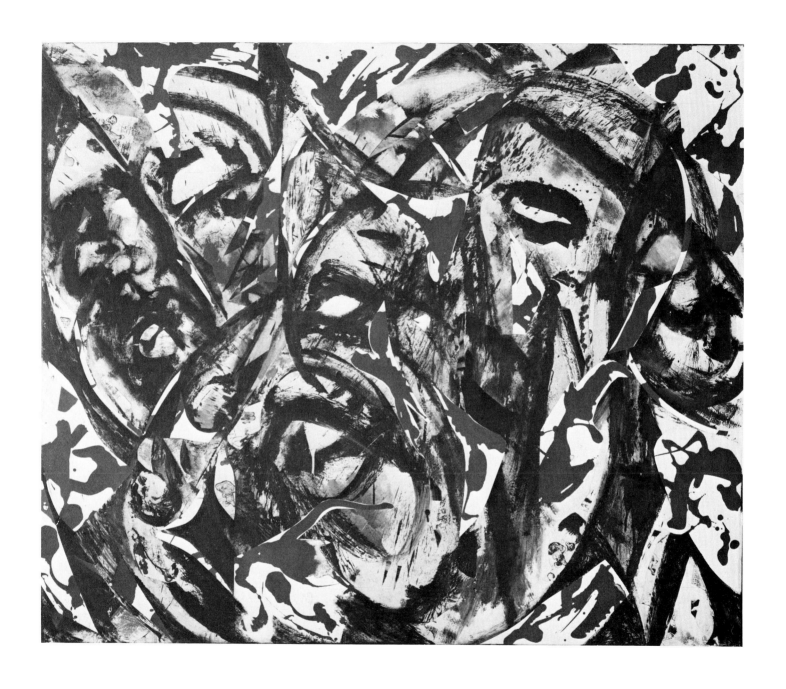

Fig. 155. *Between Two Appearances*. 1981. Oil on canvas with paper collage. 47 × 57¼″ (119.5 × 145.4 cm). Courtesy Robert Miller Gallery, New York.

Notes

[1] This photograph, originally published in *Life* magazine's issue of January 15, 1951, is reproduced as the frontispiece in Irving Sandler's *The Triumph of American Painting* (New York: Harper & Row, 1970). Sandler's explanation to the author for not including Krasner as a first-generation Abstract Expressionist in his book, which was the first historical survey of the New York School, was mainly that he identified the first generation with the "Irascibles."

[2] Lee Krasner interview in the film *The Long View*, 1977, a 16mm color film by Barbara Rose, distributed by the American Federation of Arts. All further quotes from Krasner not footnoted are from interviews with the author.

[3] Author's interviews, 1980, with Ilya Bolotowsky and Giorgio Cavallon, fellow students with Krasner at the National Academy of Design.

[4] John Bernard Myers to the author. Bolotowsky also mentioned Krasner's influence on Pollock, and Clement Greenberg refers to it in a letter to Ellen Landau, January 28, 1980.

[5] *Lee Krasner: Paintings, Drawings and Collages* (London: Whitechapel Gallery, September–October 1965).

[6] Both Krasner and Pollock collected books on all periods of art history from the cave paintings to the present and rejected any narrow vision of art. Krasner planned to visit the caves of Lascaux on her trip to Paris in 1982. However, she injured her arm and was unable to make the journey she had always wished to take.

[7] Several authors have commented on the international rather than strictly American or even Western definition of art.

[8] Robert Hobbs and Gail Levin, *Abstract Expressionism: The Formative Years* (New York: Whitney Museum of American Art and the Herbert F. Johnson Museum of Art, 1978), pp. 8–25.

[9] There are some exceptions such as Marc Chagall, Chaim Soutine, and Jules Pascin, but the emergence of Jews as important visual artists is a relatively recent development. Krasner's relationship to Judaism was complicated. Marcia Tucker has remarked on the influence of Hebrew script, which Krasner learned as a child, on her large calligraphic paintings in *Lee Krasner, Large Paintings* (New York: Whitney Museum of American Art, 1973–74).

[10] Her mother complained that she was too independent. See Ellen Landau, "Lee Krasner's Early Career, Part One: Pushing in Different Directions," *Arts Magazine* (October 1981): p. 110.

[11] However, she received a degree in art education in 1982 from Cooper Union. For a detailed account of Krasner's education, see ibid., pp. 110–16.

[12] Krasner interview in the film *The Long View*.

[13] Compare with Pollock's drawings from the nude in Francis V. O'Connor and Eugene V. Thaw, eds., *Jackson Pollock, A Catalogue Raisonné of Paintings, Drawings and Other Works* (New Haven: Yale University Press, 1978), vol. III.

[14] Author's interview with Ilya Bolotowsky, 1980.

[15] Clement Greenberg, *Art and Culture* (Boston: Beacon Press, 1961), p. 6.

[16] Ibid., p. 7.

[17] Cynthia Goodman, intro., in *Hans Hofmann 1880–1966* (New York: André Emmerich Gallery, 1981), n.p.

[18] Hans Hofmann in Sarah T. Weeks and Bartlett H. Hayes, eds., *Search for the Real and Other Essays* (Andover: Addison Gallery of American Art, 1948), pp. 40–48.

[19] Cynthia Goodman, *Hans Hofmann.*

[20] Hans Hofmann in Weeks and Hayes, *Search for the Real,* p. 62.

[21] Ibid., p. 46.

[22] Clement Greenberg, *Art and Culture*, p. 232.

[23] Hans Hofmann in Weeks and Hayes, *Search for the Real,* p. 47.

[24] Ibid.

[25] Cynthia Goodman, *Hans Hofmann.*

[26] Cynthia Goodman, "Hans Hofmann as Teacher," *Arts Magazine* (April 1979), p. 122.

[27] Ibid.

[28] A. B. Carles used Matisse's color and Kandinsky's improvisatory brushwork in his paintings of the thirties, which anticipate "action painting." See A. B. Carles in Barbara Wolanin, *Painting with Color* (Philadelphia: Pennsylvania Academy of Fine Arts, 1983).

[29]Hofmann student Lillian O'Lindsay, who later married Viennese architect Frederick Kiesler, to the author. Mrs. Kiesler provided important information regarding the Hofmann School, where she was a friend of Krasner's. Kiesler, who came to the United States in 1926, was an important stimulus in promoting enivronmental art and was friendly with both Krasner and Pollock.

[30]See "Mrs. Jackson Pollock," *Time* (March 17, 1958), p. 64.

[31]Hans Hofmann in Weeks and Hayes, *Search for the Real*, p. 57.

[32]Ibid., p. 56.

[33]Kline projected his own drawings onto a screen through a Belopticon projector, which mechanically enlarged the image to become the basis for his abstract paintings. See *Franz Kline Memorial Exhibition* (Washington, D.C.: Washington Gallery of Modern Art, 1962), p. 14.

[34]Interview with Harold Rosenberg in the film *Art/Work/U.S.A.: American Art in the Thirties* by Barbara Rose.

[35]For an extensive description of Gorky's WPA murals see Ruth Bowman, *Murals without Walls, Arshile Gorky's Aviation Murals Rediscovered* (Newark: The Newark Museum, 1978).

[36]A. E. Gallatin, *American Abstract Artists Annual* (New York, 1938).

[37]O'Connor and Thaw, eds., *Jackson Pollock*, vol. IV, p. 229.

[38]John Graham, *System and Dialectics of Art* (Baltimore: Johns Hopkins Press, 1971), p. 115.

[39]Joan Miró interview with the author, published in the exhibition catalogue *Miró in America* (Houston: Museum of Fine Arts, 1982).

[40]These photographs were made at the same time Namuth's celebrated series of Pollock painting his poured paintings. Namuth took Krasner seriously as an artist and photographed her on a number of occasions.

[41]Krasner had read the Schwartz translation and inscribed Rimbaud's words in black on her studio wall except for the phrase "What beast must one adore?" which she wrote out in blue. This two-color scheme appears in her first large field painting *Blue and Black*, 1951–53 (Museum of Fine Arts, Houston). When Tennessee Williams made derogatory remarks about the quote on a visit to Krasner's studio with Fritz Bultman, Krasner threw him out.

[42]The signature "Lee Krasner," which appears in later photographs of the painting published by Harriet and Sidney Janis, *Abstract and Surrealist Art in America* (New York: Reynal & Hitchcock, 1949), was actually put in by Jackson Pollock. Krasner had dropped the second "s" from her family name and begun to use the androgynous Lee rather than Lenore while she was working on the WPA. Nevertheless both her marriage license and Pollock's death certificate are signed with her full legal name, Lenore Krassner.

[43]O'Connor and Thaw, eds., *Jackson Pollock*, vol. IV, p. 276.

[44]Gene Baro. *Lee Krasner: Collages and Works on Paper 1933–1974* (Washington, D.C.: Corcoran Gallery of Art, 1975).

[45]B. H. Friedman, intro., *Lee Krasner: Paintings, Drawings and Collages* (London: Whitechapel Gallery, 1965).

[46]E. C. Goossen, "The Big Canvas," *Art International* (November 1958), p. 101.

[47]See Greenberg's manifesto for stained color-field painting. *Post-Painterly Abstraction* (Los Angeles: Los Angeles County Museum of Art, 1964), for a full account of his views on abstraction after Pollock. It is remarkable that Krasner's contribution is completely ignored. However, the complicated relationship between the two (Krasner introduced Greenberg to Pollock originally) soured after Pollock's death for many reasons.

[48]Lee Krasner in *The Long View*.

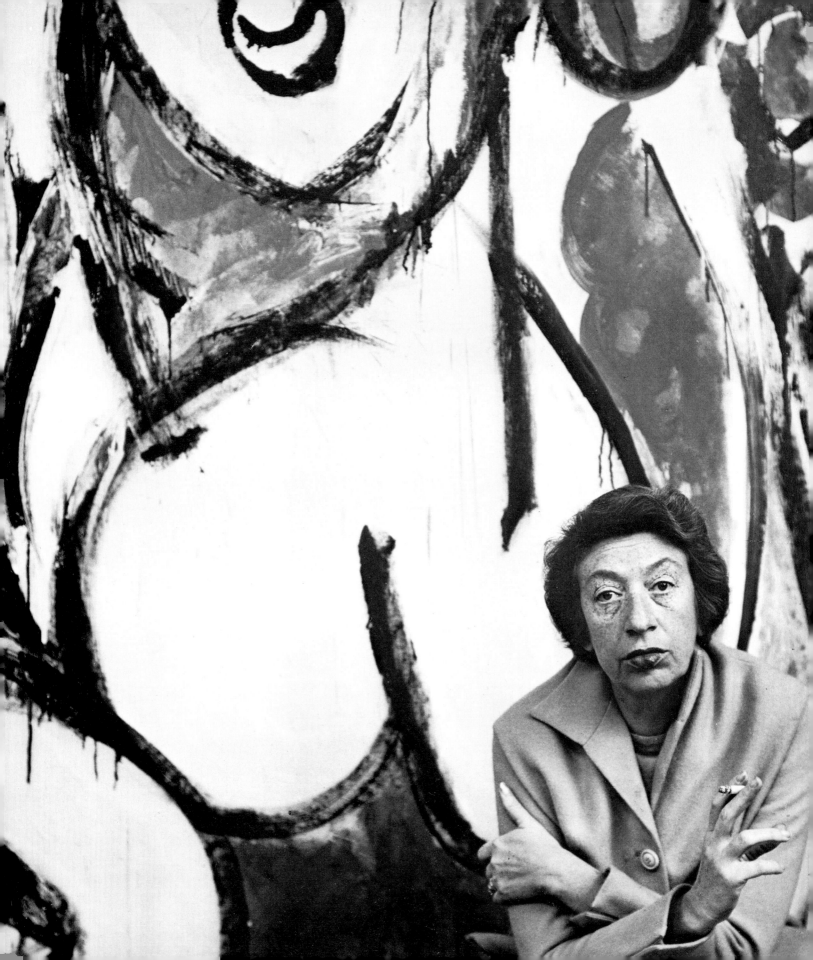

Chronology

1908	Born October 27, Lenore Krassner in Brooklyn, New York, of Russian parents.
1922–25	Attends Washington Irving High School in Manhattan.
1926	Admitted to Women's Art School of Cooper Union.
1928	Attends Art Students League.
1929	Graduates from Cooper Union. Admitted to National Academy of Design.
1932	Completes studies at National Academy.
1933	Attends City College and Greenwich House.
1934	Works as an artist on Public Works of Art Project from January to March. Begins work as an artist for the Temporary Emergency Relief Administration.
1935	Becomes an assistant on WPA Federal Art Project, Mural Division, in August.
1936	First meets Jackson Pollock at Artists Union loft party.
1937	Begins studies with Hans Hofmann.
	Group exhibition: "Pink Slips over Culture," protest exhibition sponsored by the Artists Union and Citizens Committee for Support of the WPA, ACA Gallery, New York.
1940	Leaves Hans Hofmann's studio. Exhibits with American Abstract Artists group at the American Fine Arts Galleries, New York.
	Group exhibition: "First Annual Exhibition of the American Modern Artists," Riverside Museum, New York.
1941	Is invited by John Graham to participate in show at the McMillen Gallery, New York, to be held the following January.
	Group exhibitions: "Fifth Annual Exhibition of the American Abstract Artists," Riverside Museum, New York; "Abstract Painting," organized by the WPA and circulated throughout the United States.
1942	Participates in "American and French Paintings," McMillen Gallery, New York, and as a result of show meets Pollock for second time. Sees him constantly thereafter.

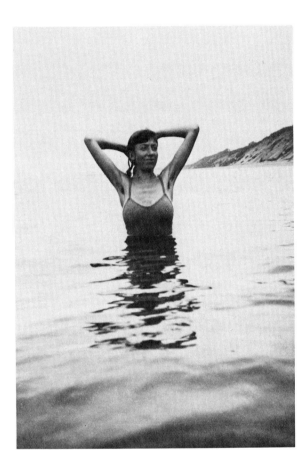

Lee Krasner, Jones Beach, c. 1939

Group exhibition: "Sixth Annual Exhibition of the American Abstract Artists," Fine Arts Galleries, New York.

1943 Group exhibition: "Seventh Annual Exhibition of the American Abstract Artists," Riverside Museum, New York.

1944 Group exhibition: "Abstract and Surrealist Art in America," Mortimer Brandt Gallery, New York.

1945 October 25, marries Jackson Pollock at Marble Collegiate Church, Fifth Avenue, New York. Shows in "Challenge to the Critic" with Pollock, Gorky, Gottlieb, Hofmann, Pousette-Dart, and Rothko, Gallery 67, New York.

1946 Little Image paintings start to evolve.

1948 Group exhibition: "The Modern Home Comes Alive—1948–49," Bertha Schaefer Gallery, New York.

1949 Little Image series terminates.

Group exhibition: "Man and Wife," Sidney Janis Gallery, New York.

1950 Group exhibition: "10 East Hampton Abstractionists," Guild Hall, East Hampton, New York.

1951 First solo exhibition, "Paintings 1951, Lee Krasner," held at Betty Parsons Gallery, New York.

1953 Begins collages.

Group exhibitions: "17 East Hampton Artists," Guild Hall, East Hampton, New York; "An Exhibition of Oils, Watercolors, Prints and Sculpture by Eight Artists of Eastern Long Island," Hampton Gallery and Workshop, Amagansett, New York.

1954 Exhibits in first group show of all women artists, "Group Show—Eight Painters, Two Sculptors," at Hampton Gallery and Workshop, Amagansett, New York.

Solo exhibition: The House of Books and Music, East Hampton, New York.

1955 Solo exhibition: Stable Gallery, New York.

1956 Travels to Europe for first time. Jackson Pollock dies on August 11.

Group exhibitions: "The 30's: Painting in New York," Poindexter Gallery, New York; "1956 Annual Exhibition: Sculpture, Paintings, Watercolors and Drawings," Whitney Museum of American Art, New York.

1957   Group exhibition: "1957 Annual Exhibition: Sculpture, Paintings, Watercolors and Drawings," Whitney Museum of American Art, New York.

1958   Solo exhibition: "Lee Krasner, Recent Paintings," Martha Jackson Gallery, New York.

Group exhibitions: "International Art of a New Era," Osaka Art Festival, Osaka, Japan; Signa Gallery, East Hampton, New York.

1959   Completes two mosaic murals for Uris Brothers at 2 Broadway, New York. Begins Umber and Off-White series of paintings.

Solo exhibition: "Lee Krasner, Paintings 1947–59," Signa Gallery, East Hampton, New York.
Group exhibition: "Arte Nuova," Circolo degli Artisti, Palazzo Graneri, Turin, Italy.

1960   Solo exhibition: Howard Wise Gallery, New York.

Group exhibition: "Opening Exhibition 1960," Signa Gallery, East Hampton, New York.

1961   Group exhibitions: "Panorama," Galerie Beyeler, Basel, Switzerland; "Modern American Painting," Laing Art Gallery, Newcastle-upon-Tyne, England; "New New York Scene," Marlborough Fine Arts, London; "Contemporary Paintings Selected from 1960–1961 New York Gallery Exhibitions," Yale University Art Gallery, New Haven, Connecticut.

1962   Umber and Off-White series terminate.

Solo exhibition: "New Work by Lee Krasner," Howard Wise Gallery, New York.

Group exhibitions: Pennsylvania Academy of Fine Arts, Philadelphia; "Women Artists in America Today," Mount Holyoke College, South Hadley, Massachusetts; "Continuity and Change: 45 American Abstract Painters and Sculptors," Wadsworth Atheneum, Hartford, Connecticut.

1963   Group exhibition: "Hans Hofmann and His Students," circulating exhibition organized by The Museum of Modern Art, New York.

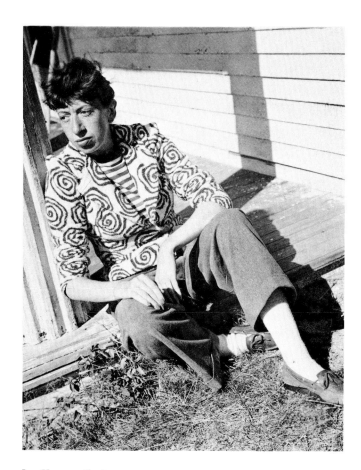

Lee Krasner, Springs

1964 Group exhibitions: "Festival of the Arts Exhibition," Guild Hall, East Hampton, New York; "American Vision," Marlborough Gallery, New York; "American Drawings," The Solomon R. Guggenheim Museum, New York; "One Hundred Contemporary Prints—Pratt Graphic Art Center," The Jewish Museum, New York.

1965 Lives and works in New York City and Springs, East Hampton, New York.

Solo exhibitions: "Lee Krasner, Paintings, Drawings and Collages," retrospective at Whitechapel Art Gallery, London (circulated the following year by the Arts Council of Great Britain to museums in York, Hull, Nottingham, Newcastle, Manchester, and Cardiff); "Lee Krasner, Gouaches and Drawings," Franklin Siden Gallery, Detroit.

Group exhibitions: "Drawing Society New York Regional Exhibition," Gallery of Modern Art, New York; "Art Festival Exhibition," Southampton College of Long Island University, Southampton, New York.

1966 Joins Marlborough Gallery, New York.

Group exhibition: "1966 Invitational Exhibition," The Parrish Art Museum, Southampton, New York.

1967 Solo exhibition: "Paintings by Lee Krasner," University Art Gallery, University of Alabama, Tuscaloosa.

Group exhibitions: "Contemporary American Artists Exhibition," Fine Arts Division, Southern Illinois University, Edwardsville; "Large American Paintings," The Jewish Museum, New York; "White House Rotating Exhibition," organized by the Smithsonian Institution, Washington, D.C.

1968 Solo exhibition: "Lee Krasner, Recent Paintings," Marlborough Gallery, New York.

Group exhibitions: "163rd Annual Exhibition," Pennsylvania Academy of Fine Arts, Philadelphia; "Selections from the Dorothy Norman Collection," Philadelphia Museum of Art, Philadelphia; "Holland Festival/Critici Kiezen Grafiek," Haags Gemeentemuseum, The Hague, The Netherlands; "1st Annual Exhibition of the Artists of the Springs," Ashawagh Hall, Springs, New York (Krasner has exhibited annually in the "Exhibition of the Artists of the Springs" since 1968); "Betty Parsons' Private Collection," Finch College Museum of Art, New York (circulated to Cranbrook Academy of Art, Bloomfield Hills, Michigan; and Brooks Memorial Art Gallery, Memphis).

1969 Solo exhibition: "Lee Krasner, Recent Gouaches," Marlborough Gallery, New York (circulated to Reese Palley Gallery, San Francisco).

Group exhibitions: "Drawings, Watercolors and Sculpture by Modern Masters," Marlborough Gallery, New York; "Contemporary American Painting and Sculpture 1969," Krannert Art Museum, Champaign, Illinois (circulated to College of Fine and Applied Arts, University of Illinois, Champaign-Urbana); "Espaces abstraits de l'intuition à la formalisation," Galleria d'Arte Dortina, Milan; "American Drawing of the Sixties: A Selection," New School Art Center, New York.

1970 Group exhibitions: "Pratt Graphics Center Benefit Exhibition and Sale," Associated American Artists, New York; "Peace Portfolio I," The Jewish Museum, New York; "Contemporary Women Artists," Hathorn Gallery, Skidmore College, Saratoga Springs, New York (circulated to National Arts Club, New York); "Drawing Society New York Regional Exhibition: 1970," Cooper-Hewitt Museum of Decorative Arts and Design, Smithsonian Institution, New York; "Artists of Suffolk County, Part II: The Abstract Tradition," Heckscher Museum, Huntington, New York; "Little Show," Guild Hall, East Hampton, New York; group exhibition, Young Collectors Gallery, Guild Hall, East Hampton, New York; "The Summer Place," The Parrish Art Museum, Southampton, New York; "Artists of the Region—Small Works," Guild Hall, East Hampton, New York; "Judy Heller Memorial Exhibition," Guild Hall, East Hampton, New York; "Exhibition of Paintings Eligible for Purchase under The Childe Hassam Fund," Academy Art Gallery, American Academy of Arts and Letters, New York.

1971 Group exhibitions: "Art in Embassies," American Embassy, La Paz, Bolivia; "Litografias de la Coleccion Mourlot," Departamento de Actividades Culturales y el Museo de la Universidad de Puerto

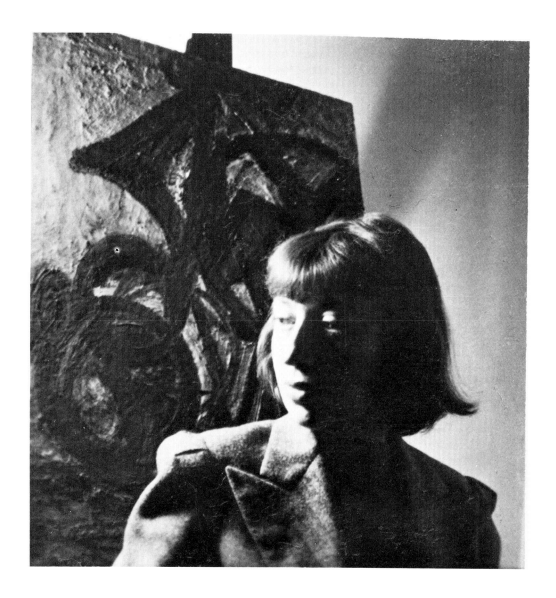

Lee Krasner, c. 1938

Rico, San Juan; "National Welfare Rights Benefit Art Sale," New York; "Aspetti dell'Informale," organized by the Ripartizione Instituzioni Culturali, Palazzo Reale, Milan.

1972   Group exhibitions: "Free Form Abstraction," Whitney Museum of American Art, New York; "Long Island Artists," Port Washington, New York; "Benefit for the New York Studio School," New York; "American Action Painting," Marlborough Galleria d'Arte, Rome; "A Sense of Place," Guild Hall, East Hampton, New York; "Artists of Suffolk County, Part VI: Contemporary Prints," Heckscher Museum, Huntington, New York; group exhibition, Young Collectors Gallery, Guild Hall, East Hampton, New York; "American Women: 20th Century," Lakeview Center for the Arts and Sciences, Peoria, Illinois; "Art for McGovern," Sidney Janis Gallery and Pace Gallery, New York; "UnManly Art," Suffolk Museum, Stony Brook, New York.

1973   Solo exhibitions: "Lee Krasner, Recent Paintings," Marlborough Gallery, New York; "Lee Krasner, Large Paintings," Whitney Museum of American Art, New York (continued through 1974).

Group exhibitions: "Labyrinths: Women and the Arts: Multi Media," London; "1973 Biennial Exhibition of Contemporary American Art," Whitney Museum of American Art, New York; "Americanishe Abstrakte Malerei," Marlborough Galerie AG, Zurich; "Twenty-One over Sixty," Guild Hall, East Hampton, New York; "14 Women," University Art Gallery, University of North Dakota, Grand Forks; "Artists' Benefit Sale for Encounter," Warren Benedek Gallery, New York; "Art on Paper 1973," Weatherspoon Art Gallery, University of North Carolina, Greensboro; "Hard and Soft," Arras Gallery, New York; "Artlift '549'—Benefit at Women's Interart Center," New York.

1974   Is given Augustus St. Gaudens Medal, awarded by Cooper Union Alumni Association, and Lowe Fellowship for Distinction, awarded by Barnard College.

Solo exhibition: "Lee Krasner: Selections from 1946–1972," Miami-Dade Community College, Miami (circulated to Beaver College, Glenside,

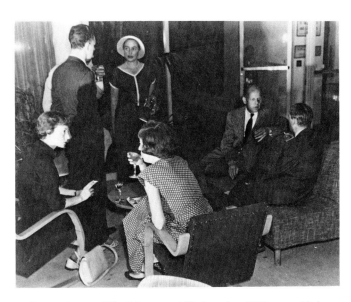

In the penthouse of The Museum of Modern Art, 1950; *seated left to right:* Elaine de Kooning, Lee Krasner, Jackson Pollock, Willem de Kooning; *standing at center:* Dorothy Norman.

Pennsylvania, and Gibbes Art Gallery, Charleston, South Carolina).

Group exhibitions: "American Self-Portraits," National Portrait Gallery, Smithsonian Institution, Washington, D.C. (circulated to Indianapolis Museum of Art, Indiana); "In Her Own Image," Samuel S. Fleischer Art Memorial, Philadelphia; "Woman's Work—American Art '74," Museum of the Philadelphia Civic Center, Philadelphia; "Contemporary Graphics: A Survey of Recent Work," Horace Mann Gallery II, Bronx, New York; "America on Paper," Galerie Beyeler, Basel, Switzerland; "Prints by Artists of the Region," Guild Hall, East Hampton, New York; "U.S. Olympic Editions 1976," Kennedy Graphics, New York; "In den unzahligen Bildern des Lebens . . . Surrealität—Bildrealität 1924–1974," Kunsthalle Düsseldorf, Düsseldorf (circulated to Staatliche Kunsthalle, Baden-Baden, Germany, continued through 1975).

1975   Solo exhibitions: "Lee Krasner: Collages and Works on Paper, 1933–1974," Corcoran Gallery of Art, Washington, D.C. (circulated to Pennsylvania State University, State College, Pennsylvania; and Rose Art Museum, Brandeis University, Waltham, Massachusetts); "Works on Paper: 1937–1939," Marlborough Prints and Drawings Gallery, New York.

Group exhibitions: "Artrain," East End Arts and Humanities Council, Long Island, New York (circulated to Riverhead, Mattituck, Greenport, and Westhampton Beach); "Artists for Amnesty," Onnasch Gallery, New York; "Subjects of the Artist: New York Painting, 1941–1947," Downtown Branch, Whitney Museum of American Art, New York; "Works on Paper," André Emmerich Gallery, New York; "Formative Years: Early Work by Prominent New York Artists," Visual Arts Museum, New York.

1976   Joins Pace Gallery, New York.

Group exhibitions: "40 Years of American Collage," Buecker and Harpsichords, New York (circulated to St. Peter's College Art Gallery, Jersey City, New Jersey); "American Artists '76: A Celebration," Marion Koogler McNay Art Institute, San

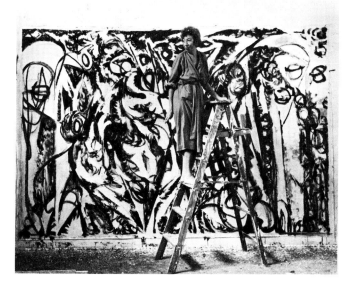

Lee Krasner, Springs, 1959

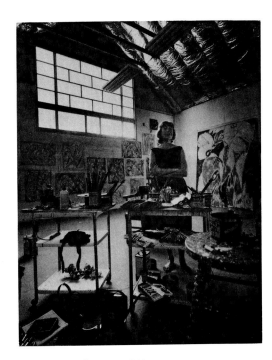

Lee Krasner, Springs, 1962

Antonio, Texas; "300 Artists to the Support of the N.Y. Studio School–Drawing Benefit," Grace Borgenicht Gallery, Leo Castelli Gallery, and Xavier Fourcade, Inc., Gallery; "Artists and East Hampton: A 100-Year Perspective," Guild Hall, East Hampton, New York; "The Modern Figure, Works on Paper," Maurice M. Pine Free Public Library, Fair Lawn, New Jersey.

1977   Is given honorary award, "Long Island Women Achievers in Business and the Professions."

Solo exhibitions: "Lee Krasner—Eleven Ways to Use the Words to See," Pace Gallery, New York; "Lee Krasner, Paintings," Susanne Hilberry Gallery, Birmingham, Michigan.

Group exhibitions: "Women Artists: 1550–1950," Los Angeles County Museum of Art (circulated to University Art Museum, University of Texas, Austin; Museum of Art, Carnegie Institute, Pittsburgh; and Brooklyn Museum, Brooklyn, New York); "Artists' Postcards—1st Edition," The Drawing Center, New York (circulated by the Smithsonian Institution Traveling Exhibition Service through March, 1980); "Points of View," Guild Hall, East Hampton, New York; "Provincetown Painters, 1890's–1970's," Everson Museum of Art, Syracuse, New York; "New York: The State of Art," Cultural Education Center, Albany; "20th-Century American Art from Friends' Collections," Whitney Museum of American Art, New York; "Recent Acquisitions," The Metropolitan Museum of Art, New York; "Extraordinary Women," The Museum of Modern Art, New York; "Contemporary Issues: Work on Paper by Women," Woman's Building, Los Angeles (circulated to Art Museum, University of Utah, Salt Lake City; and Art Gallery, University of Houston, Houston); "78 x 54," Cooper Union, New York; "New York WPA Artists, Then and Now," Parsons School of Design Exhibition Center, New York; "Twelve Americans: Masters of Collage," Andrew Crispo Gallery, New York.

1978   Solo exhibition: "Lee Krasner: Works on Paper 1938–1977," Janie C. Lee Gallery, Houston.

Group exhibitions: "Seventies Paintings," Philadelphia College of Art, Philadelphia; "Abstract

Expressionism: The Formative Years," Herbert F. Johnson Museum, Cornell University, Ithaca, New York (circulated to Whitney Museum of American Art, New York; and Seibu Museum, Tokyo); "Recent Acquisitions: Paintings and Sculpture," The Museum of Modern Art, New York; "From the Guild Hall Art Collection," Guild Hall, East Hampton, New York; "Works on Paper," Tyler School of Art, Temple University, Elkins Park, Pennsylvania.

1979   Solo exhibition: "Lee Krasner Paintings 1959–1962," Pace Gallery, New York.

Group exhibitions: "American Painting of the 1970's," Albright-Knox Art Gallery, Buffalo, New York (circulated to Newport Harbor Art Museum, Newport Beach, California); "Hans Hofmann as Teacher: Drawings by His Students," The Metropolitan Museum of Art, New York; "Art in America after World War II," The Solomon R. Guggenheim Museum, New York; "Women Artists of Eastern Long Island," Guild Hall, East Hampton, New York; "As We See Ourselves: Artists' Self-Portraits," Heckscher Museum, Huntington, New York; "Art Inc.: American Paintings from Corporate Collections," Montgomery Museum of Fine Arts, Montgomery, Alabama (circulated to Corcoran Gallery of Art, Washington, D.C.; Indianapolis Museum of Art, Indianapolis, Indiana; and San Diego Museum of Art, San Diego, California); "The East Hampton Art Colony," Pensacola Museum of Art, Pensacola, Florida (circulated to Mississippi Museum of Art, Jackson; and Museum of Art, Fort Lauderdale, Florida); "Summer Loan Exhibition," The Metropolitan Museum of Art, New York; "5 Action Painters of the 50's," Pace Gallery, New York; "The Modern Art Society: The Center's Early Years," The Contemporary Art Center, Cincinnati; "Around Jackson Pollock, East Hampton, The 1950's," Centre Culturel Américain, Paris (circulated in the following year as "17 Abstract Artists of East Hampton, The Pollock Years, 1946–56" to The Parrish Art Museum, Southampton, New York; William Benton Museum of Art, University of Connecticut, Storrs; and Zabriskie Gallery, New York).

1980   Is given Women's Caucus for Art award for "Outstanding Achievement in the Visual Arts," and the

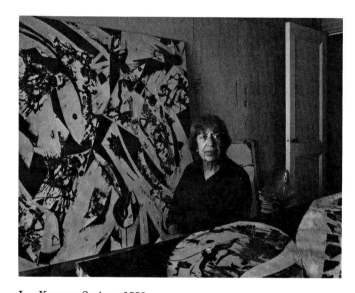

Lee Krasner, Springs, 1980

award for "Distinguished Contributions to Higher Education" given by Stony Brook Foundation, Inc.

Solo exhibition: "Lee Krasner, Recent Works on Paper," Tower Gallery, Southampton, New York.

Group exhibitions: "In Celebration of Prints: A Tribute to Lessing Rosenwald," Philadelphia Art Alliance, Philadelphia; "Prints from the Guild Hall Collection," Guild Hall, East Hampton, New York; "Originals," Graham Gallery, New York; "Pioneering Women Artists, 1900 to 1940," La Boétie, New York; "A Tribute to the Print Club: 65th Annual Exhibition," Philadelphia Museum of Art, Philadelphia; "Painting and Sculpture by Candidates for Art Awards," American Academy and Institute of Arts and Letters, New York; "Art in Embassies," U.S. Embassy, Copenhagen, Denmark; "Ten American Artists," Wildenstein Galleries, London; "The Fifties: Aspects of Painting in New York," Hirshhorn Museum and Sculpture Garden, Washington, D.C.; group exhibition, Janie C. Lee Gallery, Houston; "Portraits, Real and Imagined," Guild Hall, East Hampton, New York; *Palingenesis*, 1971, on exhibit, Vivian Beaumont Theater, Lincoln Center, New York; "From Matisse to American Abstract Painting," Washburn Gallery, Downtown Branch, New York.

1981   Joins Robert Miller Gallery, New York, at the end of the year.

Solo exhibitions: "Lee Krasner: Paintings: 1962 to 1971," Janie C. Lee Gallery, Houston; "Solstice," Pace Gallery, New York.

Group exhibitions: "Abstract Expressionists and Their Precursors," Nassau County Museum of Fine Art, Roslyn, New York; "Tracking the Marvelous," Grey Art Gallery and Study Center, New York University, New York; "Krasner-Pollock: A Working Relationship," Guild Hall, East Hampton, New York (circulated to Grey Art Gallery and Study Center, New York University, New York).

1982   Awarded the Chevalier de l'Ordre des Arts et des Lettres, awarded by the French Minister of Culture.

Solo exhibition: "The Late Fifties," Robert Miller Gallery, New York.

Group exhibitions: "Women's Art: Miles Apart," Aaron Berman Gallery, New York (circulated to Valencia Community College, Orlando, Florida); "Selected Works on Paper," Marisa del Re Gallery, New York; "Women in the Making of Art History," Art Students League, New York; "In Celebration of Age: Twentieth Century Artists in Their Seventies and Eighties," Frances Wolfson Art Gallery, Miami-Dade Community College, Miami, Florida; "A Century of Change: From the Great Collections of Long Island," Nassau County Museum of Fine Art, Roslyn, New York; "Poets and Artists," Guild Hall, East Hampton, New York; "On Paper," Edith Blum Art Institute, Bard College, Annandale-on-Hudson, New York; group exhibition, Harcus Krakow Gallery, Boston; "Landscapes," Robert Miller Gallery, New York; "The Americans: The Collage," Contemporary Arts Museum, Houston; "Carnegie International 1982," Museum of Art, Carnegie Institute, Pittsburgh (circulated to Seattle Art Museum, Seattle); "25: Namuth and Twenty-Four Artists," Phoenix II, Washington, D.C.

1983   Group exhibitions: "Artists in the Historical Archives of the Women's Interart Center of New York City," Philadelphia College of Art, Philadelphia; "Born in Brooklyn," The Rotunda Gallery, Brooklyn, New York.

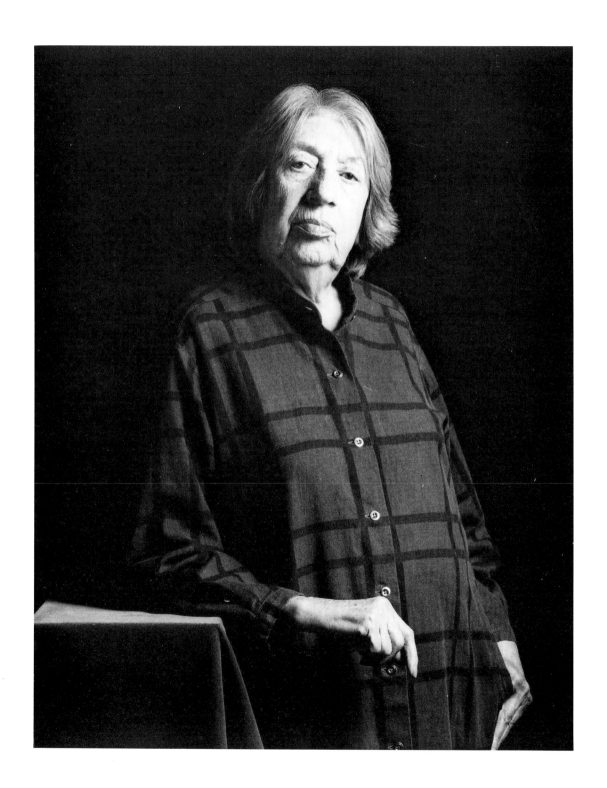

Lee Krasner, 1982

Bibliography

Books and Exhibition Catalogues

Abstract Expressionism: The Formative Years. Herbert F. Johnson Museum of Art, Cornell University. New York. 1978.

An American Collection: The Neuberger Collection; Paintings, Drawings and Sculpture. Rhode Island School of Design, Museum of Arts, Brown University, Annmary Brown Memorial; and the Smithsonian Institution, National Collection of Fine Arts. Providence, Rhode Island. 1968.

The Americans: The Collage. Contemporary Arts Museum. Houston. 1982.

Ashton, Dore. *The New York School*. The Viking Press. New York. 1973.

Ballo, Guido; Marion, Pietro; and Russoli, Franco. *Aspetti dell'informale*. Palazzo Reale. Milan. 1971.

Baro, Gene. *Lee Krasner: Collages and Works on Paper 1933–1974*. Corcoran Gallery of Art. Washington, D.C. 1975.

————. *Twelve American Masters of Collage*. Andrew Crispo Gallery. New York. 1977.

————. *Carnegie International*. Museum of Art, Carnegie Institute. Pittsburgh. 1982.

Berkson, Bill. *In Memory of My Feelings*. The Museum of Modern Art. New York. 1967.

Blum, June. *Unmanly Art*. Suffolk Museum. Stony Brook, Long Island. 1973.

————. *Women's Art: Miles Apart*. Aaron Berman Gallery, Valencia Community College. Orlando, Florida. 1982.

Cathcart, Linda L. *American Painting of the 1970's*. Albright-Knox Art Gallery. Buffalo, New York. 1978.

Cummings, Paul. *A Dictionary of Contemporary American Artists*. 2nd ed. St. Martins Press, New York. 1972.

14 Women. University of North Dakota. Grand Forks. 1973.

Freedman, Doris C. *Walking Tour Guide of Public Art in Lower Manhattan*. The Public Arts Council, Municipal Art Society, and Lower Manhattan Cultural Council. New York. 1977.

Gruen, John. *The Party's Over Now*. The Viking Press. New York. 1967.

Howard, Richard. *Lee Krasner: Paintings 1959–1962*. The Pace Gallery. New York. 1979.

Hunter, Sam. *Modern American Painting and Sculpture*. Dell Publishing Co. New York. 1959.

_____. *American Art of the 20th Century*. Harry N. Abrams. New York. 1972.

Janis, Harriet, and Blesh, Rudi. *Collage. Personalities—Concepts—Techniques*. Chilton Co. Philadelphia. 1962.

Janis, Sidney. *Abstract and Surrealist Art in America*. Arno Press. New York. 1944.

Kohlmeyer, Ida. *American Women: 20th Century*. Lakeview Center for the Arts. Peoria, Illinois. 1972.

Kozloff, Max; Ashton, Dore; and Schwartz, Constance. *The Abstract Expressionists and Their Precursors*. Nassau County Museum of Fine Art. New York. 1981.

Lee Krasner. Marlborough-Gerson Gallery. New York. 1968.

Lee Krasner. Marlborough-Gerson Gallery. New York. 1969.

Lee Krasner. Miami-Dade Community College and Beaver College, Miami. 1974.

Lee Krasner: Paintings from the Late Fifties. Robert Miller Gallery. New York. 1982.

Lee Krasner: Recent Paintings. Marlborough Gallery. New York. 1973.

Lurie, Sheldon M. *In Celebration of Age: Twentieth Century Artists in Their Seventies and Eighties*. Frances Wolfson Art Gallery. Miami, Florida. 1982.

Metropolitan Museum of Art Library Catalogue. Vol. 11. New York. 1961.

Mollison, James, and Murray, Laura, eds. *Australian National Gallery, An Introduction*. Australian National Gallery. Canberra, Australia. 1982.

Myers, John Bernard. *Tracking the Marvelous*. Grey Art Gallery and Study Center. New York. 1981.

Nature is Image and Metaphor: Selected Works by Contemporary Women Artists. Green Space. 1982.

Novak, Barbara. *Lee Krasner: Recent Work*. The Pace Gallery. New York. 1981.

Oresman, Janice. *Catalogue of the Lehman Brothers Kuhn Loeb, Inc., Art Collection*. New York. 1982.

Ossorio, Alfonso. *Exhibition of Recent Paintings by Lee Krasner*. Howard Wise Gallery. New York. 1960.

Paintings by Lee Krasner. Alabama University Art Gallery. Tuscaloosa. 1967.

Robertson, Bryan, preface, and Friedman, B. H., intro. *Lee Krasner: Paintings, Drawings and Collages*. Whitechapel Art Gallery. London. 1965.

Rose, Barbara. *Krasner/Pollock: A Working Relationship*. Grey Art Gallery. New York. 1981.

_____. *Krasner/Pollock, a Working Relationship*. Guild Hall of East Hampton, Inc. 1981.

Rubinstein, Charlotte Streifer. *American Women Artists*. Avon Books. New York. 1982.

Schoener, Allan, ed., and Namuth, Hans, essay. *Fifty-Two Artists: Photographs by Hans Namuth*. Scarsdale, New York, Committee for the Visual Arts, Inc. Scarsdale. 1973.

Springs, Harry. "Her Infinite Variety" in *Contemporary Women Artists*. Skidmore College, Hathorn Gallery. Saratoga Springs, New York. 1970.

Tucker, Marcia. *Lee Krasner: Large Paintings*. Whitney Museum of American Art. New York. 1974.

25: Namuth and Twenty-Four Artists. University Publications of America. Frederick, Maryland. 1982.

Van Devanter, Ann C., and Frankenstein, Alfred V. *American Self Portraits, 1970–1973*. Smithsonian Institution, National Portrait Gallery. Washington, D.C. 1974.

Whipple, Emez. *Poets and Artists*. Guild Hall Museum. New York. 1982.

Articles

"The Abstract Art of Lee Krasner," *The Times* (London), September 1965.

"Art in New York," *Time*, March 29, 1968, vol. 91, p. NY1.

"Artist Lee Krasner to Visit Barnard," *Barnard Bulletin*, April 11, 1974, p. 3.

Ashton, Dore. "Fifty-Seventh Street in Review," *The Art Digest*, November 1951, vol. 26, pp. 59–60.

Assur, Azmat Ahmed. "The Cover: Untitled," *Science & Technology*, September 1969, no. 93.

Baker, A. T. "Out of the Shade," *Time*, November 19, 1973, pp. 76–77.

Barkas, Janet. "Who's Who in East Hampton, Part I: Artists," (illustrated by Jack Woolheiser), *Paumanok*, July 1973, vol. 1, pp. 34–35, 99–100.

Bennett, Evelyn. "Lee Krasner: An Artist in Her Own Right," *The Bridgehampton Sun*, August 20, 1980, p. 1.

Bourdon, David. "Lee Krasner: 'I'm Embracing the Past,'" *Village Voice*, March 7, 1977, p. 57.

Brach, Paul. "Tandem Paint: Krasner/Pollock," *Art in America*, March 1982, pp. 92–95.

Braff, Phyllis. "From the Studio," *The East Hampton Star*, May 3, 1973, p. 7.

———. "From the Studio," *The East Hampton Star*, March 1, 1979.

———. "From the Studio," *The East Hampton Star*, August 21, 1980.

———. "From the Studio," *The East Hampton Star*, August 27, 1981.

Brenson, Michael. "Poets and Artists' Exhibition in East Hampton," *The New York Times*, July 16, 1982, p. C25.

Campbell, Lawrence. "Of Lilith and Lettuce," *Art News*, March 1968, vol. 67, pp. 42–43, 61–64.

———. "Reviews and Previews," *Art News*, October 1969, vol. 68, p. 17.

———. "Lee Krasner at Robert Miller," *Art in America*, no. 3, March 1983, pp. 150–151.

Cardozo, Judith Lopes. "Lee Krasner at Pace Gallery," *Art/World*, February 1977, pp. 1, 9.

Cavaliere, Barbara. "Lee Krasner: A Meeting of Past and Present," *The Soho Weekly News*, February 1, 1979, pp. 41, 44.

———. "An Interview with Lee Krasner," *Flash Art*, January–February 1980, nos. 94–95, pp. 14–16.

Conroy, Sarah Booth. "Women's Art to Get a Home," *The Washington Post*, November 4, 1982.

Cope, Penelope Bass. "Crafts Show at Art Museum Gets Help from the Arts," *Sunday News Journal*, Wilmington, Delaware, January 4, 1981, p. E4.

Delatiner, Barbara. "Lee Krasner Beyond Pollock," *The New York Times*, August 9, 1981.

DuPlessix, Francine, and Gray, Cleve. "Who was Jackson Pollock?" *Art in America*, May–June 1967, vol. 55, pp. 48–59 (includes interviews with Lee Krasner, Anthony Smith, Betty Parsons, and Alfonso Ossorio).

Ellenzweig, Allen. "The Artists," *Long Island Life*, August 1982, pp. 36–37.

Foote, Nancy, ed. *The Art Letter*, October 1972, vol. 1, no. 1, pp. 3–4.

Forgey, Benjamin. "Three Decades with Lee Krasner," *Washington Star News*, January 10, 1975, p. F3.

Foster, Sherril. "Profile: An Interview with Lee Krasner," *The Hamptons Scene*, August 2, 1980, p. 9.

Frank, Peter. "Reviews and Previews," *Art News*, summer 1973, vol. 72, p. 96.

Frankenstein, Alfred. "Review," *San Francisco Chronicle*, November 1969.

Friedman, B. H. "Manhattan Mosaic," *Craft Horizons*, January–February 1959, vol. 19, pp. 26–29.

———. "Useful Objects by Artists," *Art in America*, December 1964, vol. 52, pp. 54–61.

Gallati, Barbara. "Lee Krasner/Robert Miller," *Arts Magazine*, February 1983, vol. 57, no. 6, pp. 33–34.

Genaur, Emily. "Art and the Artist," *New York Post*, December 1, 1973.

George, LaVerne, and Sawin, Martica. "In the Galleries …," *Arts Magazine*, vol. 30, October 1955, p. 52.

"Giants of Modern Art," *Newsday Magazine for Long Island*, January 11, 1981, pp. 17–19.

Glaser, Bruce. "Jackson Pollock: An Interview with Lee Krasner," *Arts Magazine*, April 1967, vol. 41, pp. 36–39.

Glueck, Grace. "Art Notes: … and Mr. Kenneth Does Her Hair," *The New York Times*, March 17, 1968, II, p. 34.

———. "Art People: How to Recycle Your Drawings," *The New York Times*, February 25, 1977, p. C18.

———. "Art People," *The New York Times*, November 6, 1981, p. C22.

———. "Scenes from a Marriage: Krasner and Pollock," *Art News*, December 1981, pp. 57–61.

———. *The New York Times*, October 29, 1982, p. C19.

Goodnough, Robert. "Reviews and Previews," *Art News*, November 1951, vol. 50, p. 53.

Gratz, Roberta. "After Pollock," *New York Post*, December 6, 1973.

Gray, Cleve. "New Venture—The Hilton Hotel Collection," *Art in America*, April 1963, vol. 51.

"Guild Hall to Open Season with Abstract Art Show," *East Hampton*, June 29,1950.

Harris, Margaret. "Krasner Shows Her True Colors," *Philadelphia Daily News*, April 5, 1974, p. 26.

Harrison, Helen A. "Artists Find a Special Light on Lee Krasner," *The New York Times*, February 15, 1981, p. 17.

———. "Krasner–Pollock Show Traces a Partnership," *The New York Times*, September 6, 1981.

Hilton, Tim. "Filling the Gaps," *The Observer* (London), March 14, 1982.

Howe, Katherine. "Landscapes at Robert Miller," *Images & Issues*, January–February 1983, p. 65.

Hughes, Robert. "At Last the Canberra Collection," *Time*, November 15, 1982, vol. 120, no. 20, pp. 88–89.

Hutchinson, Bill. "Overshadowed by Late Husband, Lee Krasner's an Artist, Too," *The Miami Herald*, March 13, 1974, pp. C1–C4.

———. "Lee Krasner Fights Pollock's Widow," *The Boston Globe*, July 2, 1974, p. 17.

Kohn, Michael. "Lee Krasner: Paintings from the Fifties, Robert Miller Gallery," *Flash Art*, January 1983, no. 110, p. 62.

Kozloff, Max. "Art," *The Nation*, March 25, 1968, vol. 206, p. 422.

Kramer, Hilton. "2 Displays Honor Photographer, 90," *The New York Times*, April 28, 1973, p. 20.

———. "Lee Krasner's Art—Harvest of Rhythms," *The New York Times*, November 22, 1973, p. 50C.

———. "Two New Shows—Lee Krasner and Mary Frank," *The New York Times*, March 6, 1977, p. D23.

———. "Art: Elegiac Works of Lee Krasner," *The New York Times*, February 9, 1979, p. C25.

———. "Social Art and the Pollock/Krasner Connection," *The New York Times*, November 15, 1981, pp. D37–D38.

"Krasner and Pollock: Working Together," *Museum Magazine*, September–October 1981.

"Krasner/Pollock, A Working Relationship," *Grey Art Gallery Bulletin*, fall 1981, vol. 3, no. 4, pp. 1, 4.

Landau, Ellen G. "Aspects of the Fifties," *Art Journal*, fall–winter 1980, pp. 387–389.

———. "Lee Krasner's Early Career, Part Two: The 1940's," *Arts Magazine*, November 1981, pp. 80–89.

Larson, Kay. "The Old Couple," *New York Magazine*, November 23, 1981, p. 73.

Levin, Kim. "Art: Lee Krasner: Paintings from the Late Fifties," *The Village Voice*, November 16, 1982, vol. XXVII, no. 46, p. 72.

"Lively Arts," *New York Herald Tribune*, November 20, 1960, p. 21.

Lorber, Richard. "Women Artists on Women in Art," *Portfolio*, February–March 1980, vol. II, no. 1, pp. 68–69.

Lynton, Norbert. "Obstacle Race," *The Guardian* (London), September 27, 1965, p. 7.

———. "London Letter," *Art International*, November 1965, vol. 9, pp. 32–33.

McGrath, Sandra. "Out of the Shadows to Gain Recognition," *The Business Australian*, January 30, 1979.

Mitchell, Henry. "Art: Reflections on Life . . ." *Washington Post*, February 1, 1974.

Moser, Charlotte. "From Pollock's Shadow, After 40 Years of Just Painting, Krasner Has Joined Her Generation," *Houston Chronicle*, October 1978.

"Mrs. Jackson Pollock," *Time*, March 17, 1958, vol. LXXI, p. 64.

"Ms. Krasner Honored by Cooper Union," *The East Hampton Star*, February 28, 1974, p. 6.

Munro, Eleanor. "Krasner in the Sixties Free for the Big Gesture," *Art/World*, February 16–March 16, 1979, pp. 1–6.

"Myths of Sensibility," *Time*, March 20, 1972, pp. 72–77.

Nation, Pat. "The Artist Is Leading a Double Life," *Los Angeles Herald-Examiner*, August 6, 1967.

Nemser, Cindy. "In the Galleries," *Arts Magazine*, April 1968, vol. 42, p. 57.

_____. "A Conversation with Lee Krasner," *Arts Magazine*, April 30, 1973, vol. 47, pp. 43–48.

_____. "Lee Krasner's Paintings 1946–49," *Artforum*, December 1973, pp. 61–65.

Nemy, Enid. "The Big Wheels of Art Can't Get Rolling," *The New York Times*, April 26, 1980.

O'Doherty, Brian. "Review," *The New York Times*, March 14, 1962, p. 79.

Paris, Jeanne. "Lee Krasner, Adult Artist," *Long Island Press*, March 24, 1968, p. 69.

Pellicone, William. "Assessing the Krasner–Pollock Link," *The Sun*, September 10, 1981.

Perreault, John. "Art: A Breakthrough," *The Village Voice*, March 21, 1968, pp. 20–21.

Porter, Fairfield. "Reviews and Previews," *Art News*, November 1955, vol. 54, pp. 66–67.

_____. "Reviews and Previews," *Art News Annual*, vol. 26, 1957, p. 170.

Preston, Stuart. "Ten East Hampton Abstract Artists," *The New York Times*, July 16, 1950, p. 2X.

_____. "Among One Man Shows," *The New York Times*, October 21, 1951, p. 9X.

_____. "Modern Work in Diverse Shows," *The New York Times*, October 2, 1955, II, p. 15.

_____. "Art Review," *The New York Times*, November 19, 1960, p. 43.

Rago, Louise Elliott. "We Interview Lee Krasner," *School Arts*, September 1960, vol. 60, pp. 31–32.

Ratcliff, Carter. "New York Letter," *Art International*, Christmas 1969, vol. 13, p. 74.

Rattiner, Dan. "Lee Krasner, Jackson Pollock, the Legend," *East Hampton Summer Sun*, September 4, 1981, vol. XV, no. 22, pp. 1–11.

Raynor, Vivien. "In the Galleries," *Arts Magazine*, January 1961, vol. 35, p. 54.

_____. "In the Galleries," *Arts Magazine*, May–June 1962, vol. 36, pp. 100–101.

"Review," *The New York Times*, November 20, 1960, p. 21.

Richard, Paul. "Krasner: An Original in the Mainstream," *Washington Post*, January 11, 1975, pp. B1–B2.

Robertson, Bryan. "The Nature of Lee Krasner," *Art in America*, November–December 1973, pp. 83–87.

Roger, Angell. "Greetings, Friends!" (New Year's Poem), *The New Yorker*, December 27, 1982, p. 41.

Rogers, Gaby. "Three Women of Art—Citron, Krasner, O'Keeffe—Talk About Making Art in the 20th Century," *Woman Artists Newsletter*, December 1977.

Rose, Barbara, "American Great: Lee Krasner," *Vogue*, June 1972, vol. 159, pp. 118–121, 154.

_____. "The Best Game Is The End Game," *New York Magazine*, April 30, 1973, vol. 6, p. 92.

_____. "The Best Midwestern Museum in New York," *New York Magazine*, December 10, 1973.

_____. "Lee Krasner and the Origins of Abstract Expressionism," *Arts Magazine*, February 1977, pp. 96–100.

Rosenberg, Harold. "The Art Establishment," *Esquire*, January 1965, vol. 62, pp. 43–46, 114.

_____. "The Art World," *The New Yorker*, August 26, 1967, vol. 43, pp. 90, 93–97.

Russell, John. "Critics' Choices," *The New York Times Guide*, March 15, 1981, p. 5.

_____. "Lee Krasner and Pollock Painting Show in Hamptons," *The New York Times*, August 14, 1981, pp. C1, C19.

Sandler, Irving H. "New York Letter, A Selection of One-Man Shows," *Art International*, December 31, 1960, vol. 4, p. 26.

_____. Reviews and Previews. *Art News*, January 1961, vol. 59, p. 15.

_____. "Reviews and Previews," *Art News*, March 1962, vol. 61, pp. 12–13.

Sander, Marlene. "Krasner Radiant," *Working Woman*, November 1982, p. 224.

Sawyer, Kenneth B. "The Artist as Collector: Alfonso Ossorio," *Studio International*, March 1965, vol. 169, pp. 106–110.

Seigel, Judy. "Panels at the C.A.A." *Feminist Art Journal*, spring 1973, pp. 10–11, 14.

Smith, Griffin. "Lee Krasner—A Re-evaluation at Last," *The Miami Herald*, March 17, 1974, p. 10-G.

_____. "Miami Beach," *Art News*, May 1974, p. 54.

Southgate, Patsy. "The Eastern Long Island Painters," *Paris Review*, spring–summer 1959, p. 118.

Sozanski, Edward J. "The Feminine Aesthetic Is Here in Abundance," *The Philadelphia Inquirer*, March 1, 1983, pp. 1D, 6D.

"Surprises in a Woman's Life," *Vogue*, February 1979, pp. 248–250.

Tallmer, Jerry. "Scissors, Paste and Bits of Survival," *New York Post*, February 19, 1977, p. 34.

Taylor, John Russell. "United States Galleries: Resolute Eye on the Recent Past," *The Times* (London), December 1, 1981.

Taylor, Parker. "Reviews and Previews," *Art News*, April 1958, vol. 57, p. 15.

Taylor, Robert. "Lee Krasner Claims Her Place in Art," *Boston Evening Globe*, September 21, 1975, pp. A9, A12.

_____. "Lee Krasner: Artist in Her Own Right," *The Boston Globe*, May 18, 1980, p. 1.

"21 over 60 Show Talent Is Ageless," *The New York Times*, (Brooklyn, Queens, Long Island Section), July 29, 1973, p. 62.

Ventura, Anita. "In the Galleries," *Arts Magazine*, April 1958, vol. 32, p. 60.

Wallach, Amei. "Twenty-One Over Sixty—A Granddad of a Show," *Newsday*, July 22, 1973, II, pp. 3–5, 8–9.

_____. "Lee Krasner, Angry Artist," *Newsday*, November 12, 1973, pp. 4A, 13A.

_____. "Lee Krasner's Collages May Finally Put Mrs. Jackson Pollock in Her Shade," *Newsday*, February 20, 1977, II, p. 17.

_____. "Lee Krasner Out of Jackson Pollock's Shadow," *Newsday's Magazine for Long Island*, August 23, 1981, pp. 10–15, 29–31, 33–34.

Wasserman, Emily. "Lee Krasner in Mid-Career," *Artforum*, March 1968, vol. 6, pp. 38–43.

Westfall, Stephen. "The Expressionist Image," *Arts Magazine*, January 1983, p. 39.

Willard, Charlotte. "Eye to I," *Art in America*, March–April, 1966, vol. 54, p. 55.

Williams, Sheldon. "London Retrospective for Abstract Pioneer," *Herald Tribune* (Paris ed.), October 4, 1965.

Zimmer, William. "Rearranged Anatomy: Petals Made with a Compass," *The Soho Weekly News*, March 3, 1977, p. 20.

Index

Designed by Elizabeth Finger
Type set by Craftsman Type Inc., Dayton, Ohio
Color separations by L. S. Graphic Inc., New York, N.Y.
Printed by Baronet Litho Inc., Johnstown, N.Y.
Bound by Sendor Bindery Inc., New York, N.Y.